jonathan H...

Plays: 2

Guiding Star, Hushabye Mountain, Out in the Open

Guiding Star: 'This is an absorbing piece and there's an authenticity about Harvey's Scouse characters, and a vigour and humour in the way they talk, that few playwrights can match.' *Mail on Sunday*

Hushabye Mountain: 'Jonathan Harvey has more natural playwrighting talent in his camply cocked little finger than the majority of his hipper contemporaries can muster in both hands.' *Independent*

Out in the Open: 'Few playwrights can transform your tears of laughter into tears of emotional empathy, even as they run down your face. But at his best, Jonathan Harvey does exactly this, and more. His pin-sharp dialogue and wickedly accurate characterisation make his latest play a shrewdly funny comment on modern urban life . . . it is utterly irresistible.' *What's On*

Jonathan Harvey comes from Liverpool and now lives in London. His plays include: *The Cherry Blossom Tree* (Liverpool Playhouse Studio, 1987) which won him the 1987 National Girobank Young Writer of the Year Award; *Mohair* (Royal Court Young Writers Festival, London/International Festival of Young Playwrights, Sydney, 1988); *Wildfire* (Royal Court Theatre Upstairs, 1992); *Beautiful Thing* (Bush Theatre, London, 1993 and Donmar Warehouse, London/Duke of York's Theatre, London, 1994), winner of the John Whiting Award 1994; *Babies* (Royal National Theatre Studio/Royal Court Theatre, 1994), winner of the George Devine Award 1993 and Evening Standard's Most Promising Playwright Award 1994; *Boom Bang-A-Bang* (Bush Theatre, 1995); *Rupert Street Lonely Hearts Club* (English Touring Theatre/Contact Theatre Company, Donmar Warehouse/Criterion Theatre, London, 1995); *Guiding Star* (Royal National Theatre, 1998); *Hushabye Mountain* (English Touring Theatre, 1999); *Out in the Open* (Hampstead Theatre, 2001); and *Closer to Heaven* (Arts Theatre, 2001). Television and film work includes: *West End Girls* (Carlton); *Beautiful Thing* (Channel ...); ... *Gimme Gimme* (BBC); and ...

JONATHAN HARVEY

Plays: 2

Guiding Star

Hushabye Mountain

Out in the Open

introduced by the author

Methuen Drama

METHUEN CONTEMPORARY DRAMATISTS

1 3 5 7 9 10 8 6 4 2

This collection first published in Great Britain in 2002 by
Methuen Publishing Limited
215 Vauxhall Bridge Road, London, SW1V 1EJ

Guiding Star first published by Methuen in 1998
Copyright © Jonathan Harvey 1998, 2002
Hushabye Mountain first published by Methuen in 1999
Copyright © Jonathan Harvey 1999
Out in the Open first published by Methuen in 2001
Copyright © Jonathan Harvey 2001, 2002

Introduction copyright © 2002 by Jonathan Harvey

Jonathan Harvey has asserted his rights under the Copyright, Designs
and Patents Act, 1988, to be identified as the author of this work

Methuen Publishing Limited Reg. No. 3543167

A CIP catalogue record for this book is available from the British Library

ISBN 0 413 77198 9

Typeset by SX Composing DTP, Rayleigh, Essex
Printed and bound in Great Britain
by Cox & Wyman Ltd, Reading, Berkshire

Caution

Contents

Jonathan Harvey:
A Chronology

1987   *The Cherry Blossom Tree*, winner of Liverpool
        Playhouse/National Girobank Young Writers'
        Award, produced at Liverpool Playhouse Studio,
        Liverpool.

1988   *Mohair* produced at the Royal Court Theatre
        Upstairs, London, and represented the UK at the
        International Festival of Young Playwrights in
        Sydney, Australia.

1989   *Catch* produced at Spring Street Theatre, Hull.

1990   *Tripping and Falling* produced by Glasshouse
        Theatre Company, Manchester.

1991   *Lady Snogs the Blues* produced at Lincoln Theatre
        Festival.

1992   *Wildfire* produced at the Royal Court Theatre
        Upstairs.

1993   *Beautiful Thing* produced at the Bush Theatre,
        London.
        West End Girls produced by Carlton Television

1994   *Beautiful Thing* on UK tour, then at the Donmar
        Warehouse, London, then Duke of York's Theatre,
        London. Winner of John Whiting Award,
        nominated for an Olivier Award and a Writers'
        Guild Award.
        Babies produced at the Royal Court Theatre.
        Winner of the *Evening Standard* Award for Most
        Promising Playwright, nominated for Lloyds Bank
        Playwright of the Year Award. Winner of 1993
        George Devine Award.

1995   Thames Television Writer-in-Residence, Bush
        Theatre.
        Boom Bang-A-Bang produced at the Bush Theatre.

1995/6 *Rupert Street Lonely Hearts Club* produced at Contact
        Theatre, Manchester, prior to UK tour, then
        Donmar Warehouse. Transferred to Criterion
        Theatre, London. Winner of *Manchester Evening
        News* Award, Best New Play.

1996   *Beautiful Thing* released as feature film, winner of
        Best Film at the London Lesbian and Gay Film
        Festival.

1997   Swan Song produced at Pleasance, Edinburgh,
        then Hampstead Theatre, London.

1998   *Guiding Star* produced at Everyman Theatre,
        Liverpool, and subsequently at Royal National
        Theatre in a co-production.
        Gimme Gimme Gimme, six-part sitcom for Tiger
        Aspect/BBC, recorded.

1999   *Hushabye Mountain* produced by English Touring
        Theatre.
        Second series of *Gimme Gimme Gimme* recorded.

2001   *Out in the Open* produced at the Hampstead
        Theatre.
        Closer to Heaven, musical with Pet Shop Boys,
        produced by Really Useful Group at the Arts
        Theatre, London.
        Gimme Gimme Gimme, third series.
        The Lucky Ones, TV film for Yorkshire Television/
        ITV, filmed.

Introduction

In April 1989 I was living in a student house in Hull with another Liverpudlian called John. I know it was a long time ago because he wore Grolsch bottle tops on his Doctor Martens, and – what's more – I was *impressed*. John's big thing was Liverpool Football Club. My big thing was that, having moved away from Liverpool to the other end of the M62, I no longer had to pretend to like football. As I grew up I felt like the child of some bizarre mixed marriage as half my family supported Liverpool and half Everton. Every Saturday afternoon the family would congregate for their post-match tea at my nana's flat. The atmosphere was usually very strained. Particularly if one team had lost and the other won. Cheese sandwiches and angel cake would be scoffed in terse silence while watching the *Brookside* omnibus. Now I was living in Hull I didn't have to suffer this!

One Saturday John went off to a match in Sheffield. I spent the day with my other flatmates drinking tea in our filthy kitchen, saying things like . . . 'We really should get around to buying a brush.' There can't have been much on the TV as we decided to tune in to watch the game. The view on offer on the television was one of carnage and horror. The game had been abandoned. People lay dying and injured on the pitch. In all, ninety-six people died and countless others were physically and mentally scarred in a crush that afternoon after too many fans were allowed into a pen at the Leppings Lane end of Hillsborough stadium. It was difficult to believe my eyes.

This was in the days before mobile phones and so we just kept waiting for the phone to ring. Eventually it did. It was someone from home letting me know Auntie Lena was all right. (My great-aunt might be knocking eighty but has a season ticket and never misses a match.) We phoned the emergency helpline a few times for news of John but there was no news. Eventually at 7 p.m. he phoned from a call box to say he was OK.

It was a very different John who returned to our house in Hull that night. He was only twenty years old and he'd experienced people dying all around him. He'd spent the afternoon carrying the injured and dying on stretchers made from advertising hoardings. Very soon after, he 'found God'. We have lost contact now, so I don't know if he 'kept God'. But I do remember him changing a lot – from the good friend who liked the company of me and my boyfriend to the zealot who warned me each time I left the house (en route to visit said boyfriend) that, on account of my sexuality, if I was knocked over by a bus I'd be going straight to hell. My observation that, as my boyfriend only lived three doors away, I wouldn't be crossing any roads where a bus could knock me over, fell on deaf ears.

The Hillsborough Disaster opened many people's eyes to the vileness of the tabloid press. They had a field day. All the Liverpool stereotypes were dragged out of the filing cabinet and splashed over the front pages. Along with close-ups of people being squashed to death in the pens were horrific 'tales' of how fellow supporters stole wallets from and urinated on corpses. Needless to say, sales of the *Sun* plummeted on Merseyside.

Several years later I watched a documentary on some survivors of the disaster and was struck by how these people seemed to be haunted by some kind of survivor guilt. My own father, a Liverpool social worker, had been involved in the counselling of survivors and victims of the relatives. I was still aware that if Hillsborough was brought up in conversation, it appeared that some of the mud flung at those present had stuck. The facts had been marred by the rumours encouraged by the likes of the *Sun. Oh well, Liverpool hooligans strike again . . .* John was no hooligan. My Auntie Lena certainly wasn't.

I knew the reality to be different and, in *Guiding Star*, wanted to show how the tragedy affected an ordinary family. An ordinary family where in fact no one died. Yet, nearly ten years later, Terry Fitzgibbon hasn't shaken off the haunting images from that day. That day has shaped his family's development ever since.

Guiding Star was commissioned by the National Theatre. Trevor Nunn had seen the film of *Beautiful Thing* and wanted to counteract the critics who claimed that the new artistic director wouldn't be interested in new writing. It ended up being a co-production with Liverpool Everyman, a theatre where they call a spade a spade. At the dress rehearsal I asked the general manager what she thought of the show. She rolled her eyes, lit up a ciggie and said, 'It's long'!

And she wasn't wrong. I made the appropriate cuts and by opening night the play was a whole scene and twenty minutes shorter. The production was full of fantastic performances by a mostly Liverpool cast. Particularly brilliant for me was Tina Malone's heartbreaking portrayal of the next-door neighbour coping with a failed marriage and the very real tragedy of losing her child to cystic fibrosis. A counterpoint to the central character's fear of losing his sons. Thrown into the melting pot is the brash Gina, who spouts the psychobabble she has heard on daytime confessional shows while completely unaware of the very real pain surrounding her.

I was very proud of the National production. I had realised an ambition 'to be performed there'. What was most fun, though, was to watch the startled reaction of everyone else in the building when our cast arrived from Liverpool. Noisy, erring on the raucous – '*Hiya, 'elen! Y'oright, girl?!*' shouted down the corridor at Helen Mirren . . . It was the first time, to my knowledge, that actors had camped out in their dressing rooms to save the expense of renting a London flat. Well, Sir Trevor, if you stick a bed in a dressing room, what d'you expect?!

Hushabye Mountain was commissioned by Sam Mendes for the Donmar Warehouse. It's one of my favourite theatres and I'd had two shows on there before which had sold out, so they were understandably keen for a third. Sam instructed me to free my mind and take risks. My previous plays there had been one-set, five-actor plays. He told me to think bigger than this and so I did. With *Hushabye Mountain* I decided to play around with time, setting, reality, memories. By the time it was finished it seemed the Donmar were doing a season of celebrity plays (Nicole Kidman in *Educating Rita*, that sort of thing). The season had space for only one new play. A cheap play with one set, five actors. *Hushabye Mountain*'s staging was too ambitious. They plumped for a Joe Penhall play instead.

I don't think as a writer I'm that different from the next, and when I've written a play I want it on immediately, like – now! So I got my agent to show it to the Almeida, the National, the Royal Court – and they all passed on it. (A common excuse with my plays usually goes along the lines of 'We've actually done a Kevin Elyot play this season, so we've kind of "done" the gay thing.') But then my old favourites, English Touring Theatre, came up trumps, and before you could say 'Combination therapy's great!' the show was in rehearsal.

The ideas in *Hushabye Mountain* spring from an area of personal experience. After losing friends in the early nineties to AIDS I then realised with the advent of combination therapy that other friends were surviving. Amazing new feelings were being experienced. Could it possibly be that one day HIV would cease to be the black gravestone falling on top of us from the government campaign? I thought a lot about the people I knew who died, and the misfortune that they'd not been lucky enough to try any sort of effective treatment. And so I started wondering how I might explore this in a play. There was so much I had to say about AIDS. About fear. About dying. About living. I started to home in on various scenes. The dinner party where you tell your friends you're positive. Planning your funeral – the last vestige of control. Soon a story started to form. A story that could be told from shifting points of view. An elegy for a life. The chaos of the afterlife. Soon I had Just-Dead-Danny (who is very like me in a lot of ways), Connor the surviving boyfriend – grief-stricken, alone, and having experienced far too much for someone so young. And then the hope for the future is represented by Ben. Positive, and suddenly handed a plateful of hope. Instead of feasting on it, he runs, scared. Through this character I wanted to show someone who wasn't dealing well with their diagnosis and is shocked when handed a reprieve.

While auditioning for my earlier play *Rupert Street Lonely Hearts Club*, I was very taken with an actress called Rose Keegan. A unique woman who I found hilarious. Sadly the director didn't and so she wasn't cast. I struck up a friendship with Rose who, it transpired, was a neighbour of mine. (I use the word in the London sense, i.e., it took me less than an hour to get to her house.) I just knew I could write her a brilliant part and that she just *had* to be in one of my plays. Apart from anything she'd make me look good! And so I created the role of Lana for her. The ditzy posh bird with a penchant for coke and a bon mot to say about everybody. So many people who saw Rose in the play fell in love with her. My mum said she wanted to take her home with her and Neil Tennant said it was 'like seeing Marilyn Monroe for the first time'.

The genesis of *Out in the Open* was quite bizarre. I have long been a fan of the actress Ann Mitchell, since her days as the über-gangster Dolly Rawlins in Lynda La Plante's *Widows*. I've never really seen a performance by a woman on television like it, before or since. Ann once confided in me that she'd like to do a bit of comedy – and I decided I'd create a fabulous comic role for her. So I started doodling on a beach in Mykonos (as you do) and came up with Mary. One of those people who talks a lot while saying little, who covers her pain with incessant chat.

Possibly as a backlash to the teething problems of touring a multi-locational show like *Hushabye Mountain*, I decided to set *Out in the Open* in one location. And so the germ of the story was born. Mary's son has died and she can't leave his boyfriend alone.

Relationships fascinate me, as do the secrets we keep from each other. Facts that Friend A knows about me go unknown by Friend B, who may have something I can tell Friend A but not Friend C. It's some weird sort of self-protection racket. Also, we might know something about a Friend that they wouldn't *dream* of telling their lover. I've been in the position on a couple of occasions when I've been entrusted with the information that a friend is having an affair. Oh, the trauma! Oh, the cover-ups! Who's right? Who's wrong? It's a moral minefield! I am also intrigued by the rules people set in their relationships and how often in gay male relationships a certain 'openness' is condoned where it would not be in a hetero-sexual relationship.

I once went out with a guy at university who, it transpired, was living with (in the religious sense) my previous boyfriend. A therapist would have had a field day. Possibly as a result I became interested in the repercussions of a gay affair.

In the play we meet Tony and his friends Monica and Kevin. Kevin, a heavy drinker, is in denial about the extent of his feelings for Tony. Monica, a lesbian, has never actually had sex with a woman. Tony's fella Frankie died six months ago – cruising on Hampstead Heath – and now he has met someone new. What starts as a play purporting to be about his friends' reactions to his new life turns into something more complex when we learn that the new boyfriend, Iggy, was also having an affair with Frankie.

I'd been working almost non-stop with Kathy Burke for a few years on the sitcom *Gimme, Gimme, Gimme*, but my relationship with her had started as writer–director when she directed *Boom Bang-A-Bang* at the Bush in 1995. The work she did on *Out in the Open* was exquisite. I've never known such an amazing atmosphere in a rehearsal room.

Ann Mitchell, after all that eulogising, was unavailable – doing something in a mask for Peter Hall at the Barbican. Linda Bassett's performance as Mary was genuinely shattering. I learned so much from our time together, as we cut back the dialogue because she was conveying so much in the silences. Everyone in that company was slightly in awe of Linda.

The show did so well at Hampstead that after we played Birmingham they had us back for an extra month. And it's thanks to that play that I achieved a lifelong ambition. Meeting Kylie Minogue! She came to see it twice. She was our official *Out in the Open* groupie!

So, many thanks to Miss Minogue, and to all the actors, directors, designers and crew mentioned within these pages. Thanks also to Jenny Topper at Hampstead for providing such a welcoming home to my plays. Big respect to to my agent Michael McCoy for not only getting me some nice fat cheques, but also securing the board-game rights for every project I do! And big love to Richard, Dusty, Tom (the family), Kathy and Elaine.

Jonathan Harvey
December 2001

Guiding Star

Guiding Star was first performed at the Everyman Theatre, Liverpool, on 25 September 1998 and subsequently transferred to the Cottesloe auditorium at the Royal National Theatre, London, on 5 November 1998. The cast was as follows:

Terry	Colin Tierney
Carol	Tracey Wilkinson
Marni	Tina Malone
Laurence	Kieran O'Brien
Liam	Carl Rice
Gina	Samantha Lavelle
Charlie	Jake Abraham
Man in Woods	Robert Perkins
Joanne	Elaine Lordan

Directed by Gemma Bodinetz
Designed by Bruce Macadie
Lighting by Tina MacHugh
Music by Richard Harvey

Characters

Terry Fitzgibbon, *thirty-three, world-weary Liverpudlian. A good-looking fella who's let himself go in the last few years. An unassuming man who is always apologising for himself.*
Carol Fitzgibbon, *thirty-three, Terry's patient wife. Attractive and slightly built.*
Laurence Fitzgibbon, *seventeen, Terry and Carol's eldest son. A bit of a scally.*
Liam Fitzgibbon, *fifteen, Laurence's younger brother. Quiet and a bit spotty.*
Marni Sweet, *thirty-five, Carol's best friend and neighbour. A bit overweight.*
Gina, *nineteen. Pretty and loud. Laurence's girlfriend.*
Charlie Sweet, *thirty-five, Marni's husband and Terry's best mate.*
Joanne, *thirty, a beautiful prostitute from London.*
Man in Woods, *thirty-five, Welsh.*

Setting

The play is set in Liverpool, Tenby and London, 1998.

Act One

Scene One

The Fitzgibbons' back garden.

The back garden of the Fitzgibbons' council house in the south end of Liverpool. It's quite late at night. It's dark. The back door to the kitchen is open and light creeps out from inside. Two white plastic patio chairs sit near the back door. At the far end of the garden is a rubbish bin. To the right of the Fitzgibbons' garden we can see the start of their neighbours **Charlie** *and* **Marni**'s *garden, and a second rubbish bin. As the scene starts,* **Terry Fitzgibbon** *is squatting in the soil of the garden, drawing a circle in the soil around him. He turns full circle to do this. He stands up and looks up at the sky, brushing the soil away on his trousers. He is lost in thought. Eventually he walks over to one of the chairs and sits down, staring at his hands. Off, we hear their front door go and eventually* **Terry**'s *wife* **Carol** *calling for him.*

Carol (*off*)   Terry?! Terry?!

Terry   Out here.

Carol *comes to the back door in an overcoat, carrying the remnants of a chip-shop meal. She kisses* **Terry** *on the forehead.*

Carol   Hiya, love. Had a good night?

Terry   Yeah.

Carol   The kids in bed?

Terry   Er, yeah.

She walks down the garden to put her chip paper in the bin.

Carol   You'll never guess what happened at bingo.

Terry   What?

Carol   Marni won fifty pound. So it was sausage dinners all round on the way home. It's brilliant. She'll be able to get a taxi up the hospital tomorrow, she's made up.

Terry   I bet she is.

Carol   Terry, what's this?

Terry   What?

Carol   Did you do this?

Terry   I seen it on the telly. If you stand in the earth, and you draw a circle in the soil round yourself, it protects you.

Carol   What from?

Terry   I dunno. Bad luck.

Carol   You're going doolally, you are.

Terry   I think it's Celtic.

Carol   I don't care what it is, it looks a right mess. What d'you need protecting from?

Terry   I just thought I'd give it a go.

Carol   Have you started talking to the plants as well? I thought I was married to a nice riveter from Ford's. When all along I was married to Prince fucking Charles.

She looks up at the house.

Ay, Terry. I thought you said the kids were in bed.

Terry   What?

Carol   Have they taken to sleeping with the curtains wide open?

Terry   I dunno.

Carol   You'd test the patience of a saint.

Terry   Eh?

She goes inside. **Terry** *sits there. Just then* **Marni** *appears in her garden with some rubbish. She takes it to her bin.*

Marni   Are men congenitally lazy?

Terry   Oright, Marni.

Marni   I ask him to do one little thing while I'm out and he can't even be arsed. One bag of rubbish, to go in the bin. Oh no, too much like hard work.

Terry   I hear you had a win at the bingo.

Marni   Yeah I did. And what does he want? Half of it. I said, 'You can get to fuck.' I'm using that money to get a taxi up the hospital for a week. I'm sick to death of buses. I have three of them to get up to Alder Hey and it does my fucking head in. I don't know if I've got one of those faces that people feel they can just gab at, but honest to God, it's just talk talk talk all the fucking time. This woman today, she gets on the 78, and she takes one look at me and goes, 'What colour's your coat?' I said, 'What are yeh? Blind?' She goes, 'Would you say it was mushroom or brown?' I felt like saying, 'Who gives a shit?' So I just said, 'Beige.' That shut her up. I tell you, there'll be none o'that in a taxi. Though knowing my luck I'll get a driver with verbal diarrhoea.

Carol *rushes back in.*

Carol   This family's going mad. D'you know that?

Marni   Goway?

Marni *gets a ciggie out and lights up.*

Carol   The kids aren't in! Where are they?

Marni   Well, I dunno, I've been out with you.

Carol   Terry?

Terry   I've been sat out here, haven't I? I can't see the front door.

Carol   Honest to God. I turn me back for five minutes to go the bingo and the kids have done a runner. Our Laurence, fine. But our Liam?

Terry   Someone rang.

Carol   He's got school in the morning.

Terry   Who rang?

Carol   It's twenty-five to twelve.

Terry   Someone rang for Liam and he went out. I didn't notice the time go by. Don't panic, Carol.

Carol   Terry. Our fifteen-year-old son who never goes out has done precisely that. The only friend he's got round here's Wayne, and he's in the hospital.

Terry   Maybe he went to visit him.

Marni   He's not having visitors tonight.

Terry   I don't know what time he went out.

Carol   What've you been doing all evening?

Terry   Sitting here.

Carol   Ignoring the kids.

Terry   I've been thinking.

Carol   Nice one, Terry. And both your sons have disappeared.

Marni   Carol, calm down. They're probably out together.

Carol   They can't stand each other.

Marni   Doesn't stop me and my Charlie goin' the pub together.

Terry   It's not funny, Marni. Oh, fuckin'ell, where are they?

Carol   Kids take the piss, Terry. And if you don't say be in by a certain time . . .

Terry   Jesus, where are they, Carol?

Carol   I'm not so worried about Laurence.

Marni   I've got no yardstick, you see.

Terry   Bloody hell, what are we gonna do?

Marni   Coz, like, I dunno what time you're supposed to expect fifteen-year-olds back in. I mean, it's a bit different with our Wayne. D'you know what I'm saying?

Carol   You'd expect him in by now, wouldn't yeh?

Marni   Maybe.

Terry   Are you saying we're overreacting?

Marni   No. No. It's just. Well, all them kids that hang round the parade, I mean, they're younger than your Liam and they're there 'til all hours.

Carol   Coz their parents are no fucking good.

Terry   They're all on drugs.

Marni   But it's not really your Liam's style, is it?

Terry   I'm sorry, Carol.

Carol   It's them that's taking the piss.

Terry   Won't your Charlie be wondering where you are?

Marni   I've sent him to bed. Ay, we could jump in your car and drive round looking for him.

Carol   Bit tricky.

Marni   Oh yeah.

Terry   He'll be back. He will.

Carol   If you don't wanna drive it any more I don't see why you don't just sell it.

Terry   I'll get back in it one day. I will.

Carol   You keep saying that.

Pause.

Marni   Could he be round at a mate's?

Carol   What mates does he talk about?

Marni   Hasn't he got a mate in Halewood?

Terry   Surinder?

Marni   Phone him.

Carol   We haven't got the number.

Marni   Do the 1471, see who phoned him earlier.

Carol *drags the phone in from the kitchen and dials 1471.*

Terry   I've met Surinder. His parents own the paint shop by the Leather Bottle.

Marni   It's a call box. Should I phone it?

Marni   Mayslie well.

Terry   What do they call that paint shop?

Carol   They'd be in bed be now.

Marni   Rainbow Paints.

Carol   It's just ringing.

Marni   Rainbow Paints is by the Leather Bottle. I swear to God.

Terry   I'll phone 'em. Oh, Jesus. I don't fuckin' believe this!

Carol   Calm down, Terry!

Suddenly the front door goes and **Laurence** *calls through.*

Laurence (*off. American accent*)   Hi, honey, I'm home!

Terry   Thank God for that!

Marni   Oh, he cracks me up.

Terry   Laurence?!

Laurence *pops his head round the door.*

Laurence   How do?

Carol   Where've you been?

Laurence   Went for a pint in town.

Carol   Is our Liam wit yer?

Laurence   No, but he's coming up the street.

Carol   Get him out here now!

Marni   There's been murders here like you wouldn't believe!

Laurence   Jesus. Nice to see you too.

Laurence *goes back in.*

Marni   I'll get offski.

Carol   Liam! Get out here!

Terry   Carol.

Liam *enters.*

Liam   What've I done now?

Carol   Where the fuckin'ell have you been?

Terry   Don't swear at him, Carol!

Marni   See yeh.

Marni *exits.*

Liam   The Backy.

Carol   You what?

Liam   The Backy.

Carol   You've been the back field at a quarter to twelve at night?

Terry   Who with?

Liam   Judy.

Carol   Judy who?

Liam   Mrs Raymond's dog.

Carol   Mrs Raymond's dog? Why?

Liam   She's had a fall, hasn't she?

Carol   Oh, has she now? And she expects a fifteen-year-old lad to be walking round the Backy at this time o'night?

Liam   She give us a cup o'tea when I dropped the dog off. Kept me gabbing. Herbal tea it was.

Carol   I don't care if it was fucking lap song soo shong, you shouldn't be walking round there this time o'night.

Liam   I seen Mrs Raymond's daughter wit the funny eye this avvy by the Parade and she said her mum'd fell and broke her hip. And the dog wasn't getting a walk of a night so I said I didn't mind then Mrs Raymond rang this evening. She rang at half nine.

Carol   Well, how comes when I tried the 1471 it was a payphone?

Liam   Coz she's got one o'them payphones in her house. Them little ones, she has! I told yer exactly where I was goin', Dad.

Carol   But I've just rung that payphone and there was no answer.

Liam   She's dead old, it'd take her ages to get to the phone.

Carol   Oh, I feel ashamed, the poor woman.

Liam   I bet you never had a go at Laurence, did yeh?

Carol   He's earning a wage. If he doesn't get to work on time he gets money docked. You've got school tomorrow.

Liam   It's only a quarter to twelve.

Carol   I don't like you goin' the Backy this time o'night.

Liam   I was helping an old lady out. Would you rather her dog shat and peed all over her house?

Carol   Well, isn't that a lovely turn o'phrase for a fifteen-year-old boy?

Liam   God, you can talk. When you were my age you were pregnant.

Carol   Go to bed.

Liam   At least the strongest thing I've had tonight was a peppermint tea, unlike our Laurence. You have to be eighteen to drink in this country, and how old's he?

Carol   Did you have a coat on?

Liam   Ah, you're doing my head in now.

Liam *exits. Pause.*

Terry   Don't have a go at him. He's got a heart of gold.

Carol   So I was outa me mind wit worry, and all along he'd told you exactly what he was up to. Cheers, love. Nice one. Are you coming up?

Terry   I just wanna have a bit of a think for a while.

Carol   You will come to bed?

Terry   Yeah. Just wanna. You know.

Carol   It's that time of year again. I shoulda realised. Jesus, they could set clocks by you.

Terry   Ah, it's great to have them back safe, isn't it?

Carol   I'm gonna read me book.

Carol *goes indoors.*

Terry   Night, love.

The lights fade.

Scene Two

The Fitzgibbons' front room.

The next day. The room is tidy and clean and reasonably modern. A door leads off to the hall, and a window looks out on to the street. **Terry** *sits in an armchair, part of a three-piece suite which isn't that old. He is reading a book about Auschwitz. In front of him a coffee table. He wears the same clothes as he had on last night.* **Carol** *comes in carrying a bin bag of clothes.*

Carol   What's that you're reading?

Terry   It's about Auschwitz. Got it from the library.

Carol   Why?

Terry   I was just thinking about it at work, so popped in there on me way home.

Carol   You're morbid, you are.

Terry   What's in there?

Carol   I'm giving some old clothes to the Community Resource Centre. The kids' mostly. Me and Marni are going down there in a bit.

Terry   Nice one.

Carol   Terry.

Terry   What?

Carol   How are you feeling today?

Terry   Fine, girl. Cushty.

Carol   Ah, I'm made up. You're back from work early.

Terry   Yeah.

Carol   Oh, listen, you know your brown suit?

Terry   The brown one?

Carol   You never wear it no more, do yeh?

Terry   It's got flares out here.

Carol   Should I stick it in wit this lot?

Terry   Ay, I got married in that suit.

Carol   I was there.

Terry   I could get the legs taken in and the collars altered.

Carol   When do you wear a suit?

Terry   Funerals. Weddings.

Carol   You've got your nice grey Top Man one for all that.

Terry   Go'ed then.

Carol   No, it's all right.

Terry   No, Carol. Chuck it out.

Carol   I'm not chucking it out. I'm giving it to the Resource Centre. Some fella'll be glad o'that suit. You'll see him walking round the estate in it.

Terry   Someone wit no shame.

Carol   Ooh, y'little fashion victim, you!

Carol *chuckles as she goes out.* **Terry** *gets up and looks in the big bag. He roots around. He pulls out a child's Liverpool FC kit top, then shorts. He can't believe they're in there. He sits back with them on his knee, staring at them. The doorbell goes twice in succession.*

Carol (*off*)   Can you get that, Terry?

Terry *doesn't seem to hear. The doorbell goes again. Footsteps off then we hear* **Carol** *letting* **Marni** *in. They say hello then enter, laughing at the seventies brown suit that* **Carol** *is carrying on a hanger.* **Marni***, too, is carrying a bin bag of clothes.*

Carol   Can you believe it?

Marni   Oh, God, Terry, put it on and model it.

Terry   What?

Marni   Oh, come on, give us a laugh!

Terry   Carol?

Carol   He walked me down the aisle in this!

Terry   Carol?

Marni   Oh, God, the shame! D'you remember my bridesmaid's dress?

Carol   Ay, I spent a fortune on that!

Marni   Y'what? Three yards o'paisley from Speke Market? You gotta be jokin'!

As they laugh, **Terry** *stands up.*

Terry   Carol, you're not throwing these out.

Pause.

Marni   You'll have a job getting into them, Terry lad.

Pause.

Carol   All right, Terry.

Terry *sits down.*

Terry   How could you, Carol?

Carol   I didn't think.

Pause.

I didn't think, Terry.

Terry   You didn't think?

Carol   No. I didn't. I'm sorry.

Pause. **Marni** *sits down.*

Marni So what's the gossip? Where was your Liam 'til practically midnight last night?

Terry There is no gossip.

Marni Oh, goway? Your son goes missing 'til all hours and there's no gossip? Pull the other one, Terry, it's got big fat bells on it!

Terry No. There isn't any fucking gossip, all right?

Carol All right, keep your hair on, Terry. She's only having a laugh.

Terry He was walking that arl girl's dog.

Marni Which arl girl?

Terry The one from the corner.

Carol Mrs Raymond.

Marni Jewbags Raymond?

Terry D'you know she lost a load of her relatives at Auschwitz?

Marni Old Jewbags?

Terry And you just sit there on your fat arse dismissing her as old Jewbags?

Marni Did she, Carol?

Terry Yes she did. And d'you know how I know? Coz I talk to people about things that matter. Like fucking history. Like fucking losing half your family in a gas chamber. Not like where was our Liam 'til quarter to twelve last night. You can read a book about it if you want! If you can read!

Carol Terry!

Terry Just coz you haven't got anything going on in your life, doesn't give you free reign to poke your nose in other people's.

Marni   Well, excuse me, Narky Hole, but I've got plenty going on in my life thank you very much.

Carol   You know that.

Marni   Plenty.

Terry   Sorry, Marni.

Marni   So you fucking should be. And for your information I was in the top group for English at school and you were in the second!

Carol (*to* **Terry**, *about the child's kit*)   I'm not throwing that out, you know.

Terry   Good.

Pause. **Carol** *puts the suit in the bin bag then proceeds to tie it up.*

Marni   I went over the Asda today at Hunts Cross.

Carol   D'you get anything?

Marni   A fake Tommy Hilfiger T-shirt and boxies for our Wayne. It's all he can wear in the hospital, you know.

Carol   Oh, he'll be made up with that.

Marni   You wanna get yourself over there, Carol. They've got some lovely bits.

Carol   Yeah, well, you need a car to get over there, don't you.

Marni   Mm. Shame there's not a driver in the family.

Terry   I've said, haven't I? I'll get back in that car when I'm good and ready.

Carol   I'll get me coat.

Carol *exits.*

Marni   I was made up today. I got in that taxi and the driver never said a word. I said to him halfway up Mackett's Lane, I said, 'What do they call you? Silence of the Lambs?'

He said, 'You're a character.' I said, 'I know, don't tell me. Cathy from *Wuthering Heights*.' He goes, 'Is that a block of flats?' I thought, quit while you're ahead, love.

Terry   So the clothes up the Asda are good, are they?

Marni   I didn't know you were that interested in fashion.

Terry   Just being polite.

Marni   God, you don't have to be polite with me.

Terry   Well, shut your big fat winging grid then, I'm sick o'the sound o'yeh.

Pause.

I'm sorry, Marni.

Marni   What's to do wi'you, eh?

Terry   I shouldn't be havin' a go at you.

Marni   Oh, and who should you be havin' a go at?

Terry   Carol. I just dunno how she could do it.

Marni   Terry, it's in the past.

Terry   Oh, what do you know about anything?

Marni   My Charlie's doesn't half worry about you sometimes, y'know.

Enter **Carol**, *with coat.*

Carol   Ready?

Terry   There's better things to worry about than me.

Marni   Will you not give counselling another thought? It worked for him.

Terry   I'm not your Charlie.

Marni   You're missing work. They've been awful good to yeh. I mean, how many more sickies can you take? Goodwill doesn't last for ever.

Carol   Have you been taking sickies?

Terry   Well, I won't be taking any more.

Marni   If you want, Terry la'.

Terry   I won't.

Carol   Come on, Marni.

Terry   I won't coz I'm not goin' back.

Carol   See you later.

Terry   I walked out.

Carol *and* **Marni** *stand in the doorway, gobsmacked.*

Carol   You did what?

Terry   Someone'll be glad o'that job. I used to be.
Anyone can do it.

Carol   Tell me you're jokin'.

Terry *shakes his head.*

Carol   Tell me you're jokin'!

Terry   I don't tell jokes. You know that. I haven't cracked
a joke since 1989. Haven't cracked a joke, or a smile, or
been anything but morbidity itself. If I'm pissing yer off,
tough shite. I'm all right. If I'm here in this house I'm all
right.

Pause.

Marni   I'll take these.

Terry   You go an'all, Carol.

Marni   No, I can take them.

Terry   Take her with y', Marni.

Carol (*hands* **Marni** *her bag*)   I'll see you later.

Marni   OK.

Marni *goes. We hear the front door slam.* **Carol** *stands in the doorway.*

Carol   I don't *believe* you.

Terry   Believe it.

Carol   No. I don't believe *you.*

Pause.

What did you do?

Terry   I told yeh.

Carol   You know this is it now, don't yeh?

Terry   If you hurry you'll catch Marni.

Carol (*lights a cigarette*)   I don't wanna catch Marni. I wanna stay here and sort this out.

Terry   There's nothing to sort out. It's done.

Carol   Or maybe I should catch Marni. Get them clothes back. There'll be no new glad rags now. I thought we were gonna rig Liam out for his birthday. Best we get his old pullies and sweaters and tell him to make do.

Terry   I'm sorry.

Carol   No you're not. If you had any feeling left in yeh, y'wouldn't have done this.

Terry   I have got feelings, Carol.

Carol   Have yeh?

Pause.

You can only have a go at me in front of Marni, can't you? You can only answer back then.

Terry   I've got feelings.

Carol   Yeah and it's all locked up in there. With a sign, 'Keep Out'.

Pause.

I try to get to you, Terry. And you've littered yourself with a minefield. I don't know where the bombs are, but when I hit one . . . Christ, do I know it.

Pause.

Why?

Terry   You know why.

Carol   How can I know unless you tell me? You know more about Mrs Raymond from the corner than you do about me. Say you talk about things that matter. You're a liar.

Terry *lowers his head and starts to weep silently.* **Carol** *goes to him and takes the football kit from him.*

Terry   What you doing?

Carol   I'm gonna put it upstairs. In your drawer. The lads don't wannit any more.

Terry   Liam's usually back by now.

Carol   He's gone up the hospital to see Wayne.

Terry   And where's our Laurence?

The front door goes, off.

Carol   That'll be him now.

Laurence *enters.*

Laurence   Oright?

Carol   Never better. (*She exits.*)

Laurence   Has she got a cob-on?

Terry   Time o'the month, lad.

Laurence   Ay, Dad, you couldn't lend us twenty quid, could yeh? I've asked this bird out from work and when I tried to get money out the cashy it said there was nothing left in me account. Oh, go on, Dad. I get paid on Friday, I'll pay you back then.

Terry   Who's this bird?

Laurence   Gina. Ah, Dad, she's dead fit.

Terry   I've never heard you mention her before.

Laurence   She only started today, thought I better get in quick.

Terry   Where yous goin'?

Laurence   Town. Meeting her under Dicky Lewis at half eight.

Terry   I've only got fifteen.

Laurence   Ah, well, give us that then I can ask me mum for a fiver.

Terry   Oh, don't ask your mam, Laurence.

Laurence   She's not gonna deny me five fuckin' quid.

Terry   She's in a funny mood. I'll give Charlie a knock.

Laurence   But me mam won't mind.

Terry   Don't say nothing to her. Charlie's loaded. Marni had a win on the bingo.

Terry *goes out. The door slams off.* **Laurence** *switches the telly on and puts his feet up on the coffee table.* **Carol** *comes in.*

Carol   I thought you'd gone back out. Was it your dad?

Laurence   Dunno. Musta been.

Carol   Where's he goin'? (*She looks out of the window.*) He's knocking for Charlie. (*Tuts.*) Charlie's taken our Liam up to the hospital.

Laurence   Bastard!

Carol   Language! He never listens to a word I say.

She looks round at **Laurence**. *He's watching the telly. He realises she's just said something to him.*

Laurence   Sorry, what?

Carol   Take your feet off the table.

He ignores her.

Feet!

Laurence *takes his feet off the table.*

Carol   Did he tell you what he did today?

Laurence   What?

Carol   I'll leave him to tell you.

Laurence   What?

Carol   Oh, just something that's gonno affect each and every one of us in this house.

Laurence   Can we have something from the chippy for tea? I could just go a nice chiau su.

Carol   If you're paying.

Laurence   I give y'money every week, don't I?

Carol   Yeah, but a tenner every Friday doesn't stretch to chippy meals for four every Wednesday.

Laurence   It's not my fault you can't manage y'fuckin' money.

Carol   Don't you swear at me, y'cheeky little get!

Laurence   Ah, shut up.

Carol   Ay! What's got into you?

Terry *has come back in.*

Laurence   What's got into you more like! Just coz yer on y'jammy rag, don't take it out on me!

She smacks him round the head.

Carol   Your dad's packed work in. That's what's got into me.

Terry   Don't hit him, Carol.

Laurence   Don't lie! She's lyin', isn't she? Isn't she?

Terry *sits down.*

Laurence   Oh, fuckin'ell! That means we're not gonna get an 'oliday this year now.

Carol   That's right, Laurence, put everyone else before yourself as per friggin' usual.

Laurence   I hate that word, friggin'.

Pause. **Carol** *lights up a cigarette.*

Laurence   I thought we was goin' to Gran Canaria? Ah, this isn't on.

Terry   I'm sorry, lad.

Laurence   What d'you go and do that for, eh?

Terry   I couldn't hack it, lad.

Carol   Bollocks, you've been hacking it for nigh on ten years.

Laurence   Well, what we gonna do for an 'oliday?

Carol   Will you shut it, Laurence? There's more important things than holidays!

Laurence   Like what?

Carol (*smacks him over the head*)   If you wanna make yourself useful you can go and put some oven chips on.

Laurence (*jumps up*)   Yeah, well. Gotta line me stomach. I'm goin' out on the ale tonight. With me new bird.

He exits.

Carol   Not another one.

Terry   Don't hit him, Carol.

Carol   The way he speaks to me?

Terry   I'll talk to him.

Carol   Well, it's nice to know you'll talk to someone.

Pause.

Terry. What Marni was sayin' about the counselling.

Terry   No, Carol. No. Can you just leave it?

Carol   What were you knocking for Charlie for?

Terry   You're always on me fucking case.

Carol   You're not gonna get dole if you walked out the job.

Terry   I'll find something.

Carol   Get real, Terry.

Terry   I can't help the way I feel.

Carol   I'm gonna have to ask for extra hours at work. Thanks, Terry. Nice one.

Pause.

It'd be so easy. To pack a case and . . .

Terry   And what? Oh, you're gonna walk out on me now? Go on then. Prove to your mother she was right. I am a bad 'un. Rotten to the core. Well, it's true, isn't it? Isn't it?

Pause.

Carol   I'll give our Laurence an 'and wit the tea.

She gets up and goes out. **Terry** *sits there. The lights fade.*

Scene Three

The same, a few weeks later. **Liam** *is sitting watching an old film on the television. The front door goes and* **Laurence** *enters with his girlfriend* **Gina**. *They creep into the front room and are disappointed to find* **Liam** *there.* **Gina** *is dressed in red leggings and a red poncho with a red handbag and red boots. Her bizarre dress sense is quite appealing.*

Gina (*tuts*)   I thought you said . . .

Laurence   Shut up . . .

Gina   Ay! Don't tell me to shut up!

Laurence   Sorry, babes. (*To* **Liam**.) I thought you were going out wit y'mates?

Liam   They went swimming.

Gina   Couldn't you have gone wit them?

Liam   It's a free country, isn't it?

Laurence *sits down.* **Gina** *sits next to him.*

Laurence   Liam?

Liam *looks over.* **Laurence** *motions with his head to send him upstairs.*

Liam   What?

Laurence   Liam.

He motions him again.

Liam   You got a twitch?

Laurence   Get up them stairs now.

Liam   Oh, so yous two can eat face?

Gina   I'm sorry, Loll, but he's knockin' me sick.

Laurence   Liam!

Liam   Me ma said I can do what I like in this house.

Laurence   Oh, did she?

Liam   Yeah. Specially if yous two are around.

Laurence   Y'liar.

Liam   She did. Ask her if you don't believe me.

Laurence   I will.

Gina   I told you we shoulda gone to your room.

Laurence (*to* **Liam**)   Well, I'm tellin' you to move it.

Liam   I'm shitting me meself.

Gina   Oh, let's go upstairs, Loll.

Liam   Loll? (*Laughs.*)

Laurence   What's wrong wit Loll?

Liam   Nothing.

Pause.

Laurence   If Gina wants to call me Loll she can.

Gina   Laurence.

Laurence   We're staying here.

Gina   Let's go to your room.

Liam   Our room.

Laurence   My room.

Gina   Come on.

Pause.

Why not?

Liam   Coz it's got his crusty undies lying all over the floor.

Laurence *goes over and punches* **Liam**. **Liam** *hits him back. They start to fight.* **Gina** *gets the remote control and messes around with it. She lights up a ciggie as they fight. She doesn't take her eyes off the TV.*

Gina   What's on the video? Jerry Springer? D'you like him?

Laurence *lays off the fighting and sits back next to* **Gina**.

Laurence   Do you?

Gina   There's nothing worse than seeing poor white trash fighting over crap.

Liam   Turn it off then.

Gina (*she doesn't*)   He's not a patch on Ricki Lake.

Laurence   Yeah, I know. I love Ricki Lake.

Gina   She's so good wit people. And she's lost so much weight. And she's just full o'so much love, and she'd never turn yer away if you were in trouble.

Liam   Mate o'yours, is she?

Gina   No, she's American. (*Yells at telly.*) Go on! Twat her! (*To* **Liam**.) So, you didn't fancy swimmin' then, no?

Laurence   He can't swim!

Gina   Can't yeh?

Liam   Yeah.

Laurence   Don't lie!

Liam   I can!

Laurence   Y'little spaz.

Liam   I'm not a spaz. I learned to swim at Butlin's. I've got a T-shirt with it on.

Laurence   You had your feet on the floor of the pool. You were walking round doing the breaststroke with yer hands and walking with yer feet. I seen yeh.

Liam   Well, how come they give me a T-shirt then?

Laurence   Coz you robbed it.

Gina   God, fancy robbin' a smelly arl T-shirt. Feel a cunt for yeh.

Liam   Shut up.

Laurence   Ay, that's my bird you're talking to.

Liam   Oh, goway, I thought it was Ricki Lake.

Laurence   D'you know you? Yer a spazzy and a queer.

Gina   Mm, I was on the bus last week. And we stopped at that stop over the road, and I looked over at this house, and I seen you . . . dancin' in your room.

Liam   How can I dance if I'm a spaz?

Laurence   Coz yer a queer an'all, and queer spazzies can dance.

Gina   I felt ashamed. I was the colour o'that. (*Points dramatically to her red poncho.*)

Liam   I was exercising.

Gina   You were all over the place.

Liam   Ah, I'm not talking to yous two.

Laurence   Good. Let's keep it that way, shall we?

The front doorbell goes.

Gina   God, it's like Spaghetti Junction in here!

Laurence   Liam. Liam. There's someone at the door.

Liam   Well, it's not gonna be for me, is it? All my mates have gone swimmin'.

Laurence   What, both of them?

Gina *laughs uproariously. The doorbell goes again.*

Liam   It's probably that girl you got pregnant last year. (**Gina** *stops laughing.*) Come for her maintenance.

Laurence (*to* **Gina**)   Take no notice. (*Gets up.*) D'you know you? Yer a spazzy, a queer . . . and a cunt. (*To* **Gina**.) Won't be long, babe.

He exits. **Liam** *pretends to vomit at his use of the word 'babe'.*

Gina   Yeah, well, if you were in love you'd call your girlfriend babe.

Liam   I thought I was a queer.

Gina   Well, yer fella then, Jesus. You wanna wake up and smell the coffee, Liam.

Liam   You wish what?

Gina   Speak the Queen's English, it's there for a purpose.

Laurence *enters with* **Marni**.

Laurence   I dunno where she is.

Liam   Me ma? She's gone shopping.

Marni   Hiya, Gina.

Gina   Hiya.

Marni   Still goin' strong, is it?

Liam   Yeah, more's the pity.

Gina   Laurence, I'm gonna deck him in a minute.

Marni   Is the kettle on, Laurence?

Laurence   Tea?

Marni   Please.

Laurence *exits.*

Gina   No sugar for me, I've got me sweeteners here.

Marni   Yer on a diet?

Gina   Yeah. It's the selfsame diet that helped Ricki Lake lose about thirty stone. I'll lend yer it if y'want.

Marni   Oh. Thanks.

Liam   Sit down, Marni.

Gina   I mean, have you seen her lately? You'd never guess it, would yer?

Marni   What?

Gina   Well, she used to be bigger than you. She used to be bigger than Scotland.

Pause.

Ah, how's that poor son o'yours?

Marni   Oh, you know.

Liam   He's in hospital.

Gina   Goway.

Marni   Out by the weekend hopefully.

Gina   Oh, well, isn't that fantastic? Oh, you must be over the moon, are yeh?

Marni   Well, I'll believe it when I see it.

Gina   Oh no. Them doctors know what they're talking about, you know. They do all sorts o'training. It's like a mental obstacle course to become a doctor these days. Have you never seen *Peak Practice*? What's he got again?

Marni   Cystic fibrosis.

Gina   No, d'you know what? That is a real coincidence, coz only last week, I seen them collecting for that up in town. Mm, I gave them twenny pee. Y'know.

Pause.

(*About the telly.*) I tell you what, Marni, he's not a patch on my Ricki.

Marni   No?

Gina   Is it fatal? Cystic fibrosis? It is, isn't it?

Marni   Well. There are cases where CF people have lived to old age.

Gina   CF?

Marni   Cystic fibrosis.

Gina   Oh, yeah. Oh, God, what am I like?!

Marni (*chuckles*)   It's not easy, you know.

Gina   I know. They had a show on *Ricki Lake* a few months ago now about children who were really ill with childhood illnesses. Did you see it?

Marni   No.

Gina   I tape it coz usually it's on when I'm at work. But oh my God, was I weeping buckets. People don't realise how difficult it is having a sick child, do they?

Marni   Well . . .

Gina   The issues involved are staggering.

Pause.

This is a good bit. The theme is I Wanna Come Out On National TV.

Pause.

Liam   Me mum should be back soon.

Marni   Oh, good, coz I've got some news.

Gina   Is it about your son?

Marni   Not really.

Liam   She's gone the Asda in Hunts Cross.

Marni   Has your dad driven her?

Liam   Nah, she was gettin' the bus.

Marni   Where is your dad?

Liam   Dunno. He's out though.

Gina (*about telly*)   State of him. I'm sorry, but Ricki wouldn't stand for that.

Marni   He's upset.

Gina   It's the parents I feel sorry for.

The front door goes.

Carol (*off*)   Is anyone in?

Liam *and* **Marni** *get up.*

Liam/Marni   Yeah!!

Gina   In here, Carol!

Carol (*off*)   Someone give me an 'and with your dad.

Liam *goes off.* **Marni** *follows.* **Gina** *is left on her own watching the telly.* **Liam** *and* **Carol** *bring a very drunken* **Terry** *in.* **Marni** *follows.*

Carol   Get him on the couch.

Gina   Oh my God, what's the matter with him? Is he all right?

Liam   He reeks o'booze.

Marni   Where did you find him?

Carol   In the car.

They lie him down on the couch. **Gina** *stands and carries on watching the telly.*

Lying on the back seat of his fucking car.

Gina   I didn't think he could drive.

Liam   Yeah he can.

Gina   Goway.

Marni   Gina, would you put Carol's shopping away? It's all on the step.

Gina   Oh. Oh, OK then. Can I just see this?

She stands watching the telly, mouthing the words. She smiles then moves off.

(*To* **Terry**.) What are you like, eh?

She exits.

Marni   What was he doin' in the car?

Carol   He hadn't been drivin' it. He was just asleep in it.

Marni   Take the weight off your feet. Liam, get another cuppa going for your mum.

Liam *exits.*

Carol   I'm sick of it, Marni.

Marni   D'you want a ciggie?

Carol (*takes one*)   I'm walking round that fucking supermarket with a calculator. Adding it all up so's I don't go over me budget. And where's he? Getting langing drunk in the pub. I dunno where he gets the money from.

Marni   He's a popular lad. Everyone gets the ale in for Terry.

Carol   He's not popular here. I went past the pub the other day. Have I told you this? (**Marni** *shakes her head as she lights* **Carol***'s cigarette.*) And I just glimpsed through the window. And I seen him. And he was just a totally different person. Laughing and joking wit the footy crowd. I was stood there with me nose right up against the glass. It was pouring with rain. I must've looked a right prat.

Marni   And who looks a prat now?

Carol   Why's he like this, Marni? Why's he a different person here to the way he is out there?

Marni   He hasn't got to put on an act for you.

Carol   Him and his fuckin' football. I've tried, Marni. I have.

Marni   I know, love.

Carol   I've tried to understand. To be patient. To give it time. But how long does he need? Every fucking April without fail he just sinks down. And he won't talk to me about it.

Marni   Sit down, darling.

Carol   I can't go on like this.

Marni   You've got to.

Carol   Have I?

Gina *enters with a tub of ice cream.*

Gina   Oh, have you tried this? Too Good To Be True? Oh, it's marvellous this. It's like all the taste of ice cream, with hardly any fat. Should I ladle some out for everyone? Oh, go on, Carol. I think you need to take a swim in Lake You.

Carol (*shrugs*)   Whatever.

Gina   You know it makes sense.

Gina *exits.*

Marni   A marriage is for life, Carol.

Carol   How's your Wayne?

Marni   Not too good. Out by the weekend, so they say. But I think he looks shocking. I can't stay too long. I wanna get up there and take over from Charlie's mum.

Carol   Oh, get off now, Marni, d'you want me to come with you?

Marni   No. No.

Laurence *enters with their teas.*

Laurence   Ay, Mam. You can't lend us a tenner, can yeh? I promised Gina I'd take her the karaoke tonight and I'm brassic.

ol   Back seat.

ry   Liverpool won. The lads were celebrating.

ol   I've never seen you like that.

ry   I hadn't eaten.

ol   I think we should take up Marni's offer.

e.

ee holiday.

ry   It's not Gran Canaria.

ol   No. And it's not here either. I think it'd do us some
d.

ry   I dunno.

ol   I do.

kneels at his feet and kisses him.

ry   Me breath.

ol   Doesn't matter.

kisses him again.

?

se.

could just cuddle.

ry   You go up. I'll be up in a sec.

ol *gets up. She goes to the door and looks back at him.*

ol   You've got no fight left in yeh.

ry   Eh?

se.

ol   Night.

ry   Carol?

Carol   No, Laurence, I can't.

Laurence   Don't suppose you could, Marni.

Carol   No she couldn't. I dunno where your money goes
to.

Laurence   God, I only asked.

Carol   If you want karaoke, put the stereo on and sing
along to it.

Laurence   Has me dad got any money?

Marni   I think he's drunk every last penny, lad.

Laurence   He might have.

Carol *slams down her tea and goes over to* **Terry** *who is fast asleep
on the couch. She rifles through his pockets. He groans.*

Carol   Oh, well, let's see, shall we? Terry? Your son wants
a tenner. No? You got anything left? Come on, empty your
pockets out, lad. Oh, nothing for our Laurence? Oh, you do
surprise me. Oh, hang on. (*She goes in her handbag.*)

Laurence   All right, Ma.

Carol   Let's see how much we've got here. (*Empties her bag
on to the chair.*)

Laurence   I said all right.

Carol   Seventy-five? No! Seventy-eight pence. Oh, well, I
think we can all go the karaoke on that.

Gina *enters with* **Liam**, *carrying two trays of ice cream.*

Gina   Karaoke? Oh, are we's all going? Oh, yeah it'll be a
laugh that. Oh, I love the karaoke me. Dunno what I'm
going to sing.

Marni   Try 'Beg Steal Or Borrow'.

Gina (*offering ice cream*)   Too Good To Be True?

Carol   Try 'Ticket To Ride'.

Gina Oh, I'll let you OAPs do the golden oldies. I'm gonna do something bang up to date. Laurence?

Laurence Tar.

Gina Oh, don't I get a babe now?

Laurence Bad news, babe. Karaoke's off.

Gina Oh, Loll, you promised.

Laurence I know.

Gina Oh, Loll, I was looking forward to that.

Laurence I'm sorry, babe.

Gina Oh, why?

Carol Coz he's skint!

Gina Skint?

Carol Are you deaf?

Gina I lent you thirty quid last night.

Pause.

Liam What's your good news, Marni?

Gina I didn't wanna say before, but I have been practising 'What Will She Look Like With A Chimney On Her?' for weeks.

Liam Have you told her?

Marni No.

Gina And if they didn't have that I was gonna do the theme from *Titanic* and dedicate it to you.

Carol What, Marni?

Laurence I'll make it up to yeh.

Gina If it's not karaoke it's McDonald's. You're always letting me down.

Liam Will you just shut up for once in yc Marni's got something to tell me mum.

Gina God, you can't open your mouth in

Carol (*shouts*) Well, if you don't like it you can do, don't yeh?! Fuck off back to Fazack

Gina (*almost in tears*) I'm not from Fazack

Pause. **Gina** *is belittled by the roar from* **Carol**. arm of a chair.

Carol Marni?

Blackout.

Scene Four

The same, that night. **Terry** *sits up on the couch n Seltzer.* **Carol** *comes in in her dressing-gown and s washing out to dry on a clothes horse at the back of th at him as she does this.*

Terry Are the kids in bed?

Carol Liam is.

Terry Laurence?

Carol Gone to Otterspool Prom with Gina.

Pause.

Otterspool Prom. Take you back?

Terry Me head.

Carol I hope they're not doing what we use

Terry What time is it?

Carol You were in the car.

Terry The car?

Carol   Well, look at yeh! Sat in that seat while the world passes you by. I used to love you coz you were a fucking fighter.

Terry   What you tryina say?

Carol   Don't you dare twist my words, Terry Fitzgibbon, you know I still love you. Christ, would I put up with this if I didn't?

Terry   What you talking about, Carol?

Carol   Fifteen we were. Our Liam's age when we went down to Otterspool Prom. And when I got pregnant, what did we do? We fought. We fought your mam and dad and my mam and everyone on that street who said we were too fucking young. Gymslip mother, only a baby herself! When they wanted to send me away we fought. Have an abortion. We fought. Christ, when I got called for all sorts in the school playground you went round hammering the bastards who'd called me names.

Terry   Where's this coming from?

Carol (*punching her heart*)   From here! And when we had our little baby we were the happiest kids on the street, but we had to keep on fighting. When we ran away to Scotland and you made a decent woman of me, I walked back down our street with me head held high. We got the little flat, then this little house and another fucking baby and it was one long fight.

Terry   Are you saying we should have got rid of our Laurence?

Carol   No! No! I just want to know what's wrong with you, Terry. Have you fought so much that you've got nothing left? Coz I find it hard. To keep it up. But the one thing I never had to fight was you.

Terry   I don't wanna fight with you, Carol.

Carol   But I do! I need you to fight now, you bastard.
Fight for us. For something. Was it not worth it? Were they?

Terry   How can you say that?

Pause.

Carol   Oh, always this fucking silence. Well, maybe you'll
have to find some fight in you soon. Coz our baby's down
Otterspool Prom now with some slip of a girl and history
has a habit of repeating itself.

Terry   He's not daft.

Carol   No. And neither were we. But I don't fancy being a
grandma when I've not even seen thirty-five.

Terry   You don't think . . .

Carol   One day soon, Terry. The kids'll have gone. And
then it'll just be us. The last time it was just us, Terry, we
were still at school. What are we gonna be like now? With
you not speaking and me treading on eggshells.

Terry   They won't go just yet.

Carol   I'm gonna go on this holiday. I'm gonna take the
kids and we're gonna go. It'd be nice, for them, if you came
as well. We'll have our own caravan, Terry. And in the next
one'll be Marni, Charlie and their Wayne.

Terry   I love you, Carol.

She's frustrated by his lack of response.

Carol   I'm gonna take me make-up off.

Carol *exits.* **Terry** *sits there. He gets up and puts the light off and
goes and sits down again, drinking his Alka Seltzer. The front door
goes. The hall light goes on and* **Laurence** *and* **Gina** *come in and
close the door, snogging at the back of the room.* **Terry** *watches, not
knowing what to do with himself.* **Laurence** *pushes* **Gina** *against
the back wall to kiss her. Her head bangs against the light switch and
the light comes on. They see* **Terry** *sitting there.*

Gina   Ah me head!!

Laurence   Oh, oright, Dad?

Terry   I'm just off to bed.

Gina   Oh, God, I bet you've got a hangover and a half. Is yer head pulsating?

Terry   Something like that.

Gina   Night, Terry.

Terry   Yeah. Night, girl.

He exits.

Gina   It was Christmas Eve and all in the house there wasn't a sound, not even a mouse.

Laurence   Apart from your big fucking hole.

She sits on the couch.

Gina   You wish what?

Laurence   D'you wanna Bacardi?

Gina   No.

Laurence   I'm having one.

He gets a bottle from the sideboard and pours one.

Anyway, it's not Christmas Eve.

Gina   Goway. Ah, aren't yer excited?

Laurence   What about?

Gina   This holiday. I know I am.

Laurence   Why?

Gina   I think it's marvellous.

Laurence   I don't know whether me ma'll let you come.

Gina   I'm your girlfriend, aren't I? I always go on holiday wit me boyfriends.

Laurence   You don't wanna go to Wales, Gina. A caravan site.

Gina   You mean *you* don't want me to go.

Laurence   I didn't say that.

Gina   There might be a forest in Tenby.

Laurence   So?

Gina   If you could lose your virginity again, where would it be?

Laurence   Er, again? Dunno.

Gina   I do.

Laurence   Where?

Gina   In a forest.

Laurence   You mean . . .

Gina   Best yer have a word wit yer ma.

Laurence   I bet there's loads o'forests in Tenby.

Gina   I know.

Laurence *comes and sits next to her.*

Gina   Oh, isn't that a beautiful clothes maiden?

Laurence   Gina.

Gina   My mum just puts things on the radiator.

Laurence   I don't wanna drink this from the glass. I wanna drink it from you.

Gina   Y'what?

Laurence   Go on.

Gina   All right but make it quick. I don't wanna miss me last bus.

She takes a swig of the Bacardi. She keeps it in her mouth then kisses him, transferring the Bacardi to his mouth. He swallows it.

Laurence   I can't wait for Tenby.

She repeats the process.

Gina   Where did your mother get that clothes maiden?

Laurence   Dunno.

Gina   One more and that's your lot.

Laurence   I could find out for you.

As they do a Bacardi kiss the phone rings.

Gina   It's a bit late for phone calls, isn't it?

Laurence *gets up and answers the phone.*

Laurence   Hello? No, she's in bed. So's he. Are you all right, Marni?

Pause.

Jesus Christ.

Pause.

Yeah, I'll tell 'em. Where are yeh now? They'll probably wanna come. Oh, OK. Fine. Jesus, Marni. OK. Trar.

He puts the phone down. Pause.

Gina   Marni?

Laurence   It's their Wayne.

Gina   It's not what I'm thinking, is it?

Laurence *(nods his head)*   I've got to tell me mum.

Gina   D'you want me to do it?

Laurence *(shakes his head)*   You go for your bus.

Gina   Are you sure?

Laurence   I'll see yer in work.

Gina   I could make cups o'tea.

Laurence *shakes his head.*

Gina   How old was he?

Laurence   Same as our Liam.

Gina   See you tomorrow.

Laurence   I'll walk you to the stop.

Gina   It's only across the way.

She kisses him.

Trar.

Laurence   Trar.

Gina *leaves.* **Laurence** *pours another Bacardi and lights a fag.*

Carol (*off*)   Who was that on the phone?!

Laurence   Er . . . Marni!

Carol (*off*)   What's the matter?!

Laurence   Stay there, I'm coming up.

Carol (*off*)   Laurence?!

Laurence *knocks back the Bacardi, stubs the ciggie out and exits. The lights fade.*

Scene Five

The back garden.

A week later, **Terry** *and* **Charlie** *sit drinking, in funeral gear. Cans litter the coffee table. They're smoking.* **Charlie**'s *more pissed than* **Terry**. *From next door, the sounds of a party.* **Liam** *comes in in his school uniform.*

Terry   Oright, son?

Liam   Me mam sent me.

Terry   Oh aye?

Liam   She said when are yous thinking of coming back over?

Terry   When Charlie's ready.

Liam   Can I have a swig o'that?

Terry *hands him the can.* **Liam** *has a swig.*

Terry   We'll make a man of you yet.

Liam   Tar.

Terry   Is everyone still there?

Liam   Yeah. I'll get back to the do.

Liam *exits.*

Charlie   D'you think your Liam's a puff?

Terry   Y'what? Liam?

Pause.

He's a big girl's blouse but he's fuckin' sound.

Charlie   D'yer ever think Carol dotes on him a bit much?

Terry   I dote on him more than her. She's dead strict with him.

Charlie   Our fuckin' Marni. Doted on Wayne. Spoilt him rotten. The lad never heard the word no from her. Can't blame her, like. But. He was never gonna be a man. I seen it from the word go. Knew it. I just knew. You can't hurt a sick kid but. Oh, Terry, I loved him. You know that, don't yeh?

Terry   You fuckin' idolised that lad.

Charlie   I did. I did. Bloody . . . going to violin lessons. Violin? The happiest I ever saw him was when he got *My Fair Lady* out the video library. It's not right, is it?

Terry   Ay, it won a shitload of Oscars.

Charlie   He was never into all that rave music. I was more into it than him. Sitting in his room listening to all the old songs off the tapes his grandma had made him. She had him sussed. When I'd put me music on he'd be like, 'Dad. Turn it down. Three hundreds beats a minute and no tune.' Sometimes I thought he was a bird in a lad's body but. (*Shrugs.*)

Terry   Ay, he was a crackin' kid.

Charlie   I know.

Terry   You idolised him.

Charlie   I know.

Terry   Ay.

Charlie   What?

Terry   He was all right.

Pause.

Kids are gifts to us, Charlie.

Charlie   Death doesn't scare me.

Terry   After all . . . that little lad. When we . . . I could tell he was a young lad coz of his voice. Shouting for his mam. Me foot was on his chest. I couldn't see him. Then the safety barrier went and we all ended up on top of him. The life squoze out of him. Don't be funny about your Wayne, when . . . that poor fucking kid.

Charlie   I hate meself, Terry.

Terry   Your Wayne was all right.

Charlie   It was Marni that made him like that.

Terry   Ay, she only done what she thought was best for the lad. I'm the same.

Charlie   No, you're not.

Terry   I am.

Charlie   I don't hate you.

Pause.

Terry   You're bevvied.

Pause.

I climbed over some arl fella's shoulders to get out that cage. Hands lifting me over. And the first things I heard was our Liam's voice. 'I've lost me dad.' Screaming. I turned round and he's there with this busy. It took thirty-three minutes to find our Laurence. Kept lookin' at me watch. Felt like for ever. Lying on the pitch. He'd pissed and shat hisself. I got them home, back here. And all Carol could do was say, 'I told you. I told you they were too young for an away game.' Eight and six.

Charlie   You were lucky. Try to get our Wayne interested in the match and he'd laugh in your face.

Terry   We'd had such a battle to have them in the first place and then that. I'm sorry, Char.

Charlie   You don't know how lucky yer are.

Terry   I don't care what they are. I've got 'em. Don't be angry with your Marni. Be angry with the cunt up there who lets this happen.

Pause. **Liam** *enters again.*

Liam   Me mam says she wants you to come over.

Charlie   We're not ready yet, Liam.

Terry   Liam.

He hugs **Liam** *to him.* **Liam** *wrestles away.*

Liam   Are y'gonna come?

Terry   Soon.

Liam *exits.* **Charlie** *is crying.*

Charlie   Oh fuckin'ell. I never cry.

Terry   You're a top fella, Charlie.

Charlie   I hate . . . I haven't felt like this since Hillsborough. It's brought it all back. The nightmares. Just when I thought I was over it. I know I'm a twat.

Terry   I don't give a shit about you cryin', Char.

Charlie   Well, I do.

Pause.

It's not Wayne's fault.

Pause.

Three weeks ago. That day I took them machines over to New Brighton. Our Marni made us a packed lunch. I'm eating it on the front there. Top day. And there's this girl on the next bench down. Dirty, y'know. Smackhead. And she's got this mini-skirt on. And she's spreading her legs. Looking over. And I'm getting turned on.

Pause.

I shagged her in the back of the van and give her ten quid. Said her name was Donna. She was sixteen.

Pause.

A dirty fuck. I dunno what's happening to me.

Terry   Stress.

Charlie   I don't suppose you've ever . . . (**Terry** *shakes his head.*) I can get a hard-on just thinking about it.

Terry   I thought everything was OK wi' yous two.

Charlie   OK? Yeah it's OK. But OK's not, you know. I'm not leaving her or anything like that, Te'. Don't fret. Nah, stuck with the fat bitch now. If I could get out I would. But. Ah, never mind.

Pause.

I feel better for that.

Terry   Yeah. Don't take it out on your Wayne.

Charlie   There's so many evil cunts around. Why couldn't it've happened to them lads that killed Jamie Bulger?

Terry   I dunno.

Charlie   I gotta get away, Terry. I need a break, mate.

Terry   There's always Tenby.

Charlie   You know I hate the fresh air. Marni's brother said I could go and work with him if I wanted.

Terry   In London?

Charlie   Do four days a week down there and back here for weekends. Col's a foreman. Hires and fires. Always said no up 'til now on account of hospital trips. But now.

Terry   Doesn't Marni mind? (**Charlie** *shrugs*.) I think she will, y'know.

Charlie   I wouldn't do it for long.

Terry   She needs you now.

Charlie   Women are good copers.

Terry   Bullshit.

Charlie   Look at your Carol.

Terry   What about our Carol?

Charlie   Well, she's had to cope with you and all that for ... nine years now. She doesn't need that. But she's got it, and she's coping. I mean, when was the last time you and her ... ?

Pause.

I'm being way outa line here, Te'. It's none o'my business. She talks to Marni about it and you know Marni. Forever going on.

Terry   At least I don't have to go looking for it somewhere else. Like New fucking Brighton.

Charlie   Ah, come on, Te'. We're mates.

Terry   I know, like, y'know. But. Ay, you don't think she's . . . ?

Charlie   Carol? No.

Terry   No.

Charlie   She'da told Marni.

Terry   Ay, this if off its chunk.

Charlie   You'd be able to tell.

Pause.

Women cope with whatever you throw at them. If I do just two weeks in London, in me time off from work, she can go to Tenby, I can make a nice bit o'cash and get a break all into the bargain. Ay, you could come an'all.

Terry   Ah no.

Charlie   Col'd take yer on for a fortnight.

Terry   Nah, I couldn't. Carol's really looking forward to Tenby.

Charlie   Women love nothing better than getting rid o'their arl fellas for a few days.

Terry   Two weeks?

Charlie   Even better. She'd have Marni there.

Terry   I know but.

Charlie   It's not Carol, is it?

Terry   What?

Charlie   It's you.

Terry   Me?

Charlie   Ah no, Te'. I understand, like.

Terry   What?

Charlie   You're, like, agoraphobic an' all that.

Terry   I'm not.

Charlie   Forget it, Te'. I'll go on me own.

Terry   I'm not an agoraphobic. I'm not.

Charlie   S'all right, Te'. I've been there.

Terry   But I'm not.

Charlie   Ah, but think about it. You in London? A city you don't know? The pace? The people? Tubes an' all that? Nah, Te'. You wouldn't hack it.

Pause.

Terry   We should be gettin' back.

Charlie   Ay, don't say nothing to *her*, will yeh?

Terry   I won't.

Pause.

Where would you stay?

Charlie   In London? Colin's pad. It's massive.

Terry   And there'd definitely be a job?

Charlie   I've told yer, haven't I? Why?

Terry   Nothing. I'm pissed.

Marni *comes in wearing a black dress. She tidies away their lager cans.*

Marni   Charlie. Y'mam's givin' me all sorts o'grief in there. Keeps askin' where yer are.

Charlie   We're comin' now.

Marni   His teacher's pissed. Crying her eyes out in the corner. I could do without that.

Charlie   Come on, Terry lad. Time we faced the music.

Marni   Your Liam's being an angel. Filling everyone's drink up.

Terry   Yeah, well. He's a good kid. Wayne was his best mate.

Charlie   Ay! Marni Sweet!

Marni   What, Three-Piece?

Charlie *gets up and sings to her, holding his can aloft. He starts to sing 'My Special Angel' by Malcolm Vaughan.*

He stops singing.

Marni (*upset*)   You soft prick. That was his song.

She exits.

Terry   See? You can't help but love her, can you?

Charlie *shrugs and the tears pour.* **Terry** *doesn't know what to do. Eventually he stands up and hugs* **Charlie** *to him. The lights fade.*

Scene Six

The lounge.

A few weeks later. **Carol** *is hoovering.* **Terry** *is reading* **Liam**'s *school report.* **Liam** *is spark out on the couch.* **Carol** *is looking at him. She switches the Hoover off. The telly and video have disappeared.*

Carol   Listen to him, he's snoring.

Terry   PE . . . F! 'Hard to comment. Liam never brings correct kit and is sullen and uncooperative when forced to participate.' That can't be true!

Carol   You'll have to have a word with Mrs Raymond. She can find someone else to walk her dog so late.

Terry   He loves sport.

The doorbell goes. **Liam** *wakes up.* **Carol** *looks out of the window.*

You love games.

Liam   What?

Carol   Get the door, it's Marni.

Terry   Footy. The match.

Carol   Terry.

Terry   What?

Carol (*now* **Liam***'s gone out*)   He hates games.

Terry   Don't be daft.

Enter **Marni**. *She has an apron on. She stands there.*

Carol   Hiya, love. Oh, God, is it all getting a bit on top of you?

Marni   Yer haven't got a ciggie, have yeh?

Carol   Sit down.

Marni   I've come out without me Consulate.

Carol   Terry, pass us . . . tar.

Marni   Tar.

Carol *is signalling for* **Terry** *to get out.*

Terry   Think I'll put the kettle on.

Marni   I think you better stay, Terry. This involves you.

Carol   What's happened?

Marni   Oh, I'm standing there, in the back kitchen, putting his tea on. I'm just cracking an egg and watching it sizzle nicely in the pan, when he drops the most massive, almightiest clanger I've ever heard in me life.

Carol   Charlie?

Marni   Only reckons he's not going to Tenby.

Carol   What?

Marni   Oh no. Reckons him and Terry here are going off to London for a fortnight to work for our Colin.

Carol   What?

Marni   Oh, so Terry hasn't told you?

Carol   Terry?

Terry   It's nothing definite.

Carol   Say that again.

Marni   Charlie and Terry aren't coming to Tenby. They're going to do two weeks in London helping my brother do up some toff's mansion.

Carol   No. No! This is . . . it's stupid.

Marni   It's more than stupid, it's fucking ridiculous.

The doorbell goes.

Carol   But . . .

Terry   I didn't say I would.

Marni   Tell me it's just another of Charlie's hare-brain schemes. Pie in the sky. Like when he was gonna buy that plot of land and turn it into a city zoo.

Terry   He'll come to Tenby. You'll see.

Enter **Charlie**.

Charlie (*to* **Marni**)   Ay, you, the tea's ruined.

Marni   Oh, piss off, you, cunt.

Charlie   Well, that's the pot calling the kettle black.

Carol   Don't you wanna come to Tenby, Charlie?

Charlie   Of course I wanna come to Tenby.

Carol   Well, that's settled then.

Charlie   It's just . . .

Marni   See?

Charlie   It's just, you know. I'm not one for holidays, you know that. The only reason we was getting that caravan in the first place was to give Wayne a nice break.

Marni   It was very kind of our Colin to give us his caravan for the fortnight.

Charlie   But now Wayne's not here . . .

Marni   Oh, but your wife doesn't need a break, does she? I'll just sit in staring at the four walls like something out of *One Flew Over the Cuckoo's Nest*.

Charlie   I know you need a break. I'm not daft.

Marni   Imagine how I'd feel in a caravan all on me own knowing our Wayne was supposed to be there an'all.

Charlie   I just thought. Oh, forget it. Come on, you.

Carol   What? What did you think?

Charlie   I know things is hard for you and Terry. Not working. It just seemed ideal to take up Col's offer.

Marni (*to* **Carol**)   Will you listen to that? Mother Fucking Teresa of Calcutta's godson. (*To* **Charlie**.) Col doesn't offer a thing unless you put it into his head. The extra caravan for this lot was your idea. Christ, you think more of Terry than you do me.

Carol   And it's a nice thought, Charlie, but . . . you can't leave Marni on her own. Not now.

Charlie   I realise that. I do. Come on, you. I'm hungry.

Marni   You're not getting so much as a Pot Noodle out o'me tonight.

Charlie   Come 'ed, girl. I'll cook.

Marni   I'm not that keen on salmonella and chips tar, babe.

Charlie   Now who's being unreasonable? I've said I'll come to Tenby. We both will, won't we, Te'?

Terry   Yeah.

Pause.

Marni   Go to London. See if I care. If that's what you want, go! I don't want you hangin' round a perfectly good caravan for a fortnight if you don't wanna be there.

Carol   Marni, you don't mean that.

Marni   D'you wanna bet?

Charlie   No. I'll ring Col. Tell him to call it off.

Marni   Don't try and make me feel guilty.

Charlie   Snap.

Marni   I've done nothing wrong.

Marni *gets up.*

Charlie   Where you goin'?

Marni   The toilet. Why? D'you wanna wipe me arse?

She exits.

Charlie   I'm sorry about this, Carol. We'll get outa your way in a minute.

Carol   Terry. Did you wanna go to London?

Terry   No.

Charlie   Oh, cheers, mate.

Terry   Well, I don't now.

Carol   You'd actually go down there. And work?

Terry   Ah, forget it, Carol.

Carol   Forget it? I'm fascinated.

Terry   I got us into this mess. I thought I could try and get us out.

Carol   I don't believe you sometimes.

Terry   I reckon I'd be all right with Charlie.

Charlie   Carol. We're looking at the best part of a grand for two weeks' work. Now you can't knock that, can yeh?

Carol   I don't believe you either. Just upping and leaving Marni so soon after Wayne.

Charlie   I hate having time to meself. I need to keep going. Take me mind off things. If I have too much time on me hands I go on a downer. I know that coz o'the counselling. I'm being dead selfish, I know. But, me and Marni's different in that respect. If I have two weeks with her with nothing to do, she'll wanna keep goin' on about Wayne, and . . . I know she needs that, but . . . I'd rather not think about it.

Marni*'s come back to the doorway. He's not seen her.*

Charlie   I know I'm being selfish, but I just wanno hang on to me sanity. I've lost that once. I don't wanna lose it again.

Marni *is crying.* **Liam** *comes to the door and puts his arm around her.*

Liam   You all right, Marni?

Marni   You can say it to them but you can't say it to me.

Charlie   If you'd given me time I would. But you came storming round here. I thought you were goin' the loo.

Marni   There's no toilet paper.

Carol   Isn't there? Oh bloody'ell.

Marni   It's all right. I can hang on 'til I get home.

Carol   Oh, for God's sake. We're living off beans on toast. We've sent the TV and video back today. And now there's no bog roll. I'll have to go the shop. Terry, have you got a couple o'quid?

Terry *shakes his head.*

Carol   No?

Charlie   Eeyar, Carol.

Carol   Liam?

Charlie   Carol . . . (*He's holding out some money.*)

Carol   It's OK.

Liam   In me piggy bank.

Carol   Will you get it?

Liam *exits.*

Terry   I'm sorry, Carol. I'm sorry, Marni.

Marni   Ay, Carol. How d'you fancy sharing a caravan with me? Give the kids one to themselves?

Carol *sighs desperately, then throws her head back and starts to laugh.* **Marni** *joins in, shaking her head. The doorbell goes.*

Liam (*off*)   I'll get it!

Carol   If it's Christian Aid, rob the buggers!

She and **Marni** *laugh.* **Gina** *enters with* **Liam** *who is carrying his piggy bank.* **Gina** *is dressed head to toe in turquoise; leggings, boots, poncho and Alice band. She carries a video cassette and a newspaper.*

Gina   Hiya! Hiya, Marni, ah. Laurence not back yet no?

Carol   No, love.

Gina   Oh, it's nice to see you having a giggle, Marni, love. Takes more muscles to frown than to smile, you know. Now, does anyone mind if I watch this afternoon's *Ricki Lake* 'til he gets back? I'll only have it on quiet, only I haven't had a chance to watch it yet, and you know what I'm like.

Carol   Feel free, go right ahead.

Gina   I know yous all think I'm stupid.

Carol   Well, you can't be more stupid than us.

Gina   Oh, I can't wait for Tenby, you know. Us girls are gonna have a right giggle. I had this dream the other night. And us three were sitting round a camp fire, just pissing ourselves. I couldn't get over it. Video.

She moves to where the telly usually is. She sees it's gone.

Oh.

Liam   Mum?

Liam *has got a couple of pounds out of his piggy bank.*

Marni   Give it him back. Gina? Could I borrow your paper?

Gina   Sure, Marni, yeah, you go right ahead. We're gonna have to get used to share and share alike when we're on our hols!

Carol   It's a caravan we're going to, you know, not the friggin' outback.

Gina   Oh, you know what I mean, Carol.

Marni   Any particular section you don't like, Gina?

Gina   Telly reviews. They've been slagging my Ricki, cunts.

They all giggle at her turn of phrase. **Marni** *takes the paper and goes to exit to the loo with it.*

Marni   Well, if it was good enough for my arl girl in the war, it's good enough for me!

She exits. **Carol** *starts to laugh again. Eventually her laughter turns to tears.* **Liam** *goes and hugs her. He starts crying too.* **Terry** *and* **Charlie** *look fed up.*

Gina   Oh, listen, stop it. Oh, will yous stop it?

They keep crying.

God, feel ashamed for yous.

Terry *stars to cry.*

Gina   What are yous like?! Smile, kidders, it might never happen!

Liam   Shut up, will yeh.

Gina   Are yous all mad or something? We're going on our holidays!! Jesus.

She sits down on the arm of the chair. Just then **Laurence** *comes in. He sees everyone crying.*

Gina   Don't look at me.

Laurence   I got a taxi back. Can anyone lend us a tenner?

Blackout.

Act Two

Scene One

A forest in Tenby.

Pitch black and approaching midnight, there is just a hint of moonlight shining down through the trees. **Laurence** *enters shining a torch ahead of him.* **Gina** *follows him eating chips. She wears a yellow poncho, leggings and platform trainers. She is trying to eat, but can't see where she is going.*

Gina Laurence!

Laurence Com 'ed.

Gina I've got platform trainees on, I'm gonna go arse over tit.

He shines the torch so she can see where she is going.

Up here. I can't see me chips.

He shines the torch so she can see her food. They stop where they are.

I'm having to force these down. Christ knows how much weight I'm going to put on.

He puts his hand between her legs. She slaps him off.

Do I look really fat?

Laurence Huge.

Gina Do I?

Laurence No.

Gina Best I get on that *Ricki Lake*. I'll be sat on that chair and on the screen it'll say 'Gina: She's ballooned.'

Laurence I'll have to go an'all.

Gina Yeah?

Laurence And it'll say 'Laurence: His knob's aching.'

Gina   Ricki wouldn't stoop so low.

Laurence   It's only when you're around.

Gina   Mm, well, I'll be very around if I'm eating chips every night. You'll have to spin me round to get out the house. Can't believe it.

Laurence   What's got into you?

Gina   Fat's a feminist issue, gobshite.

Laurence   And I can't help being a man, with a man's needs.

Gina   God, you're obsessed, you.

Laurence   You have this effect on me, Gina.

Gina   God, if I had a pound for every time someone had said that to me.

Laurence   You'd be fuckin' skint.

Gina   I'd be as rich as Ricki.

Laurence   Will you stop goin' on about her?

Gina   Well, you stop goin' on about y'knob then.

Laurence   So who else's said it to you?

Gina   Everyone. Jammed up against the bus shelter aged thirteen with some big fat hairy monster from the youth club tryina stick it between me legs . . . 'You have this effect on me, Gina.' Bending over the photocopier at work: 'Photocopy this, love.' 'Fuck off, Phil.' 'But Gina, you have this effect on me!'

Laurence   Phil who?

Gina   I've seen more erections than a master scaffolder. I'm sick of it.

Laurence   Phil who? Who said that at work?

Gina   It was before I was transferred to your branch.

Laurence I'll fuckin' deck him.

Gina Deck yourself, you're all the same.

Laurence Is that why you were moved to our branch?

Gina I kicked him in the bollocks with me Spice Girl trainees and the bastard put in a grievance procedure.

Laurence Sit down.

Gina I'm not sitting down there, the filth of it!

Laurence *takes his coat off and spreads it on the floor.*

Laurence Madam?

She sits down on his coat. He remains standing.

But I'm allowed to say it to yeh, coz I'm your fella.

Gina I'm gonna kill you if we're lost.

Laurence Aren't I?

Gina And don't be whipping nothing out.

Laurence We're not lost.

Gina Well, where are we then?

Laurence Caravan's about ten minutes that way.

Gina How do you know?

Laurence Coz look up there.

They look up into the sky.

Gina Mm?

Laurence They're the exact same stars that y'see from the caravan.

Gina (*tuts*) They're the exact same stars you can see from my bedroom window at home. What do you know about stars?

Laurence I know where we are.

Gina   Well, what's that one called? The big bright fuck-off one at the top.

Laurence   That's the guiding star.

Gina   The what? Never heard of it.

Laurence   So me dad says.

Gina   Your dad? And you believe him? Feel a cunt for yeh.

Laurence   I can believe him if I want.

Gina   And I suppose you believe that there's fairies at the bottom of the garden. Stars don't have names like that, Laurence. They have names like 'The Plough' and 'The Bear' and 'Orion's Belt'. Guiding star me arse.

Laurence   My dad said if yer ever got lost, you could look up into the sky and one of two things would happen.

Gina   Surprise me.

Laurence   You'd either see one of the Liver Birds off the Liver Buildings flying in the sky, and it'd fly back to Liverpool so's you could follow it.

Gina   Or?

Laurence   Or you'd see that bright star, the guiding star, that'd get yeh home, coz it shines right above our house.

Gina   Who does he think you are? Jesus?

Laurence   I like it.

Gina   Your dad's soft in the head, it's common knowledge.

Laurence   No he's not.

Gina   And as for that mother o'yours. She was the one who said I could share a caravan with you and your Liam in the first place. But you shoulda seen the daggers she give me this morning when I comes out the caravan in me nightie.

Like we'd been shaggin' in front of your Liam. I felt ay-fuckin'-shamed.

Laurence No danger o'that with your attitude.

Gina I can't help being on me period.

Laurence I don't mind, you know.

Gina Good. Coz I never come away to have sex wit yer, Loll. I came away to have valuable time wit yeh.

Laurence No. I don't *mind*.

Gina What?

Laurence A bit o'blood.

Gina Y'know, you?

Laurence What?

Gina Y'dead romantic.

Laurence D'y'reckon?

Gina Well, put it this way, if I was on *Ricki Lake* now it'd say 'Gina: She's bein' sarky.'

Laurence I dunno why you bothered comin'.

Gina I've told you why. This is *our time*. We can give each other feedback. And check out, y'know, if we've got a future. This isn't a dress rehearsal, Laurence, this is the real thing. I wanna find the real me in this relationship. You wanna find the real you. We wanna find the real each other. Yeah?

Laurence Yeah. But . . .

Gina Are we agreed on that?

Laurence Yeah.

Gina Talk through y'feelings on that one, Loll, coz I need to know. Zero talk means zero communication, yeah?

Laurence Yeah.

Gina   So talk.

Laurence   Erm. I think. We've gotta . . . listen to each other. And . . . hear each other.

Gina   And listen to your heart?

Laurence   Oh, God, yeah.

Gina   Like your inner voice?

Laurence   Like the inner child.

Gina (*nodding*)   With yeh, with yeh.

Laurence   Coz like . . . zero contact . . . means zero everything, really.

Gina   When you say contact . . . d'you mean like on a spiritual level?

Laurence   Well, spiritual and . . .

Gina   Psychological?

Laurence   Yeah. And, y'know, I think . . . sometimes . . . words aren't enough.

Gina   That's why classical music's so popular with old people.

Laurence   Exactly.

Gina   Right, so can I do a recap here? What you're saying is . . . sometimes, verbal communication doesn't reach far enough.

Laurence   That's exactly it.

Gina   Goway, so like, y'talking . . . psychic powers here?

Laurence   Well, that sort o'communication where, between a man and a woman, you can sort of reach out and . . . have a shag.

Pause. **Gina** *eventually stands up.*

Laurence   Tell me what y'feeling, love.

Gina   Caravan's this way you say?

She's walking away.

Laurence   I thought we were talking!

Gina   Give us that torch!

She snaps the torch out of his hands and storms off, fuming.

Laurence   Yeah, well, you said I'd get me hole in Tenby and look at yeh! I'm sick o'the sight o'you flirtin' with anything in a tracksuit. I've seen you with them lads from Kirkby in the third caravan down. You'll put a stop to that!

Gina   They're dead spiritual!

Laurence   I've seen yeh!

Gina   Drop dead!

Laurence   Gina! Wait for me! I said . . . ay, you!

He follows her off. Blackout.

Scene Two

The same, a few nights later. It is a bit lighter now, though still late at night. We can now make out a wire-mesh fence halfway down the stage. Lights flash past indicating a passing train on a railway line beyond the fence. **Liam** *comes on and walks slowly along. A* **Man** *enters in jogging gear. He half jogs and walks, then stays jogging on the spot.* **Liam** *freezes. The* **Man** *speaks with a broad Welsh accent and looks like he could be in the army.*

Man   Lost something?

Liam   Er, me dog.

Man   I haven't seen no dogs. Not from round here?

Liam   No.

Man   Holiday?

Liam   Yeah.

Man   Bring your dog on holiday, do you?

Liam   She's brown. 'Bout this high. Judy.

Man   Judy?

Liam   Yeah.

Man   It's not a good idea bringing dogs up here this time o'night. You wanna stick to the road.

Liam   I was on the road but I let her off the lead. She ran into the trees.

Man   Where's the lead now then?

Liam   Sorry?

Man   Dog lead.

Liam   In me pocket.

Man   Bit late for dog walking, init?

Liam   She needed a crap.

Man   I like the peace and quiet this time o'night. No cars on the road. No one to see you, jogging like. I can just run and run and . . . maybe she's gone down by the railway line. There's a hole in the fence. Maybe she's gone through there, had a bit of a sniff around and can't find the hole again.

Liam   D'you think so?

Man   It's easy enough to do. You've gotta know the fence, haven't you?

Liam   I hope she's all right.

Man   She won't be mown down by a train. There's another fence next to the line. Wire-mesh. No holes in that.

Liam   Perhaps I better look.

Man   It's only an idea. She could be anywhere, couldn't she?

Liam   Yeah.

Man   D'you want me to show you where the hole is?

Liam   Go 'ed then.

Man   I don't mind. It's better if you're with someone, don't you think?

Liam   Suppose so.

Man   It's down here.

He shows him the hole in the fence. They go through to the other side.

Liam   Can't see her, can you?

Man   What's your name, lad?

Liam   Wayne.

Man   Scouser?

Liam   How d'you guess?

Man   I used to know Liverpool.

Liam   Yeah?

Man   Staying up the caravans?

Liam   Yeah.

Man   With your mates?

Liam   Family.

Man   Still at school?

Liam   Just left.

Man   Which one?

Liam   Pope John Paul the Second.

Man   Good Catholic boy?

Liam   Dunno.

Man   Do much sport?

Liam   No. She's not here, is she?

Man   I don't think so.

Pause.

Ah, I need a slash, you know.

Pause.

Think I'll have one. Don't mind, do you?

Liam   No.

The **Man** *turns his back on the audience. He walks up a bit.*

Man   Good thing about tracksuits, no flies to mess about with. You wanna get it out, you can. No problem.

Pause.

Here, look at this.

Liam *slowly approaches him.*

Man   Look.

Liam   Where?

Man   Is that a tenner down there?

Liam   It's just a bit of paper.

A train goes past. They are momentarily lit up. **Liam** *stares at the train in panic.*

Man   What d'you think of that?

Liam   It's all right.

Man   Yeah?

Liam   Yeah.

Man   Not bad, is it?

Liam   No.

Man   You shy, Wayne?

Liam   No.

Man   You sure?

Liam   Yeah.

Man   Well, go on then.

Liam   What?

Man   Let's see yours.

Liam   I've gotta find me dog.

Man   Fuck your dog.

Liam   Me mam'll kill me.

The **Man** *puts his dick away and turns round. He starts to walk away.*

Man   You had your chance, lad. No Scouser messes me around. Can't afford to be choosy with a face like that. Hanging round here. Bet you lose your dog every night.

Liam   She just ran off.

Man   Fucking Catholics.

Liam   Hang on!

Man   Why? What's keeping me here? You shouldn't play games with me, I've told you.

Liam   I've never . . .

Man   Never what?

Liam   I mean, I've watched. There's this field back home. I've seen. But. Never. I mean. I want to. But.

Man   But what?

Pause.

Eh?

Liam Don't go.

Man Why not?

Liam *undoes his trousers and pulls them down.*

Liam Well, what are you waiting for?

Blackout.

Scene Three

A flat in London.

Joanne's *flat in Earls Court. A big old room in a converted house. The only features are a sofa bed, opened out into a bed, and a window.* **Joanne** *is a woman* **Terry** *has met in the pub that night.* **Terry** *comes in and stares at the bed. He sits on it.*

Terry Nice flat.

Joanne *comes in with two drinks. She's a good-looking thirty-year-old with a north London accent. She hands him a drink.*

Terry Couldn't you afford a couch?

Joanne Oh, sorry, it folds away into a settee. I weren't expecting to bring anyone back. Come on, give us an hand.

She goes to put the bed back into a settee. **Terry** *stays sitting there.*

Terry No, it's fine.

Joanne Right. It's vodka and orange, it's all I had in.

Terry So what do they call this then?

Joanne According to the letting agency it's a spacious pied-à-terre for a single person or couple in the heart of cosmopolitan Earls Court. But as far as I'm concerned it's a room in a house on the fourth floor with no lift. And as for Earls Court being cosmopolitan, that means that every other person you meet is a queen, a brass, a backpacker, or a nut-nut.

Terry   And what are you?

Joanne   Pissed. Hopefully. The amount you've spent on me tonight.

Terry   But how would you describe yourself?

Joanne   To who?

Terry   In that little list.

Joanne   Well, I aint a queen.

Terry   Are yer a brass?

Joanne   You know exactly what I am, Terry.

Terry   Why d'you think I come back?

Joanne   Why? Well, the way I remember it was, we was having a laugh in the pub with your mate Charlie and us two wanted to keep on drinking.

Terry   He's all right, Charlie.

Joanne   Suppose.

Terry   No he is.

Joanne   Yeah, well, you aint seeing it from my perspective. As soon as a bloke finds out what I do for a living he just can't let it drop. 'You're beautiful! You're too intelligent.' Load of old wank. Whereas you. You spoke to me like I was a human being.

Terry   Fuck, are yeh?

Joanne *smiles.*

Joanne   Come on. Let's make the bed into a couch. I can't get comfy.

Terry   I'm all right.

Joanne   Oh, well, that's all right then.

Terry   Have I missed the last tube?

Joanne   No. Why, d'you want to?

Terry   I like you, Joanne.

Joanne   But?

Terry   I haven't been honest with you.

Joanne   I know you're married.

Terry   No, it's not that.

Joanne   If you miss the last tube there's a cab office downstairs. There's buses all through the night. You're not in Liverpool now.

Terry   You can say that again.

Joanne   I'm not making you stay. (**Terry** *has finished his drink.*) My my, we were thirsty. Care for another?

Terry   Go 'ed then.

Joanne   I love your accent.

Terry   I haven't got an accent. I talk proper me.

Joanne   Yeah, yeah.

Joanne *exits.* **Terry** *gets up and goes and stands at the window. He puts his hand in his pocket and pulls his wallet out. He gets a bundle of money out of the wallet and goes and lays it on the bed. He puts his wallet back in his pocket and goes and stands at the window.* **Joanne** *comes back in with another drink. She hands it to him, then goes and sits on the bed.* **Terry** *remains standing looking out of the window, his back to her.*

Terry   Cheers.

Joanne   So what d'you make of London then?

Terry   S'all right, yeah.

She finds the money on the bed.

Joanne   Terry, you've dropped . . .

Pause.

Terry?

Terry   I don't know how much you charge.

Pause.

I couldn't believe it when I first got here. Every phone box you went in just full of all these cards and numbers. Cards and numbers. Up for a good time? Dial this number. Yeah, I'm up for a good time. But I never had the bottle to dial. So I goes in another box and another box. And I just kept phoning our house. Which is pointless coz they're all away. So I just listen to it ring. And tonight. I goes in another box. Only this time I dial. Some fucking bird with big tits in Bow. I don't even know where Bow is. And she answers. And I hang up.

Joanne *is starting to cry, silently.*

Terry   I'm a shithouse, Joanne. I can't even get that fucking right. So I meets Charlie for a drink and you're there with your mates. And when you say what to do for a living, I'm like . . . Jesus. It's being handed to me on a plate. What am I gonna do? Only I can't even get this right. I'm looking at yer all evening like a moth to a flame. Only when a moth gets to a flame it's two steps forward and ten steps back.

Joanne   Look at me.

Terry   Only moths don't take steps, do they? They fly.

Joanne   Look at me!

Terry   I can't get nothing right!

Joanne   No you can't. Some punter you are if you can't even look at me.

He turns round.

See this? (*She holds the money up.*) I don't want this! I don't want jack shit from you!

She throws the money down on the floor.

Terry   Don't cry, babe.

Joanne   Don't you dare tell me what to do. Jesus, d'you think I brought you back here for . . . Make up your mind, Terry. What am I? An easy lay at the end o'the night? A mate? I'm certainly not Big Tits in Bow.

Terry   Please. Let me fuck yeh. I haven't fucked our Carol in six months.

Joanne   Good. And when was the last time you made love to her?

Terry   I'll make love to you then.

Joanne   D'you wanna know how I'd really describe myself? Stupid. I'm so stupid! I meet blokes like you all the time. You're just like all the rest.

Terry   I'm not.

Joanne   Well, what d'you call that then? You don't have to buy me, Terry. Why d'you have to go and spoil it?

Terry   I'm sorry.

Joanne   But I certainly aint giving it you for free now.

Terry   Can we start again?

Joanne   D'you know what makes me stupid? What makes me really stupid? I don't fancy many people. And tonight. Christ, why didn't I just say I worked in a shop?

Terry   D'you want me to go?

Joanne   Be a fucking man!

Pause.

Terry   What shop d'you work in?

Pause.

Joanne   Boots.

Pause.

Terry   Which counter?

Pause.

Joanne   Rimmel.

Terry   Worked there long?

Joanne   Since I left school.

Pause.

Terry   What's it like?

Joanne   I love it.

She's crying again now. **Terry** *takes her in his arms and kisses her. She responds.*

Terry   I'm sorry.

Joanne   You're a good man, Terry.

Terry   I'm a waste o'fucking space.

Joanne   Bet Carol don't think so.

Terry   You're beautiful.

Joanne   Don't.

They kiss again and fall on to the bed. It looks like they're going to have sex. **Joanne** *undoes* **Terry**'s *belt and starts pulling his jeans down. He panics and tries to pull away from her. She doesn't let him go without a fight. He sits away from her.*

Terry   Leave me alone. Leave me. Don't touch me.

Joanne   It's all right.

Terry   No it's not.

Joanne   You're just pissed.

Terry   I wish I was. I wish that was all it was.

Joanne   Let's just lie here.

Terry   I really do.

Joanne   Well, what is it? Drugs? I don't have that effect on too many people.

Terry (*laughs*)   You haven't got a fucking clue, have yeh?

Joanne   I've only just fucking met you!

Terry   I wouldn't worry. I've known our Carol most o'me fucking life and she doesn't know.

Joanne   What?

Terry   Me.

Joanne   I don't know what you want.

Joanne *tries to push him again. He brushes her off gently.*

Terry   What's that park called near Buckingham Palace?

Joanne   St James?

Terry   I was down there this avvy. And there was this duck there trotting along, with all its baby ducks following behind. Every turn it took the babies followed like a shadow. And he's heading for the lake. Only there's this fence. And he can't get through. He's too big. And he's looking for a gap, only he can't find one. And the babies just follow. And then the babies cotton on and they squeeze through. And he tries and he tries and he's just stuck there, watching the babies. And people are gathering round, tryina help it over. But he spreads his wings out and they can't get hold of him.

Joanne   And?

Terry   What?

Joanne   What happened then?

Terry   I couldn't look any more. That's me. The kids following. Then going on ahead. And you can't do nothing about it. And you're just stuck behind the fence and they're out there swimming. And people are tryina help you. But it's no fucking good.

Joanne   Sorry to disappoint you, Terry, but that duck was probably their mother.

Terry   And if that was our Carol she'da been all right. Let them go on ahead. Not panicking. I nearly lost me lads one day. But she doesn't understand. Coz she wasn't there. What's it gonna take for her to understand?

Joanne   I think you're asking the wrong person. Look. Why don't you stay? We don't have to have sex. Come on, it'll be really expensive in a cab.

He sits there. She takes his shirt off. She presses her glass to his chest to cool him.

Terry   OK.

Joanne   Nightcap?

He nods. **Joanne** *takes his glass and exits.* **Terry** *lies back on the bed. Something under a pillow is making it uncomfortable. He looks underneath it and finds a* Sun *newspaper. He is shocked. He jumps up and starts getting dressed again as* **Joanne** *returns with another drink for him.*

Joanne   What's up?

Terry   You read this crap?

Joanne   For the stocks and shares.

Terry   The lies they printed about Hillsborough.

Joanne   Oh shit.

Terry   D'you know what they said we did? They said we robbed dying kids of their money. Said we pissed on them.

Joanne   I'm sorry.

Terry   Have you ever seen anyone die?

Joanne   Me mum.

Terry   I bet you never robbed her.

Joanne   Terry . . .

Terry   Or pissed on her.

Joanne   Terry, stop it.

Terry   I seen so many people die that day. Right before me eyes. When a Scouser sees that he goes into shock. But Scouse shock doesn't mean you rob or piss on people. We're not an alien nation.

Joanne   I know.

Terry   Yet you still buy this filth?

Joanne   It was a long time ago.

Terry *gives a long pained laugh.*

Terry   And I've just got a scally working-class Liverpool chip.

He stands up.

Terry   Thanks for the drink.

Joanne   Don't I even get a kiss?

Terry   I'll see meself out.

He goes. **Joanne** *lies back on the bed as the lights fade.*

Scene Four

The beach at Tenby.

A few days later. **Marni** *sits in a deckchair on the pebbly beach. She has a summer dress on. There is another deckchair empty next to her.* **Carol** *walks towards her along the beach in a sarong and bikini top, carrying a big straw beach bag.*

Marni   Any sign?

Carol   They've gone out for a walk. I've done something terrible.

Marni   What?

Carol   I went in their caravan when they'd gone.

Marni   Oh, God. Call the police.

Carol   Well, it's a good job I didn't, coz I found this.

She opens her beach bag. **Marni** *pulls out a tin. She opens it and pulls out a joint.*

Marni   Where?

Carol   Is it what I think it is?

Marni   Where was it?

Carol   In our Laurence's toilet bag.

Marni   What were you looking in there for?

Carol   I wanted to see if he'd brought any johnnies.

Marni   And has he?

Carol   Thirty. Oh, what am I gonna say to him?

Marni   Slip it back later and he'll be none the wiser.

Carol   Is it pot?

Marni   One way to find out.

She lights it.

Carol   Marni! What are you doing?

Marni   I think it's skunk.

Carol   Oh, Marni, don't. It's a slippery slope.

Marni   Oh, goway! Queen Victoria used to smoke this stuff all the time.

Carol   Did she?

Marni   Didn't get her itching for a bit o'smack, did it?

Carol   What was wrong with her?

Marni   Nothing. She was always off her tits on this stuff.

Carol   Have you done it before?

Marni   Years back. When I was courting Col's mate Lenny McVitie from the Tate 'n' Lyle.

Carol   You never told me.

Marni   I never told you he tried to give me one up the arse but he did.

Carol   No, you did tell me that.

Marni   Did I?

Carol   You told everyone.

Marni   Will you relax, Carol?

Carol   Some kids out in a dinghy there, look.

Marni   I'll roll another one in a minute, then he won't know we've taken it.

Carol   We?

Pause.

Did you think it was tight of me not to give the kids money for a dinghy yesterday?

Marni   It's fucking good skunk this.

Carol   Just coz everyone else at the site was hiring them.

Marni   Paul McCartney smokes this stuff, you know.

Carol   I'm not made o'money.

Marni   Thirty johnnies? (*Giggles.*)

Carol   You don't think they're at it in the caravan, do you?

Marni   With your Liam front row in the audience? I don't think so.

Carol   I hope to God she's on the Pill. I should ask really. Me of all people.

Marni   They probably nip down here to the beach of a night. I did that when I was their age. (*Lights the joint.*)

Carol   I remember.

Marni   You and Terry in one bed. Me and Charlie in the other. The babies in the carry cots. We were too embarrassed to even kiss in front of yous. I got bruises on me bum from all these pebbles. Charlie used to say, 'It's you, me and the stars, baby.' Like he was Jimmy Cagney or something. He'd lie on top o'me. And he'd just look down into me face like I was the most beautiful thing he'd ever laid eyes on. In awe of me.

Carol   Ah.

Marni   Now we can't have so much as a light on. If there's a chink in the curtains he has to get up and mess about wit them. Can't bear to look at me.

Carol   Marni.

Marni   It's true. He doesn't even kiss me any more. Just sticks it in. When he can find it. And gets on with it. I'm like that: 'Pull me nightie down when you've finished.'

Pause.

Carol   It's hard when you have kids though. Keeping the noise down. Sorry.

Marni   No. I was just thinking. If someone had come to us, when we first come here. When our Colin first found this caravan site. If someone had come to us and said, y'know, in twenty years' time . . . all this is gonna've happened to you. And shown us. I'd never've believed it.

Carol   No.

Marni   And yet. All this has stayed the same. The caravan's still olive green.

Carol   Vile.

Marni   The trees are still there. The sea's still there. Nobody's changed all this. Yet. Some bright spark with a clipboard hasn't gone, 'Ooh, y'know what'd go lovely there? A nice tower block.'

Carol *chuckles.*

Marni   But we've changed.

Carol   Have we? I still feel eighteen. I look at that Gina and wonder why I don't remember her from school. Get a fucking big shock when I look in the mirror.

Marni   I don't think I'll ever be the same again. All them miscarriages. Then Wayne. Wayne loved all this. I'm trying real hard, y'know. To be me normal bubbly self. Not to be mopy. I always knew that one day I'd sit on this beach, and look at that view, and not have him here. I always knew that one day we'd have an extra room gathering dust and not know what to do with his things. And I always knew realistically it'd be during his teens. I just suppose I thought that when I sat in this chair and looked at that view I'd have Charlie with me. Oh, I'm glad you're here. I want you here. I just thought he'd be here too.

Carol   Silly prick.

Marni   He was wrong, my Charlie. It's not me, him and the stars. It's just me. Why haven't I broken down yet, Carol?

Carol   You will.

Marni   What if I don't?

Carol   You will.

Marni   If I didn't know meself better I'd say I was one hard-faced bitch.

Carol   Am I gonna get a drag on that or what?

Marni   Druggie. (*Passes the joint to her.*)

Carol   So? (*Takes a drag.*) D'you think those kids are all right over there?

Marni   Where?

Carol   They're miles away now.

Marni   They're probably local kids. Do it all the time.

Carol   God, it's heavy on your lungs, isn't it?

Marni   That's better.

Carol   Good. I can't remember the last time me and Terry even touched each other.

Marni   I can. A peck on the cheek when he said trar at the train station.

Carol   I feel like some old spinster. I should take up knitting.

Marni   Solitaire.

Carol   And yet. There was this time. We'd been married about a year. And he'd got his first car. You and Charlie babysat for us. And he drove us down to Otterspool Prom. And we made love in one o'them shelters on the front.

Marni (*shocked*)   It's dead open there!

Carol   I was shameless. I was in love. And we got back in the car. All blushes and giggles. And he put the radio on. And this song was playing. And he stuck the car in reverse and he drove me all the way down the Prom, backwards. And when we got to the end, the song finished. And he took my hand and kissed it and said, 'You'll always be my sex goddess.' And I knew he was full o'shite. And I knew we'd never do all that again. And I knew that moment had passed. But I didn't care. Coz we *had* done it. And we *had* driven backwards. And he *had* said it. Daft, isn't it? And I always thought he'd forgotten that. 'Til the week before Hillsborough. We went for a drive out on the Wirral. And we come across this sort of arts and crafts centre. And they had a record sale on, y'know, second-hand tapes and records. And I saw him buying this tape. And he sticks it in me handbag. And he whispers in me ear. 'Track four's for you, sex goddess.' And I looked at the back of the tape, and track four was . . . the John Lennon song 'Woman'. It's what had been on the radio that day. And . . . I felt so daft. Coz I thought only I'd remembered how special that day was. And I was wrong. It'd meant a lot to him too.

Marni   Stop hoggin' the joint.

Carol   I think you better roll another one.

Marni *chuckles. The lights fade.*

Scene Five

A dinghy in the sea.

Laurence, **Gina** *and* **Liam** *are in a dinghy in the middle of the sea. The lads are in trunks and T-shirts.* **Gina** *is in a swimming costume with a T-shirt over the top.* **Laurence** *is rowing with two oars, but having some difficulty.* **Gina** *is smoking.*

Gina   I can see yer ma over there, look.

Laurence   Don't let her see us.

Gina   Scared o'your own mother? Feel ashamed for yeh.

Liam   Is she looking?

Gina   Too busy gasbagging. With that mountain range she calls a friend.

Liam   Don't be vile, you.

Gina   Well, she does my swede in.

Liam   Oh, shut it, you.

Laurence   It's not her fault her son died, is it?

Gina   Not unless she sat on him.

Liam   Er, that's my best mate you're talking about there.

Gina   Well, you've gotto admit, she could do with losing a few pound. You're not peddling fast enough.

Laurence   It's rowing.

Gina   They're made up with the beach them two, they're never off it. K'nell.

Liam   You're made up wit the sound o'your own voice. You use it often enough.

Gina   Well, maybe that's because I know that one day, this country is gonna be listening to it, when I've got me own discussion programme. *The Gina Carmichael Show.* And I tell you one thing, *you'll* never be a guest on it. (*To* **Laurence**.) Yer ma's gettin' smaller, row faster. (*Tuts.*) Feel ashamed.

Liam   Why?

Gina   Eh?

Liam   Why d'you feel ashamed?

Gina   I just do, all right?

Liam   And what d'you feel ashamed of?

Gina   Oh, Laurence, will you tell him? He's doin' my swede in.

Liam   What d'you feel ashamed of?

Gina   You, if you must know.

Liam   You're in the middle o'the fucking sea. There isn't another person for miles. Who is there to feel ashamed in front of?

Gina   The fish. All right?

Liam   Ay, Laurence. Me ma's tiny now.

Gina   I've told him to row faster, he's just ignoring me. What's new?

Laurence   I'm rowing as fast as I can.

Gina   We must be miles away from the shore now coz that Marni one looks like a stick insect.

Liam   What y'doin', Lau'?

Laurence   It's dead hard.

Liam   You'll never have yer own show.

Gina   Wanna bet?

Liam   Yeah, I do.

Gina   Well, let's see the colour o'your money. See? You know I'm right. I met this DJ once from Radio City, and he said I had more than enough to . . . in his words . . . 'make it in this business'.

Liam   The perfect face for radio. (*To* **Laurence**.) Let's have a go.

Gina   Oh my God, where are we?

Laurence   Oh, shut up, woman.

Gina   But . . .

Laurence   Shut up!

Liam   We're drifting out.

Liam *is now having a go at rowing.*

Gina   Y'know what this is, don't yeh? It's karma. I knew we shoulda paid for this dinghy.

Liam   It wasn't my idea to rob it.

Pause.

You have a go.

Gina *takes over the oars.*

Gina   I thought the beach was looking a bit quiet.

Laurence   What are y'tryina say?

Gina   The fucking tide's goin' out, isn't it? And us with it.

Laurence   It was your idea to come out in this fucking dinghy.

Liam   No wonder me ma said we couldn't.

Gina   So it's my fault, is it? Ah, well, fuck y'fuckin' oars then!

She throws the oars into the middle of the boat. **Laurence** *picks them up and rows again.*

I'da tried anything to keep you out o'them woods. Y'dirty bastard. You've had one thing on your mind this holiday. It rhymes with kex, and when you do it, you don't wear 'em. Why d'you think I suggested Liam came an'all. To keep you off me!

Laurence   We could swim back.

Liam   You know I can't swim.

Laurence   I could get in and try and pull the boat back as I'm swimming.

Gina   A cunt y'maybe but I don't want you drowning on me, Laurence.

Liam   What are we gonna do?

Gina   HELP!!!

They all scream 'Help' for a while.

Gina   It's so quiet.

Liam   They say that just before a plane crashes it goes deadly silent.

Laurence   What you sayin' that for?

Gina   There isn't even any seagulls.

Liam   I can still see me mum. MUM!!!!

They all call 'MUM!'

Laurence   We're gonna be all right. She's seen us.

Gina   What's she gonna do? Row out on her friend?

Laurence   Just keep calm.

Liam   She hasn't seen us.

Laurence   She has, look, she's running down the beach.

Liam   Has she?

Gina   What if she's just goin' for an ice cream or something?

They call 'Mum' again.

Gina   What do we do now?

Laurence   Just wait. (*To* **Liam**.) Stop cryin', you.

Liam   I'm not.

Laurence   Y'big pufta.

Liam   Shut up, you.

Gina   He's scared.

Laurence   I'm fuckin' scared but I'm not cryin'!

Pause.

Gina   Scared o'dyin' a virgin?

Laurence   Scared o'dyin' a slut?

Liam   Will yous two stop it?

Laurence   Just coz you're gonna die a virgin.

Liam   We're not gonna die. Me mum's seen us.

Gina   Can't even see her now.

Liam   She'll get help.

Laurence   Little virgin fuckin' cryin'.

Liam   I'm not a virgin, all right?

Laurence   Oh and who've you fuckin' knobbed?

Liam   Mind your own.

Gina   I've heard stories about you.

Liam   I've heard stories about you.

Gina   Off my mate Yosemite who lives by the Backy. She's seen you hanging round with the queer boys of a night. On the mound.

Laurence   Well, she's fuckin' lying then.

Gina   Oh, you go sticking up for him, why don't yeh?

Laurence   She's speaking bollocks, he never even goes out hardly.

Pause.

Liam   Well, I've heard you. In the middle of the night. Stuffing your face. Then making y'self sick.

Pause.

Gina   I think there's something wrong with your hearing, love.

Liam   Don't love me.

Gina   Don't worry, Liam. I'll never love you.

Pause. She sings.
    In my Liverpool home
    In my Liverpool home
    We speak with an accent exceedingly rare
    Meet under a statue exceedingly bare.
    If you want a cathedral, we've got one to spare
    In my Liverpool home.

Laurence   What d'you sing that for?

Liam   Me ma's gonna kill us.

Laurence   I know.

Pause.

Gina (*sings*)
   In my Liverpool home
   In my Liverpool home
   We speak with an accent

Liam (*joining in*)
   exceedingly rare
   Meet under a statue exceedingly bare
   If you want a cathedral, we've got one to spare

Laurence (*joining in*)
   In my Liverpool home.

They start to sing it again. The sound of a helicopter arrives overhead. It starts to drown them out. They look above them and stop singing, happier now. As the lights fade a rope ladder descends towards them from above.

Scene Six

The Fitzgibbons' lounge.

A week later. **Carol**, **Laurence** *and* **Terry** *sitting snugly on the couch watching the television.* **Laurence** *is in the middle.*

Carol   Not seeing Gina tonight?

Laurence   No.

Carol   Seeing her tomorrow?

Laurence   At work.

Carol   What about in the evening?

Laurence   I've got a driving lesson.

Terry   I suppose we should be grateful we don't have to listen to her wittering on about Ricki bloody Lake.

Carol   Oh, you should've heard her at the caravan, Terry. Every day we got a detailed description of what Ricki eats for breakfast, what Ricki eats for tea, or rather what she doesn't eat.

Laurence   I don't think she'll be happy 'til she's licked Ricki Lake out.

Carol   Don't be disgusting! Oh, that's horrible!

Laurence *and* **Terry** *are laughing.*

Terry   You dirty bastard!

Carol   Don't encourage him, you! You're as bad as each other! Eugh! God, I've got a really vivid picture in me head now.

Laurence (*about a woman on telly*)   She's a dyke.

Carol   Who?

Laurence   Her.

Terry   No she's not. Is she?

Carol   Is she, Lau'?

Laurence   Yeah.

Carol   No she's not. She's married to thingy. Him off what d'you call it. Shite thing wit vets.

Laurence   Nah, it just looks like her.

Carol   God, I wish you hadn't said that about Ricki Lake. Is she lesbian?

Laurence   Dunno. Probably.

The doorbell rings twice.

Carol   That's Marni's ring.

Laurence   She's another one.

Carol   You can answer the door for that.

She laughs as he leaves the room.

He's got a filthy mind on him. Aren't you shocked?

Terry (*not convincing*) Yeah.

Carol Yeah, thought you might be.

Terry He's got a fucking brilliant sense of humour, our Laurence.

Marni *and* **Laurence** *re-enter.* **Laurence** *slumps back on the sofa,* **Marni** *sits in an armchair.*

Carol Hiya, Marni love. (*To* **Laurence**.) Switch that off.

Laurence I'm watching it.

Carol Well, turn it down then. Ah are yer all excited, love? Got your Charlie coming home from the Big Smoke. Ah, are y'cooking him a nice tea?

Marni No.

Carol Are yous getting a Chinese? Spend his money.

Marni I'm a cooking a nice tea, but he's not having any.

Carol Why? What's happened?

Marni Not unless I stick it in a Jiffy bag and post it to him in London. Waste o'good food.

Carol Don't tell me! He's pissed in a bar and he's missed his train.

Marni No.

Carol Marni, what?

Marni He's staying down there another week.

Carol Goway!

Marni Bastard.

Carol Why?

Marni They didn't get all the work done what with Terry coming back early so it's gonna take them longer. So he says.

Carol Don't you believe him?

Marni I wanna believe him.

Terry It's possible.

Carol Terry knows, y'know.

Marni My brother is employing him as a favour. My brother would willingly pay him ten million quid and let him come home tonight.

Carol Oh, have your tea with us.

Marni No, I've got enough food to sink a battleship.

Carol The money'll be good, love.

Marni Who's side are you on?

Terry She's not on anyone's side.

Carol I'm on her side!

Laurence Has he squared it with work up here?

Marni Compassionate leave.

Carol Maybe he wants some space. I don't mean from you.

Marni Well, who from then?

Carol From his head.

Marni And what about me? I'm sick to death of space. I had a beach full of space in Tenby. I've got four walls and two floors of space through there. I need him here with me. That house has been empty for ages. Wayne only had about a week in his own bed the last six months. It's like nothing's changed. I get me coat on and me bus fare out and I get to the door and I look out to the bus stop and it's only then I remember. I can't go the hospital. I need Charlie here to make it real.

Carol Oh fuckin'ell.

Marni   It's not too much to ask, is it?

Carol   No, it's not, Marni.

Terry   He's an arlarse, Marni.

Marni   Terry. I want you to be honest wit me now. Has he met someone else?

Carol   Don't be daft.

Marni   Has he?

Terry   No.

Marni   Swear on your Laurence's life.

Terry   I swear to yeh, Marni, no. I don't know what he's playin' at.

Carol   Marni, I'm quite sure.

Marni   I wouldn't blame him. I mean, look at me.

Carol   You're gorgeous, you.

Marni   I was once. Didn't realise it at the time. Now when I look at photos of meself when I was twenty I think, 'God, girl, you really had something.' Now I see a camera and I run a mile.

Carol   I'll kill that fuckin' Charlie. It's him that's made you feel like this. He doesn't know how lucky he is.

Marni   Well, I'm making lamb tonight if anyone fancies it. Roast potatoes, carrots, turnips, sprouts, mint sauce.

Carol   Oh, sounds gorgeous, count us in.

Marni   Diet starts tomorrow.

Carol   D'you fancy some o'that, Laurence?

Laurence   Yeah. You're a cracking cook, Marni.

Carol   And it better be dripping in fat or there'll be murders!

Marni   I'm so jealous o'you sometimes, y'know.

Carol   Oh, shut up.

Marni   I look at yous two and I'm green. You've got the kids. You've got each other. You've got a gorgeous figure, Carol.

Carol   D'you want a hand peeling the spuds?

Marni   And d'you know what the worst thing is? I know that in a week's time he's gonna ring up and say he's got to do another week.

Carol   Come on.

Marni   Will your Liam want to eat?

Carol   I suppose so. He's out walking Mrs R's dog.

Marni (*suddenly illuminating*)   I knew there was something I had to tell you!

Carol   What?

Marni   Guess who I got speaking to in the Asda today?

Carol   Who?

Marni   Mrs Raymond. Can she talk for England or what? Well, you know you say your Liam's walking her dog right now?

Carol   Yeah. He does it most nights.

Marni   Well, I don't know whether he is actually.

Carol   You what?

Marni   I'm pushing some serious trolley round the Asda, getting all the bits in for arlarse's tea. When who should corner me in Home Bake but her.

Carol   Mrs Raymond?

Marni   I give her a quick nod, but you know how I've got one of those faces that people feel they can just gab at?

Carol   Did you give her an inch and she took a mile?

Marni   She goes, 'Scuse me, love, but don't you live next door to that nice Liam Fitzgibbon?' I goes, 'So?' coz, you know, I'm tryina get the tea in for *him*. She goes, 'Could you give him this?' (*Gets a tenner out of her pocket.*)

Carol   Bloody'ell.

Laurence   Bastard!

Marni   I felt like saying, 'Give it him yourself, love. Who d'you think I am? The Royal Mail?' but then I caught sight of her zimmer frame and thought, anything to help an elderly neighbour . . . you know.

Carol   Oh, isn't that lovely? Oh, he'll be made up with that.

Marni   I haven't finished yet! Then she goes, 'I wanna thank him for making Judy's final days so special.'

Carol   Judy the dog?

Marni   Can you believe it?

Carol   It's dead?

Marni   Well, by this stage I'm thinking she's a bit barmy Miss Babs, so I goes, 'Let's get this straight, love. You're telling me that your dog is no longer with us?' She goes, 'Didn't Liam say? Run over on the bypass Tuesday last.' Then she bursts out crying. I had to leave me shopping where it was and help her to a cup o'tea in Beryl's Pantry. I got that fucking dog's life history. I felt like saying, 'Listen, love, I don't know what you see when you're twitching at your nets morning, noon and night, but I happened to have buried me son two months back.'

Terry   The dog can't be dead, he's walking it right now.

Marni   Did you know the dog was blind?

Carol   No.

Marni   No. Neither did her from 34. She took the dog out while we were in Tenby, let it off the lead and, next thing you know . . .

Carol   So where's our Liam been going?

Marni   Spuds?

Carol   Wait 'til I get my hands on him.

The phone goes. **Laurence** *answers it.*

I'll ring his bloody neck.

Laurence (*on phone*)   Hello? Who is it? Hang on.

Carol   Who is it?

Laurence *shrugs as he hands her the phone.*

Carol   Hello? Speaking. Which station? I'll come and collect him.

She puts the phone down.

Terry   Who was that?

Carol   Police.

Terry   What?

Carol   Liam's been arrested.

Terry   Eh?

Marni   What for?

Laurence   Fuckin'ell.

Carol   They said they'd tell me when I got there.

Marni   Terry, drive her.

Carol   I'm all right.

Terry   I'll walk you.

Carol   I'll go on me own.

Terry   Sure?

Carol   You wait here. I'll phone you when I get there, let you know what's going on. Where's me bag?

Marni   No, Carol, someone should go with yeh.

Carol   Still jealous?

Marni   Come on.

The women exit.

Terry   What's all that about?

Laurence   Dad?

Blackout.

Scene Seven

The same, two hours later. **Laurence** *is looking out of the window.* **Terry** *is sitting staring into space in the armchair. The telly is on.* **Laurence** *suddenly hurries back to the couch. The front door goes.* **Liam** *comes in.* **Carol** *follows with a brolly, putting it down.* **Liam** *sits on the couch.* **Marni** *follows on behind. They all stay there in silence.* **Laurence** *breaks it.*

Laurence   You all right?

Liam *shrugs.*

Marni   Listen, I'll get the tea on.

Carol   No, stay, Marni.

Carol *is annoyed that* **Terry** *hasn't said anything. She switches the telly off, stands behind his chair and pushes it round so that he has to look at* **Liam**.

Terry   What did they say?

Laurence   Are they going to prosecute?

Pause.

Liam   Got let off with a caution.

Pause.

Terry   Well, that's good, isn't it?

Marni   That's what I said.

Terry   He's not been right since Hillsborough.

Laurence   This has got nothing to do with Hillsborough, Dad!

Marni   Look, I should go.

Terry   That put yer off y'footy.

Laurence   It's got fuck all to do with that!

Carol   Don't you swear at your father.

Liam   It's to do wit me.

Carol   Oh, so yer enjoy it, do yeh?

Pause.

Marni   I'll give yer a knock later.

Terry   Yeah, always sticking your fucking oar in.

Carol   Ay, you! She's more use to me than you are!

Liam   I never enjoyed footy.

Terry   Yes you did.

Marni   I'm not standing for this.

Liam   Stay, Marni!

Terry   You used to love football!

Liam   I never!

Terry   Yes you did! I used to take you up that Backy and have a kickabout and you loved it!

Liam   I just enjoyed spending time with you! I didn't care what I was doing!

Terry   Your face in the car down to Sheffield.

Laurence   For Christ's sake, our Liam's been doing it with fellas up the back field of a night. That's what this is about! Not football.

Carol   It's about him lying through his back teeth about walking some arl woman's dog.

Marni   Dead dog.

Liam   You know then.

Terry   Why did you do it, son?

Carol   At last!

Terry   Why did you do it?

Liam   Dunno.

Terry   Eh?

Laurence   Coz he enjoyed it probably.

Carol   Stop tryina help him out, you.

Liam   What's so wrong with that?

Carol   You're sixteen years of age! That's what's wrong with that!

Laurence   You fucking hypocrite!

Terry   Ay! Less of the swearing!

Laurence   Well, you were pregnant with me when you were his age!

Marni   That was an accident!

Liam   So he was an accident, was he?

Terry   No!

Laurence   Well, thanks a fucking bunch!

Carol   We weren't flying in the face of nature.

Marni   Yeah, your mother certainly didn't go traipsing round the Backy having it off with lezzies, did she?

Laurence I dunno, do I?

Carol You cheeky bastard!

Marni You're a bright lad!

Laurence D'you have to be thick to be queer?

Terry He's not fucking queer!

Liam Aren't I?

Pause.

Marni Jesus Joseph and Mary.

Carol (*to* **Terry**) This is your fault, coz you weren't strong enough as a father.

Marni Yeah!

Terry Ay, what's it got to do with you?

Carol Stop having a go at her!

Terry Take a look in your own backyard first!

Marni Meaning what?

Pause.

Meaning what?

Liam No one did this to me.

Laurence There's nothing wrong with him. You gotta stop using Hillsborough as an excuse.

Terry I don't.

Carol At least he's got an excuse.

Liam He hasn't though.

Laurence He doesn't need an excuse!

Liam We're both alive.

Marni (*to* **Terry**) You fucking bastard!

Terry   Well, your Charlie spotted it years back!

Liam   You thought you'd lost us.

Marni   He never! He woulda told me!

Terry   I'm not surprised he hasn't come back!

Liam   You thought you'd lost us but yer hadn't.

Marni   Our Wayne was the nicest lad on this planet!

Carol   What are you gonna do, Terry?

Liam   We never died!

Terry (*to* **Carol**)   D'you want me to go mad? Kick him out? What is it you want, Carol?

Carol   Oh, since when has it mattered what I want?

Liam (*a roar*)   Will somebody just fucking listen to me?!

They all go quiet.

Liam   Please.

Carol   Well, say something then.

Marni *has broken down crying.*

Terry   I heard him. Yous all think I just sit here in me own little world. But I hear you. All of yous.

Laurence (*pointing out* **Marni**'*s distress*)   Mum.

Terry   You've hit the nail on the head, Li'. I thought I'd lost yous and I hadn't. And I vowed to meself that day that I wasn't gonna fucking lose yous if I could help it. So I won't be kicking no one out.

Carol   I'm not saying kick him out.

Liam   I'm sorry.

Laurence   Don't fucking apologise, Li'.

Terry   But I'll be fucked if you think you're going that Backy again.

Carol   Hallelujah!

Liam   You can't stop me.

Terry   D'you wanna bet?

Marni   Liam, you can't.

Liam   I bet Wayne would.

Carol   Liam, I think you better get to bed.

Liam   Oh, I'm sick o'living in this house.

Terry   Eh?

Carol   You what?

Laurence   You're not the only one, mate.

Liam   Living under your roof and his cloud.

Carol   I think it's your bedtime actually, Liam.

Liam   April comes and he's depressed.

Carol   Get to bed.

Liam   Can't bear the truth in this house. That's why you're always getting me to shut up.

Liam *goes to leave the room.*

Terry   Come back, you. Got something to say, Liam? Then say it.

Liam   You feel guilty.

Terry   Eh?

Liam   You blame the police. You blame the *Sun*. You blame everyone but yourself.

Terry   So Hillsborough was my fault, was it?

Liam   No!

Laurence   Let him finish. Jesus.

Liam   And . . . not getting over it. It's like you are blaming yourself.

Carol   Oh, I've had enough of this.

Laurence   That's precisely what he's saying, Mum. Open your gob in this house and someone has to jump down it.

Liam   And that's what they want. The police. The *Sun*. You slag them off to anyone who'll listen, Dad, and I know why.

Terry   Coz they're fucking bastards, the lot of them.

Liam   No. Coz you've let them get to you. Coz you were scared.

Terry   So?

Liam   And you tried to get out that cage. And when you did you stood on a kid. And you feel you killed him.

Pause.

Terry   I did.

Liam   Dad, you never. I never. He never. They did.

Terry   I did.

Marni   No you never, Terry.

Terry   Will you fucking shut it?

Pause.

Liam   And you think me ma doesn't understand coz she wasn't there. Well, where were you in Tenby, Dad? You'da seen she understood then.

Terry   I came as soon as I could!

Carol   Don't bring that up.

Laurence   Why not?

Carol   Just don't!

Laurence   Why not?

Liam   I thought you were going to kill us in Tenby, Mum. But you never.

Carol   Drop it!!

Terry   Carol?

Carol   Just drop it, Terry.

Marni   D'you wanna ciggie, Carol?

Carol   Do I? Do I? What do I want? I dunno what I want any more. I don't want this. But I've got it. I don't want to feel like me heart's about to explode but I've got it. I don't want you thinking I don't know me arse from me elbow but I've got it.

Terry   I don't think that!

Carol   And d'you know something else, son? You're right. I do know how your father feels, and d'you know what? It's sick. It's scary. And it frightens the living daylights out of me. All I ever wanted was a nice home, good kids, and enough money to see us through. Not much to ask, is it? I can't even manage that. Coz every now and again something comes along and smacks me round the face. I don't know what it is. But it says: You stupid cow. How dare you want that? I'm gonna take your kids away from you. Your nice home. That fella who said he loved you. I'm gonna take that all away from you coz you're a stupid bitch to want it in the first place.

Pause.

Marni   I want Wayne.

Liam   I'm sorry. About tonight. The Backy. I'm sorry.

Carol   Bed.

Liam *exits.*

Marni   I want Wayne!

She runs from the room.

Carol   Yous two are thick as thieves all of a sudden.

Laurence   Ah, I'm going to bed.

Carol   What for? So you can take some drugs?

Laurence   I'm surprised I'm not a smackhead having you as a mother.

Laurence *exits.* **Carol** *runs to the door.*

Carol   You cheeky little bastard! (*To* **Terry**.) Are you just gonna sit there and let him talk to me like that?

Pause.

Well, are yeh?

Suddenly **Terry** *jumps up out of his seat, he rushes to the door.*

Terry   Ay, you! Get back in here. I said get back in here! And you an' all, Liam!

Laurence *re-enters, closely followed by* **Liam**.

Terry   Got something to say to your mother, Laurence?

Laurence   She's the one who was kickin' off.

Terry   Have you got something to say to your mother, Laurence?

Laurence   But . . .

Terry *smacks* **Laurence** *round the face. It stuns him. Pause.*

Laurence   I'm sorry.

Terry   Open your fuckin' mouth!

Laurence   I'm sorry.

Terry   Say it like you fucking mean it!

Laurence (*yells*)   I'm fuckin' sorry!! All right?!

Terry   Up them stairs.

Laurence *exits.* **Liam** *is cowering.*

Terry   And you? D'you know how it feels to get a phone call from the police? Oh no, didn't think about that before you went off gallivanting, did yeh?

Liam   I've said I'm sorry. I am. And I'm sorry I said that about Wayne to Marni. But it's the truth. Wayne was me best mate. I knew him better than any of yous.

Terry   OK, OK, your mother's been through enough for one night. But bear in mind you're grounded.

Liam   How long for?

Terry   Till I say. Now up them stairs. And if I were you I'd be saying your prayers.

Liam   Marni's locked herself in the bog.

Liam *exits.* **Carol** *sits down.*

Terry   Give us one o'them.

She gives him a cigarette. He lights it up and they both sit there a while, smoking.

Carol   I better get up there and get her out.

Terry   Give her five minutes.

Pause.

Carol   What?

Terry   Is that how you feel?

Pause.

When was the last time that car was used?

Carol   I dunno. Monday? Frankie from the Heights took Laurence out for a lesson.

Terry   So there's petrol in it?

Carol   I dunno. I suppose so. Why?

Terry   Streets'll be quiet this time o'night.

Carol   Don't tell me you're gonna get behind the wheel o'that car. You'll be too scared o'knockin' some insomniac toddler over.

Terry   Come here, you.

Carol   Why should I?

Terry   Coz I'm yer husband and I say so.

Carol   It doesn't suit you, Terry.

Terry   Carol. For once in my life I'm fucking trying!

She gets up and goes over to him.

Closer.

She steps closer. He pulls her to him. He snogs the face off her. His hands are all over her.

Carol   Bloody'ell.

Terry   Get your coat.

Carol (*she still has it on*)   Are you blind?

Terry   The crap'll still be here when we get back.

He goes to the sideboard. He gets a tape out. He throws it to her.

Catch!

Carol   What's this?

Terry   Sounds.

Carol   John Lennon?

Terry   Where are the keys?

Carol   On the hook in the hall. Where they always are.

Terry   Come 'ed then.

Carol   Where are you takin' me?

Terry   Where d'you think?

He holds the door open for her and she goes out. He follows. Presently we hear the front door go. **Laurence** *comes down from upstairs and runs into the lounge and looks out of the window. Off, we hear* **Terry** *trying to start up the car.*

Laurence   Liam! Liam! Look out the window!

Outside, the car won't start.

Liam! Liam! Are yer awake?

Liam *appears in the doorway. He's got a coat on and he's packed a sports bag.* **Laurence** *is quite shocked.*

Laurence   Have you seen this?

Liam *stays where he is. Outside, we hear the car start up and then drive off.* **Laurence** *looks back.*

Laurence   Where are yeh goin'?

Liam   Never you mind.

Laurence   D'you need some money?

Liam   Please.

Laurence   Tenner do yeh?

Liam *nods.* **Laurence** *gets a tenner out of his pocket and gives it to him.*

Laurence   It's mad, isn't it?

Liam   I know. Tar.

Laurence   Well, if you're going, go. Marni'll be back down in a minute.

Liam   Why you being so nice to me?

Laurence   If I was being nice I'da give yeh twenty.

Liam *goes to the door.*

Laurence   Are yeh goin' off wit one o'them fellas?

Liam   Dunno yet.

Laurence   Was you and Wayne?

Liam   No.

Laurence   I don't know nothing about this, all right?

Liam   Yeah. See you, Laurence.

Laurence   See you, Li'.

Liam   Thanks. For the money.

Laurence *looks out of the window.* **Liam** *exits. The front door goes.* **Laurence** *watches* **Liam** *walk down the street. He gets a cigarette out and lights up. As he smokes, 'Woman' by John Lennon starts to play and the lights begin to fade.* **Laurence** *is keeping watch at the window, occasionally dragging on the cigarette.*

Hushabye Mountain

Hushabye Mountain was first performed at the Lyceum Theatre, Crewe, on 3 February 1999. This was followed by a national tour. The cast was as follows:

Beryl/Judy/Julie Andrews/ Virgin Mary/Bird Woman	Elizabeth Estensen
Connor/Attendant	Stuart Laing
Danny/Priest	Andrew Lincoln
Lana/Spirit of Esther Finnegan/ Attendant	Rose Keegan
Lee/Sister Bernadette/ Dead Person	David Kennedy
Ben/Kevin/Dead Person	Nick Bagnall

Directed by Paul Miller
Designed by Jackie Brooks
Lighting by Andy Phillips
Music by Terry Davies

Characters

Danny May, *thirty, a waiter from Liverpool who has recently died from an AIDS-related illness.*
Connor Bond, *late twenties, Londoner. Danny's boyfriend.*
Lee Bond, *early thirties, Connor's brother. A cycle courier.*
Lana Bond, *thirty. Liam's middle-class wife. A red-haired, anxious PR assistant.*
Beryl May, *fifty. Danny's mum.*
Ben, *twenty-three, northern gardener and part-time actor. Diagnosed HIV-positive in his late teens.*
Judy Garland, *a dark-haired actress and singer who could be thirty or sixty. Currently employed as the Keeper of the Stars in Heaven.*
Kevin, *early twenties, Glaswegian. Beryl's nurse.*
Julie Andrews, *a hotel chambermaid with exquisite diction.*
The Virgin Mary, *a chain-smoking Irish celebrity mum.*
Sister Bernadette, *an elderly deaf nun.*
Priest
Spirit of Esther Finnegan, *a stern primary school teacher.*
Bird Woman, *a character from* Mary Poppins.
Two Pearly Gates Attendants
Two Dead People, *recent arrivals in heaven.*

This can be achieved with six actors with the following doubling:
Actor 1: Beryl, Judy, Julie Andrews, Virgin Mary, Bird Woman.
Actor 2: Connor, Pearly Gates Attendant.
Actor 3: Danny, Priest.
Actor 4: Lana, Spirit of Esther Finnegan, Pearly Gates Attendant.
Actor 5: Lee, Sister Bernadette, Dead Person.
Actor 6: Ben, Kevin, Dead Person.

Act One

Scene One

Pearly Gates.

As the lights start to dim, 'Feed the Birds (Tuppence a bag)' from
Mary Poppins *starts to play. We listen to it in darkness for a bit
then a light falls on the* **Bird Woman**, *dressed in Edwardian rags,
sitting with bags of crumbs. Whereas in the film she was head to toe in
black, she is now in the same apparel, but it is all in white. The light
spreads and we are in the clouds. As the song progresses, we become
aware of a grand pair of silver gates behind her. Two people appear at
them, the* **Pearly Gates Attendants**. *One has a clipboard, the
other guards a silver clothes rail from which hang three pairs of wings
on coat hangers. The attendants are dressed in all-white imperial
robes, and have white hair.*

*Downstage, a queue of three people enter. They are dressed in white
hospital operating gowns. At the end of the queue is* **Danny**. *They
stand and wait. The clipboard* **Attendant** *nods and one by one,
slowly, they approach the* **Bird Woman**, *hand her a silver coin and
she hands them a bag. They each put a hand in their bag and sprinkle
the contents in the air. Instead of crumbs, it is silver sparkly angel dust.
They then approach the gates where they are ticked off on the list by one
of the* **Attendants**. *The second* **Attendant** *then puts on their
angel wings and they pass through the gates and into heaven.*

Danny *is looking behind him and almost misses his turn. They nod
to him to come. He repeats what the others have done, thoroughly
enjoying it. As he stands at the gates he looks back and smiles at the*
Bird Woman, *who smiles back. He then goes in. The lights fade.*

Scene Two

Psychiatric hospital.

Beryl May *sits at a table cutting star shapes out of silver card. She is wearing a hospital gown with a bedjacket over it.* **Kevin**, *a nurse, enters and is immediately annoyed.*

Kevin   Who said you could wear a bedjacket, Beryl? Personal items of clothing are banned in the art room coz of the scissors. (*He is brusquely stripping* **Beryl** *of her bedjacket.*) It just has to be one little nick and the next thing you know you've got relatives shouting abuse. Now I'm not confiscating it. I'm just taking it away. (*Beckons to the door.*) Come in!

Connor *enters with a bunch of flowers.*

Kevin   Now we've got a visitor for you, Beryl. He's called Connor. You remember Connor?

Connor   Oright, Mrs May?

Kevin   You won't get any sense out of her. She hasn't spoken for two years.

Connor   I know.

Beryl *pushes all the star shapes on to the floor.*

Kevin   Now was there really any need for that? (*He's down on his hands and knees picking them up.*)

Connor   Oright, Mrs May? Bought you these. (*Holds out flowers.*)

Kevin   Oh, isn't that fantastic, Beryl? Flowers.

He puts them on the table. **Beryl** *looks at them.*

Connor   Making Christmas decorations in September? Aren't they confused enough?

Kevin   Even sane people start early these days.

Beryl *starts to convulse.*

Kevin   Oh, Jesus Christ, she's having . . .

Connor   Mrs May?!

Kevin   Some sorta . . .

Connor   What is it?

Kevin   Oh, maybe not.

Connor   Is she all right?

Kevin   Beryl? Beryl?

The fit ends. **Beryl** *opens her eyes.*

You put the fear o'God in me then, Beryl.

Connor   Oright, Mrs May?

Kevin   It's Connor.

Beryl *speaks with an American accent.*

Beryl   Connor?

Kevin   Fuck me, she spoke. Have a Rolo. (*Gives her a Rolo out of her pocket. To* **Connor**.) You gottie reward good behaviour, see. Careful with your teeth there, Beryl.

Beryl   Beryl? What kind of a name is that?

Kevin   It's your name.

Connor   She's speaking with an American accent.

Kevin   Oh, it'll be that thing they taught us at night school.

Connor   But she's from Liverpool!

Beryl   I am here, you know.

Kevin   Echolalia. See, reruns of *Hart to Hart* were on in the day room.

Beryl   Stop looking at me like that.

Kevin   That's American, isn't it?

Connor   Oright, Mrs May?

Kevin   Coz they've got a dog called Freeway.

Beryl   Boy, can he talk for England or what?

Kevin   Which is American for motorway.

Beryl   Yes we know what a fuckin' freeway is, mister!

Kevin   Och, well, that's charming, eh? It took me two buses to get here, and I'm only voluntary.

Connor   Well, at least you're speaking today, eh?

Beryl   Sometimes I don't speak? That's too bad.

Connor   Why are you . . . speaking like that?

Kevin   Echolalia.

Beryl   How do you mean?

Connor   Well, with that accent.

Kevin   Echolalia. The illness of repetition.

Beryl   Well, you beat me hands down on that score.

Connor   It's great . . . that you're finally talking. It's brilliant.

Beryl   You're Daniel's friend, aren't you?

Connor   Yeah.

Beryl (*gets up*)   That's what we said in the vaudeville days. 'Oh, that's his friend.' Backstage, the choreographer. His friend hovering on opening night. 'Who's the guy in the double-breasted suit, Susie?' 'That's Peter's friend.' The nasty people in box office said that daddy had a friend. (*To* **Kevin**.) Don't believe a word of it. (**Kevin** *looks flummoxed. To* **Connor**.) You and me have to talk. I am not Daniel's mother. Do you understand me?

Kevin   Well, who the hell are you, then?

Beryl   Let's just say . . . I'm in showbusiness.

Connor   Oh, fuckin'ell.

Kevin   I knew it was a bad idea to let them watch *Stars In Their Eyes*. Maggie over there thinks she's Cher.

Beryl   I am not Cher!

Kevin (*shouts offstage*)   Put some clothes on, Maggie!

Beryl   Did Cher traipse from New York to the City of Angels with nothing to keep her from starvation but her mother's promises of fame? A thousand dreams in a travelling trunk. An agent's address on the back of a cigarette box. My poor sisters' faces when the agent said it was me who had it. Me they wanted. Me who'd make it.

Connor   Mrs May. Please. Sit down.

Beryl   I am not Daniel's mother.

Connor   Maybe I should go.

Beryl   No!

Connor   She don't even know who I am.

Beryl   You're Connor! Daniel's friend!

Connor   I was his boyfriend!

Kevin *looks shocked.*

Connor (*to* **Kevin**)   What?!

Kevin   I didn't say a word.

Beryl   Yes, they say that, don't they? These days. Oh, he's my . . . boyfriend. 'Who's this?' 'My boyfriend.'

Connor   I'll get off.

Beryl   My body is being inhabited by the spirit of another. Say you believe me. You don't.

Connor   Look, I dunno.

Beryl   Do you?

Connor   Well, yeah.

Beryl   Good. Coz there's not much time. (*To* **Kevin**, *about flowers.*) Honey? I think these need a drink.

Kevin *tuts, takes the flowers and scissors, then heads for the exit. As he does he calls to someone, off.*

Kevin   Maggie! Maggie! Put that hairbrush down!

He exits. Off, we hear Maggie burst into a gutsy rendition of 'Gypsies, Tramps and Thieves'. **Connor** *and* **Beryl** *look off.*

Beryl   She used to be an embalmer. It's very sad.

We hear a slap offstage, then Maggie is silent.

Connor *sits down.*

Beryl   Don't be blue.

Connor   You said we needed to talk.

Beryl   I don't like people being sad.

Connor   Yeah, well. You don't always get what you want, do you.

Beryl   I have news of Daniel.

Connor   What?

Beryl (*touching* **Connor**'s *face*)   Such pretty skin.

Connor   Have you been hearing voices? In your head?

Beryl   If that's what makes you happy, think that.

Connor   You've been talking to him?

Beryl   I know it sounds stupid.

Connor (*fighting tears*)   Has a medium been round or somin?

Beryl   Are you ready to listen to me?

Connor *nods.*

Blackout. 'Northern Lights' by Renaissance plays, leading us into the next scene.

Scene Three

Hotel bedroom.

Lana *in wedding dress and veil,* **Lee** *in morning suit. They're standing by the door to the bathroom.* **Connor** *has locked himself inside, crying.* **Lana**'s *veil is back.* **Lee**'s *holding a drink.*

Lana   Don't cry, poppet!

Connor (*off*)   He should be here! He should fucking well be here!

Lee   Come out here and have some of your drink.

Connor (*off*)   Go back to the party!

Lee   Should I get my mum?

Connor (*off*)   Why d'you have to play that record?

Lee   Weren't me or Lana running up to the DJ's box, was it? I seem to remember it was you. You asked for it. Probably because you knew you'd end up like this. You big drama queen.

Lana   That's not very helpful, Lee.

Lee   Well, it's my wedding day, all right?

Connor (*off*)   He'd've wanted to be here coz he fucking loved you two.

Lana   Please come out, Connor.

Connor (*off*)   Your big day and what do I do?

Lee   Fuck it up.

Connor (*off*)   You should be downstairs.

Lee   I know we should be downstairs, but it's a little bit tricky at the moment.

Lana   Come out of the closet!

Lana *and* **Lee** *laugh.*

Connor (*off*)   Don't be homophobic.

Lana   I could ask them to play 'YMCA'?

Lee   Come on, babe. Leave him.

Connor (*off*)   Yeah. I ain't committing suicide or nothing.

Lana   I've got some coke in my going-away bag.

The bathroom door opens and **Connor** *stands there, his face wet with tears. He too is dressed in a morning suit.*

Connor   Chop us a line out then.

Lee   No! That's for tonight.

Lana   Just do it!

During the following, **Lee** *finds the coke and chops three lines on a mirror.*

Connor   I'll be all right in a minute.

Lana   Look on it as the best man's present.

Connor   I'd expect a gram for that.

Lee   You are. You're a big fat drama queen. I told you to steer clear of the gin. Maudlin cunt.

Lana   Come on. (*Hugs* **Connor**.)

Connor (*crying again*)   Seeing all those people down there looking at me with fucking sympathy or disgust. I'll be all right in a minute. And then this stupid story come in my head.

Lee   I didn't see no one looking at you in disgust.

Connor   He'd been to Blackpool for the illuminations. He was only about eight or somin. Back at school his teacher said, 'Danny May. Where would you find the aurora borealis, better known as the northern lights?' Well, it was a doddle for him, weren't it? And he said, 'Blackpool, miss. We've just spent a weekend looking at 'em.' (*Cries.*) D'you know what his teacher said?

Lee   Does it matter?

Lana   Yes.

Connor   She said, 'You've never seen the northern lights and you never will.' And the bitch was right. What time is it?

Lee   Why?

Lana   Calm down.

Lee   Five past fucking seven, all right?

Connor   One minute I think I'm OK. I kept it together through the service and then.

Lee   Sniff up, we're in the country. (*Passes him the mirror.*)

Connor   Best man. Best man at making a cunt of himself.

Lana   You haven't.

Connor (*does his line*)   This is supposed to be your day.

Lee   Right an'all.

Lana   Well, it's everybody's day really. Getting married . . . hold my veil back . . . (**Lee** *holds her veil back as she snorts her line.*) it's public affirmation . . . (*Sniff.*) of our love . . . (*Sniff.*) so in order for it to be public . . . (*Sniff.*) that involves everybody. (*Dabs the rest.*)

There is a knock at the door.

Who is it?

Lee   It's me mum. Hide the charlie.

Lana   Hello?

Ben (*off*)   Is Connor in there?

Connor   Oh, fuck.

Lee   Who is it?

Connor/Ben (*off*)   Ben.

Connor   Hang on! (*To* **Lee**.) He's all right.

Lana   Have we met him?

Connor   I invited him down for the do.

Lee   Hurry up.

Connor *lets* **Ben** *in. He is dressed in overalls and carries a sports bag.*

Connor   Oright?

Ben   Hiya.

They peck cheeks.

You oright?

Connor   Fine. Er . . . This is Ben. This is me brother Lee.

Lee   Oright, mate? (*Snorts his coke.*)

Connor   And my now sister-in-law Lana.

Lana   Hello, Ben.

Ben   How'd it go?

Lee   Woulda been all right if this prat hadna kept bursting into tears every five seconds. D'you want some o'this?

Ben   I wouldn't say no. Thanks. Sorry bout the way I look.

Lee   You ain't that ugly.

Ben   I've come straight from work.

Lana   Oh, what do you do?

Connor   Ben works for the Royal London Borough of Kensington and Chelsea.

Ben   Parks and gardens department.

Lana   I love topiary. All that greenery. Just out there, sort of, I dunno, nature, isn't it? You can get those really tiny trees, can't you?

Ben   Bonsai.

Lana   They're fantastic, aren't they? They're just like, sort of, gardens for . . . really tiny people. What was that film?

Lee   Which one?

Lana   With those really little tiny people in it.

Connor   *The Borrowers.*

Lana   That was great, wasn't it? Although we didn't see it at the pictures, we saw it on the video, so the effects weren't as startling. What were we talking about?

Ben *snorts a line.*

Ben   Cheers. Better jump in the shower then get changed. I'll see yous all downstairs for a lambada, yeah?

Lana   Yeah, we could sort of talk about gardening and stuff.

Connor (*giving him the key*)   It's just next door.

Ben (*kisses him*)   Smile.

Ben *exits. Pause.*

Lee   How long's this been going on?

Connor   A week?

Lee   He looks about twelve.

Lana   He seemed really interesting.

Connor   When he's not gardening, what he really wants to do is act.

Lee   Where did you meet him?

Connor   Mum'll wonder where we are.

Lee   Fuck me mum. I'm interested.

Connor   Yeah and I know why.

Pause.

Consummate your marriage. (*He makes to go.*)

Lee   Woi! I've just given you a line o'charlie. The least you can do is stay here and talk to me.

Lana   Danny's been dead six months, Connor. Would he want you sitting in every night like . . . I dunno . . .

Lee   A boring cunt?

Lana   An old maid!

Connor   We're not sleeping together.

Lee   Wouldn't matter if you were, mate.

Connor   I just don't know what to do. No one tells you how long you leave it after your bloke dies and you start seeing someone else.

Lana   I suppose when it feels right. I don't think there's any right or wrong.

Connor   He scares me.

Lee   Why? Is he some sort of axe murderer?

Connor   I'm scared of how he makes me feel.

Lana *hugs him.*

Connor   The day before yesterday. I went up to Yorkshire. To see Danny's mum.

Lana *sits on the bed.* **Lana** *and* **Lee** *are both gobsmacked by this.*

Connor   I thought I was all right. Thought I was moving forward. Finally getting somewhere. Thought Danny was at peace. Wherever he was. Till she opened her big mouth. She said he weren't.

Pause.

Lana   She spoke?

Lee   She's talking bollocks, mate. And you're a cunt for believing it.

Lana   Lee . . .

Lee   You shoulda fucking punched her.

Connor   Oh, and that woulda made everything so much better.

Lee   I'm gonna get downstairs. You coming?

Lana   I'll get changed.

Lee   I dunno what she said to you, Connor. And I don't care. But I know this much. You're doing all right for yourself and I'm proud o'you. Don't let her banjax that.

Lee *exits.*

Connor   He don't understand. No one does.

Lana   Well, that's not strictly true.

Connor   Yeah?

Lana   He was my best friend.

Connor   I better get next door and see Ben.

Lana   What exactly did she say?

Connor   It was a bit weird.

The sound of **Ben** *chanting the Buddhist 'nam yo ho' comes through from the bedroom.*

Ben's a Buddhist. 'Nicheron shoshu.' (*Posh Oscar Wilde voice.*) I love a working-class boy who's really made something of his life!

'Northern Lights' plays again, leading us into:

Scene Four

Beyond the pearly gates.

Danny *sitting on a cloud in his gown and wings. A small boat sails by beneath him. In it is a woman in a black shawl –* **Judy**. *She's*

American, is getting on a bit, but has a youthful quality that endears her to many. She has a pile of shining stars in her boat.

Judy   What's the weather like up there?

Danny   OK.

Judy   You warm enough? I can throw you a bedjacket. I've got one in here somewhere.

Danny   I'm all right.

Judy   What, you're used to hanging about on clouds?

Danny   Not really. How come you're in a boat in the middle of the sky?

Judy   I guess I can't afford an aeroplane. You OK?

Danny   I dunno. I've been told to wait here.

Judy   Uh-ho. That means you ain't been passed yet.

Danny   Passed?

Judy   Passed for passing on. Or is it over? I never can remember.

Danny   Oh.

Judy   Nervous?

Danny   A bit. They gave me my wings and then they called me back. Ran through a load o'questions with me then said they'd be back later. They've been gone for ages.

Judy   What seemed to be the problem?

Danny   Well, first they were going on about me not being religious. They seemed to have everything written down in a book. And then they wanted to know did I get on with my parents.

Judy   And did you?

Danny   Not really. And then they were going on about whether I'd lived me life to the full. They said there was this thing called the Forecast for the Unseen Future. It's what I'd imagined would happen to me after my death. But they weren't sure whether I was entitled to go through all that yet. They said they had to make a few decisions. I'm not sure what those decisions are exactly.

Judy   You'll be OK, Danny.

Danny   You know my name?

Judy   Don't state the obvious, it's very unbecoming.

Danny   How d'you know my name?

Judy   I know everybody's name.

Danny (*the stars in her boat*)   What are they?

Judy   Stars. Want one?

Danny   Can I?

Judy   Actually, no. Not 'til you've been passed for passing on. Or is it over?

Danny   How come you've got so many? Did you nick 'em?

Judy   Excuse me but I'm the Keeper of the Stars. This is my job. Mind if I knit? I like to keep busy.

She gets some wool and starts to knit.

Danny   What's your name?

Judy   Well, that would totally give the game away.

Danny   You seem dead familiar.

Judy   It'll come to you.

Danny   Are they hot?

Judy   Kinda hot and kinda cold. So. Anyone else been by since they left?

Danny   No. You're the first one. To be honest with you it's a bit boring stuck up here. One advantage is I don't need the loo. I had a terrible weak bladder when I was alive, but that seems to have gone.

Judy (*shrieks*)   Are you dead?!

Danny   Erm . . .

Judy (*laughing*)   Only joking. Join the club.

Danny   Oh. And I'm not hungry or thirsty so . . .

Judy   You'd have a much better time about three miles due east.

Danny   Why? What's over there?

Judy   Hey, I'm dangling a carrot, not a turnip. Pumpkinhead.

Danny   I don't understand.

Judy   Good. I like to feel intellectually superior.

Danny   What are you knitting?

Judy   It's just a shape at the moment. It could go either way. I might even knit a new country, they ain't discovered one o'those in years! (*Pretends to throw the wool.*) Splat! Alkamania!

Danny   It's very kind of you to keep me company.

Judy   I'm a very kind person. Tell you the truth, it can get a bit boring sailing around with a boat full of stars all day too.

Danny   What d'you do with them?

Judy   That's a trade secret. (*Laughs.*) Got you that time too! No, these little babies are lost stars. It's kinda like fishing. Did you ever fish?

Danny   No.

Judy   Me neither, but hopefully the analogy isn't lost on you. I go around and I hawl 'em in. Then I go round handing 'em out to folks who get passed.

Danny   So if I get passed, I'll get a star?

Judy   Bet you can't wait.

Danny   And then what?

Judy   And then I'll take you three miles due east.

Danny   What do they have to decide?

Judy   This and that.

Danny   And what if I don't get passed?

Judy   You go three miles due west.

Danny   What's there?

Judy   Think east.

Danny   When will I know?

Judy   You ask a lot of questions, Danny May.

Danny   It's not hell, is it?

Judy   Do you believe in that shit?

Danny   Now who's asking questions?

Judy   We just gotta stay put for a few hours more. By then this passing shit'll be as clear as the nose on your face. You do have a nose, don't you?

Danny   Yes.

Judy   Good.

Danny   And you'll stay with me.

Judy   It's my job, isn't it?

Danny   Thanks.

Judy   Don't mention it.

Danny   I already did.

The lights fade.

Scene Five

Hotel bedroom.

Lana *sitting on the bed in pyjamas.* **Lee**'s *in the bathroom.*

Lana   Lee? What are you doing in there?

Lee (*off*)   Hang on.

Lana   Don't make a smell.

Lee (*off*)   I ain't on the bog!

He comes out in matching pyjamas.

D'you think this is Connor's idea of a joke?

Lana   He said that now we're respectable we had to wear them.

Lee   Look at you. You beautiful doll.

Lana   I know how Connor felt today.

Lee   Come on, babe. It's our night.

Lana   What were you doing in there?

Lee   Oh. Wait up.

He goes into the bathroom and returns with a box, wrapped up with a ribbon.

For you. Mrs Bond.

Lana   The name's Lana. Lana Bond. What is it?

Lee   Open it and find out.

She opens the box. Inside is a pebble, varnished, pretty big.

A pebble. From your favourite beach. I thought what d'you get the woman who has everything? Gorgeous husband. Flat. Knick-knacks to die for. D'you remember last week when I said I was going to see me mum? I got a train. And I went to the seaside. And I got that for you. Hold it up to the light. It's engraved. Ever so faint. Our wedding date.

Lana *is crying.*

Lee   Hey, eh, eh, what you crying for?

Lana   It's beautiful.

Lee   It's yours, babe. Our beach. Our pebble.

Lana   I'm sorry. It just reminds me of. That beach. It.

Lee   Yeah, it's supposed to.

Lana   No. I need to go to the toilet.

She runs in and shuts the door.

Lee   Have I done somin wrong?

Lana   No!

Lee   Well, don't make a smell!

Pause.

Don't you like it?

Pause.

It's special.

He sits there. He gets up and goes to the door.

What you doing in there? Lana?

From behind the door we hear **Lana** *and* **Danny** *singing 'Feed the Birds' starting at the line 'All around the Cathedral'. The lights change and the door spins round to reveal:*

Scene Six

Cottage bathroom.

New Year's Eve, several years ago. **Danny** *and* **Lana** *sit clothed in the dry bath, one at either end facing each other. They each have a bottle of champagne in their hands, bladdered. They're both singing 'Feed the Birds'. They have also had some E's.*

Danny (*speaking*)   Where is he?

Lana   Lee?!

Danny   He's gonna miss midnight.

Lana   Why were we singing that?

Danny   Coz it's a fucking excellent song.

Lana   Oh you were talking about. What were you talking about?

Danny   Fuck knows. Does he know where we are?

Lana   Lee?! Come and sit in the bath with us!

Danny   Lee!

Lana   Oh, isn't this lovely?

Danny   Who needs to be stuck in some sweaty oven of a club when you can sit in a bath in a country cottage in the middle of nowhere.

Lana   Usually when I have taps rubbing into my back it really gets on my tits. But this feels really nice. (*Rubs her back against the taps.*) Oh, that feels fantastic. (*Funny voice.*) It's really beautiful actually.

Danny (*funny voice*)   It's fantastic.

Lana   D'you want to swap ends so you can have a go?

Danny   No, my end's really beautiful too.

Lana   I remember now. We were singing it because you said, when you first moved to London, you sang it.

Danny   God, what's that?

Lana   What?

Danny   Something in my pocket.

Lana   What is it?

He pulls out a pebble.

Danny Off the beach.

Lana God, you could take it home and varnish it. You could set up a stall.

Danny No. I didn't sing it when I first moved to London.

Lana Really?

Danny Well, not all the time.

Lana Imagine that.

Danny I went to St Paul's Cathedral, and I stood on the steps, and I played that full blast on me Walkman. Coz I'd always wanted to live in London. And I thought it'd be just like it was in *Mary Poppins*.

Lana Gosh. That's incredible actually.

Danny When I was a kid and I saw that film. All those films set in nostalgic London. I thought that's what it'd be like. I could climb on any rooftop and see scores of soot-faced sweeps flick-flacking their hearts out. Push some smoke from a chimney top and it'd turn into a staircase to a cloud. It was a real let-down to find out it wasn't like that. I should've known. We didn't have a nanny.

Lana Nostalgic London. I like that. 'Where do you live? North London? South London?' 'No, Nostalgic London.'

Danny I used to look at me mum and think. Why couldn't we have a nanny like Julie Andrews? Why couldn't we live in a big posh house?

Lana What a shame your parents died.

Danny D'you love Lee?

Lana Yes.

Danny Is the sex still fantastic?

Lana Yeah, it's great.

Danny Is it?

Lana Yeah.

Danny D'you use condoms?

Lana Yeah, use 'em and abuse 'em.

Danny Do you?

Lana I'm on the Pill. You know I'm on the Pill.

Danny Don't you worry about HIV?

Lana I'm forever going on about how it's gone to my hips. HIV?

Danny Do you worry about it?

Lana Do you?

Danny You know I do.

Lana You'll be all right.

Danny Well, I'll soon know one way or the other.

Just then he yelps in pain and jumps up. He's getting cramp in his leg.

Ah! Me leg!

Lana Oh God, what?

Danny Cramp!

Lana Sit on the thing!

He climbs out and sits on the side of the bath, rubbing his leg.

Is that better?

Danny I think I was lying funny.

Lana God, this bath's really dangerous. Are you all right?

Danny Yeah.

Lana What were we talking about?

Danny It doesn't matter.

Lana Are you going for the test?

Danny   I've already been.

Lana   When?

Danny   Last week.

Lana   Shit. You should've told me. Why didn't you tell me?

Danny   Some things you have to do on your own.

Lana   When do you get the results?

Danny   Next Thursday.

Lana   Oh, I wish you'd've told me.

Danny   Look. I'm gonna be fine. You know me.

Lana   God, you must've been so worried.

Danny   Well, I didn't want to worry you.

Lana   Listen. You are my best friend.

Danny   And you're mine.

Lana   I love you, Danny Dominica.

Danny   I love you, Lana Lasagne.

Lana   Blow me a kiss and I'll catch it.

He blows her a kiss. She mimes catching it in the air and then wiping it on her lips.

Danny   My turn.

She blows him a kiss. He catches it too.

Lana   Anything you go through I go through too.

Suddenly she yelps in pain.

Danny   What?

She pulls the pebble out of the bath.

Lana   Your pebble. Knelt on it.

Danny   D'you mind not telling Lee?

Lana   Danny, you'll be all right. You're not going to die.
You can't die.

Danny   Where is he? He's gonna . . . (*Looks at watch.*) Shit!
We've missed it. Come on.

*He climbs into the bath. they join hands and start singing 'Auld Lang
Syne'. Neither of them are shit hot on the words.*

Danny/Lana   Lest old acquaintance be forgot
And never bought to mind.
Lest old acquaintance be forgot
For the sake of Auld Lang Syne.

Lana   Happy New Year!

Danny   Happy New Year, darling!

Lee *enters. He too is drinking from a bottle of champagne.*

Lee   Woi! You get your hands offa my bird.

Danny   Try and make me!

Lana   Lee! Catch this!

She blows a kiss for him to catch.

Lee   Oh, that's getting on my tits that game.

Lana   Lee! Happy New Year!

Danny   What happened to you?

Lee   Well, I forgot where the E's were, then I
remembered, then I seen the phone, right, and I thought I'd
ring me brother and leave a message on his machine
wishing him a happy new year and that. Anyway, he
answers and it turns out he's sat in on his own. So I told him
to drive down here first thing tomorrow.

Lana   Oh, brilliant.

Danny   Fab.

Lee   Well, I can't have him on his own on New Year's, can I? He's all right, Danny. You will like him.

Lana   Well, he's gay.

Lee   No he ain't.

Lana   Oh no, he's not.

Danny   But you think he is.

Lee   If he was, he'da told me.

Danny   Sometimes it's hard to tell your family.

Lee   Nah, mate, we're dead close.

Lana   Did you get the pills?

Lee   Here.

He hands out three E's. They neck them with their champagne.

It's gonna be a good year. I can feel it.

Danny   Good.

Lee   Fucking love you, mate.

Danny   Love you too.

Lee *and* **Danny** *hug.*

Lana   Can I use some of your face freshener, Danny?

Danny   Sure.

Lana *gets out of the bath and roots around in a toilet bag on the floor. She sprays herself with a small bottle of eau de toilette. as she does she finds a piece of paper in the bag and unfolds it and reads it.* **Beryl** *enters with a letter to post.*

Beryl   'Dear Daniel, Got your letter. No time to chat at present. Few problems round here at the moment. Glad to hear you're satisfied with new dentist. Wish I was. Mum. PS Enclosed is recipe for corned beef hash. Simple, quick and tasty.'

As she exits, **Lana** *puts the letter back and the lads break from their hug.*

Lee   Merry New Year!

Danny   Merry New Year!!

Lana (*beat*)   Merry New Year!

Scene Seven

Hotel bathroom / bedroom.

Connor *on the phone in a kimono.* **Ben** *comes in in his undies. He watches him for a while.*

Connor   Hello, can you put me through to housekeeping please? Oh, hi. Yeah, it's Connor Bond in 238, I need another bath towel. OK. Right, thanks.

He puts the phone down.

Julie will be up with a new towel shortly, sir.

Ben   What's that?

Connor   What?

Ben   You a tranny?

Connor   It's a kimono. Thought you'd love it.

Ben   You think I'm gonna shag you coz you look like Buddha?

Connor   Get somin from the minibar.

Ben   I've had enough for one night.

Connor   Get us a brandy.

Ben   Dutch courage?

Connor   It's quite a while since I've done this.

Ben   Not trying to avoid me, are you? Hiding in here, fretting over towels.

Connor   Don't be daft.

Ben   Your Lee reckons I look like a rent boy.

Connor   If someone said that to me I'd be flattered.

Ben   D'you fancy me then?

Connor   Ben.

Ben   I know. And I'm sorry.

Connor *looks at him.*

Ben   That I've not been very forthcoming.

Connor   Maybe we're better off just being mates.

Ben   You reckon?

Pause.

Are you ready for this?

Connor   Get us a brandy.

Ben   You don't talk about him much.

Connor   You don't wanno hear all that.

Ben   You haven't even told me how he died.

Connor   How does anybody die? Their heart stops beating.

Pause.

No, you're right.

Ben   Is it so obvious that I should've guessed?

Connor   You can say it.

Ben   Did he have AIDS?

Connor   What do you think?

Ben   You could say it.

Connor   Yes he did.

Pause.

Ben   I'm sorry.

Connor   When Danny got ill. Everything with Danny . . .
I . . . I just thought that was it. I'd never get involved with
anybody else. And now. When I curl up with you, part of
me is so relieved to have someone to hold me that I could
cry. And the other part says, what am I doing? It's Danny's
bed. And I feel sick.

Ben   That's not Danny's bed. It's Trusthouse Forte's.

Pause.

We don't have to get involved. We could just have a bit
o'fun.

Pause.

Are you positive?

Connor   Would it make any difference if I was?

Ben (*shrugs*)   Might do.

Connor   Oh well, cheers, mate. Well, since you ask. No.
Jesus. I've just lost any respect for you that I had. Well done.

Ben   Would it make any difference to you if I was?

Big pause.

Connor   You're too young.

Pause.

Aren't you?

Ben *shakes his head. There is a knock at the door. A woman's voice
from off,* **Julie**.

Julie (*off*)   Housekeeping!

Ben   Perfect timing.

Ben *exits.* **Julie** *comes in shortly. She's played by the actress who plays* **Beryl**. *She's dressed as Mary Poppins and carries a carpet-bag and umbrella. She speaks like Julie Andrews.*

Julie   One fresh bath towel for you, sir.

Connor   Thanks. Stick it anywhere.

Julie   That's no way to keep an orderly nursery now is it, sir?

Connor   Sorry?

Julie   Close your mouth please, Connor, we are not a codfish.

She puts the carpet-bag down and gets out a large bath towel.

I always say the best place to hang a towel is on a towel stand. Head up, Connor, don't slouch.

Connor   Who the fuck are you?

Julie   Never judge things by their appearance, Connor, I'm sure I never do.

Connor   Have we met before? Oh, shit.

Julie   My my, we are swearing a lot this evening. Guilty conscience?

Connor   No, he's just a friend I've got staying for the night.

Julie   Are you feeling all right, sir?

Connor   Thanks for the towel, you can go.

Julie   Best foot forward now. Spit spot. Incidentally, (**Beryl***'s voice.*) I bought Danny that kimono. I certainly never envisaged it being used to woo a Buddhist. (**Julie***'s voice.*) Good day to you, sir.

She exits.

Connor   Ben? Ben?

Ben *enters with a brandy.*

Connor   That chambermaid. Did she really have a carpet-bag?

Ben   What?

Connor   Did she?

Ben   Thanks a lot. I've just told you I'm positive and you're prattling on about the chambermaid's accessories.

Connor   Sorry?

Ben   Good. (*Hands him the brandy.*) I'm going to bed.

He gets into bed. **Connor** *stands there. The lights fade.*

Scene Eight

Settle.

Beryl *comes on, holding a letter to post.*

Beryl   'Dear Daniel, Please note our change of address. Your father had to shut up shop in Liverpool after a few incidents which culminated in him throwing Percy Littlewood through a plate-glass window. The result was a customer boycott. His nerves are very bad as you can imagine, what with the upheaval you caused with your bold exclamations and upping and leaving. The past year is one I'd care to forget actually. Anyway, we decided to get away from Livepool and are currently settled in Settle, minding Auntie Jan's cottage while she continues to make a fool of herself travelling round the world with a man half her age and twice as dim. It's very picturesque. I'd invite you to come and stay but there is your cousin Raymond to consider. He's very young for thirteen and I'm not sure I want him seeing too much of you yet. He's a little wary of homosexual people, being a teenager. That's not to say I disapprove because I know there are lots of single men in all walks of life. I hope you sort yourself out soon anyway. You must excuse my train of thought and handwriting as your father wasn't too keen on me writing so I've come to a little lake down the lane from the cottage and there's quite a breeze blowing. Don't forget it's Joanne's birthday on the fifteenth. Don't bother with anything flash as she's just been diagnosed colour blind and is easily confused by anything but the primaries. Hope you are well. There was a documentary on ITV on Wednesday about some women in London who were on a rent strike or something. I always find London a very grey and dreary place full of drug peddlars and ladies of easy virtue. Did you see it? I switched over halfway through because Dave Allen was on. But it looked interesting. Love and God bless, Mum. PS I know you're a vegetarian. I am very sorry.'

Scene Nine

Hotel bedroom.

The early hours of the morning. **Connor** *spark out in the bed.* **Ben** *stands looking out of the window in the kimono.* **Connor** *stirs.*

Connor   Danny?!

Ben   It's me.

Connor   Oh. What you wearing that for?

Ben   I was cold. Sorry.

Connor   Couldn't sleep?

Ben   It's my favourite time of the day.

Connor   You're weird.

Ben   So quiet. The gardener at this place must be second to none.

Connor   Good. It's costing me an arm and a leg to stay here.

Ben   I'll chip in. I'm not a rent boy.

Connor   I never said you were.

Ben   How d'you feel?

Connor   Fine. You?

Ben   Yeah. Fine. Need a wazz.

Ben *exits to the bathroom.* **Connor** *settles down to go back to sleep.* **Danny** *enters in the kimono, smoking.*

Danny   Connor. (*Louder.*) Connor. Connor.

Connor   What time is it?

Danny   Half one.

Connor   What's the matter?

Danny   I can't sleep.

Connor   It's half past two.

Danny   I was talking to Lana earlier.

Connor   Danny! What did the doctor say? He said do something constructive if you can't sleep. And that don't include waking me up. Do the washing up or something.

Danny   I've done it.

Connor   Well, take a Valium!

Danny   I was thinking we could tell them on Friday.

Connor   What are you talking about?

Danny   Go back to sleep.

Connor   I'm awake now.

Danny   We're seeing Lana and your brother on Friday and I thought we could break the news.

Connor   Couldn't it wait 'til the morning?

Danny   Well, I knew you had to be up early so I thought I might not catch you. I feel terrible I've never told Lana, she's me best mate. Usually, when I got the results she'da been the first one to know. But I'd just met you, and I was caught up in . . . me fucking life's based around lies.

Connor   Light us a fag.

As **Danny** *does this he starts to cry.*

Connor   What? What's the matter?

Danny   I've just been lain here thinking.

Connor   What?

Danny   I'm scared, Connor.

Connor   Oh, you dickhead. Come here. (*He hugs* **Danny**.) What you scared of?

Danny   I saw Marshall today.

Connor   That poisonous queen?

Danny   Connor, I hardly recognised him. He had KS all over his face.

Connor   Where was he?

Danny   Soho. Having a drink. I'm going to end up like that, aren't I?

Connor   I don't know.

Danny   Well, you should fucking know!

Connor   You might not get that.

Danny   I'd rather be dead than have you wheeling me down Old Compton Street half skeletal and covered in lesions. I'm not afraid of dying.

Connor   Good.

Danny   Just suffering.

Connor   Right.

Pause.

Everything seems worse at night.

Danny   Oh, I'll just sit here and wait for the sun to come up. It'll all be fine then.

Pause.

A letter'll come saying my test results last year were a false alarm. Someone fucked up at the clinic. It's just pure coincidence that my T-cells have been dropping at a rate of knots and the fact I get nightsweats's just hormone imbalance. Wouldn't that be nice? I'll sue them to the hilt and we can retire to that house in the country we've always dreamed of.

Pause.

Connor   Take a sleeping tablet.

Danny   I've already taken two. You're not getting rid of me that easily.

Connor *spies a piece of paper on the floor.*

Connor   You been reading her letters again? It's no wonder you can't sleep. Burn it.

Danny   You would say that.

Connor   Cut the apron strings. She did.

Connor *stubs out his cigarette and turns over to go to sleep.* **Danny** *stays sitting on the bed, staring into space.*

Scene Ten

Beach.

Ben, **Lana**, **Lee** and **Connor** *having a boozy afternoon on a picnic rug on the beach. They are all in good spirits, but* **Ben**

especially is drunk and has become pretty loud and occasionally camp. There are empty bottles of wine and a small tub of olives.

Ben   Have you heard the latest? They invented AIDS.

Lana   Who did?

Ben   It's the latest theory.

Lee   Someone with a sick sense of humour.

Ben   What's my drug?

Connor   AZT.

Ben   They invented AZT way way back in, I dunno, the fifties or something. And then they had to invent the illness for it to treat.

Connor   Do you really believe that?

Ben   I don't believe it, I just read it.

Lana   You're getting sand in the olives.

Lee   Where d'you read that?

Ben   In a magazine.

Connor   It's quite an old theory.

Ben   Is it?

Connor   And probably complete bullshit.

Lana   How did your audition go?

Ben   OK.

Lana   Just OK?

Ben   Yes. Just OK.

Lee   What was it for?

Ben   A theatre-in-education company.

Connor   It's for a play about . . . AIDS.

Ben   *Whoops There go My T-Cells!*

Lee   It's not called that. That is sick!

Connor   No, it's not. Is it?

Ben   I made it up. It was a joke.

Lana   How is your count, Ben?

Ben   Three hundred and ten.

Lana   Oh, that's fantastic.

Connor   What is the play called?

Ben   Oh, *Positive* . . . something or other. But I don't give a shit. They asked me if I was drunk.

Connor   And were you?

Ben   What I really wanna do is more TV.

Lana   Oh yes! I told everyone in the office. I said, 'My friend Ben's on the telly tonight!' They were all really impressed.

Lee   What were you in?

Ben   I posted a letter in *Hollyoaks*.

Lee   Who invented AIDS?

Connor   It's a sort of conspiracy theory.

Lana   Oh, I'm not keen on those.

Ben   AZT!

Lee   What's that actually stand for?

Ben   Dunno. I just take it. When I can remember. Thank heavens I'm a Catholic, I'd be hopeless on the Pill.

Lana   I thought you were a Buddhist of some repute.

Lee   A pisshead of some repute.

Ben   I'm allowed, I've got AIDS.

Connor   Have you fuck.

Ben   I had 250 T-Cells in November. If I lived in the States that'd be a diagnosis.

Lana   Were you really upset when Princess Diana died?

Ben   No.

Lee   She had the common touch.

Ben   Oh, don't get me started.

Lana   Olive, Connor?

Ben   I fucking hate the royalty.

Lana (*olives*)   Lee?

Lee   They're a bit bitter for my liking.

Connor   Isn't he just.

Ben   I used to go out with this bloke called Steve, right? Now, I know blame isn't a particularly politically correct term as far as HIV's concerned. But when I've had a drink, I don't feel particularly PC. Anyway, he's the one to blame.

Pause.

He used to work. Tell 'em where he used to work, Connor.

Connor   Buckingham Palace.

Ben   Buckingham Palace! You'd walk round his house and he'd be like that . . . 'Oh, the Queen give me that', or 'Princess Anne give me that, she's the only one with manners. She'd never let a door slam in your face.'

Connor   He'd been a footman. And reckoned he contracted the virus at the palace.

Ben   Life was one long gay orgy beneath stairs.

Connor   I mean, it was years ago.

Ben   They'd never heard of HIV, had they? And AIDS were a packet of slimming biscuits.

Lana   Sorry?

Connor   You used to get these slimming biscuits called
Ayds.

Lee   That's fucking sick.

Ben   But when I don't blame him, Steve, I blame her, the
Queen. Having all that going on under her roof.

Pause.

Lana   Do you want the last olive, Ben?

Lee   How old are you?

Ben   Nearly twenty-three.

Lana   No?

Lee   Right, well, I'm thirty, right, and I was thirteen when
I first heard of AIDS. So you'da been what, 'bout six. So
therefore I'm assuming you've known all your sexual life
that you've been at risk.

Ben   Risks are there to be taken.

Lee   So the only person you can really blame . . . is
yourself.

Lana   Lee.

Lee   I don't believe in pointing the finger, Lana. He does.
I was just getting him to shut up.

Ben   I seen this documentary the other night about the
Crown Jewels.

Connor   Oh, here we go.

Ben   She's got crowns worth millions of pounds and she
calls 'em fucking hats! If she had any moral fibre, she'd
fucking sell a couple off and put it into research. Coz if he
hadn'ta worked for her, I wouldn't be going to that fucking
clinic once a fortnight. And I always thought that when I
did get ill, I'd be lying in some hospice somewhere and her
fucking ex-daughter-in-law'd be coming in and patting me
on the head.

Lee   Well, she can't now, can she? Have some fucking respect.

Ben   Hey, Connor. Maybe your Danny should have had it branded on his forehead like a packet o'fags. By appointment to Her Royal Highness the Princess of Wales.

Connor *punches him.*

Pause. **Ben** *shields his face and makes out it didn't hurt.*

Lana   I always liked Princess Di.

Lee   Yeah, coz you see the good in people, babe, unlike some.

Lana   We camped out on the funeral route, didn't we?

Ben   D'you want a fucking medal?

Lee   Do you mind not being so rude to my wife?

Lana   You sound like someone who's given up.

Connor   He's given up work.

Ben   Fuck 'em.

Lee   Who?

Ben   Everyone. I'm taking all I can from this disease. Fuck 'em.

Lee   Like what?

Ben   Council flat, £187 a week living allowance, mobility allowance, washing machine, free drugs . . .

Connor   Legal . . .

Ben   Support groups, aromatherapy. I've been rebirthed twice, and every now and again they wheel me out to have me picture taken looking maudlin for the *Guardian*. Didn't he do well?

Lee   Well, I hope it makes you very happy.

Ben   I thought it would. I really did. There's no more drink.

Connor   I wonder why.

Ben   Where's the nearest offy?

Lee   Up on the front.

Ben   Can I have some money? Please.

Connor *gives him a ten-pound note.* **Ben** *is now standing up.*

Connor   Get one of each.

Ben   You can talk about me behind me back.

He walks up the beach then stops.

And another thing.

Lee   Oh, here we go.

Ben   Can you seriously stand there, Lee . . .

Lee   I'm sitting down, wanker!

Ben   . . . and tell me that every time you've had it off that you've used a condom? So why should I be any different to you?

Ben *exits.*

Lana (*funny voice*)   Now would you say he was a bit fucked up?

Connor   What?

Lee   You're pissing on Danny's memory bringing him.

Lana   You could have any man you wanted.

Connor   Could I?

Pause.

Lee   You wanna tell him to get lost, and find yourself some fucking dignity.

Connor   I already have.

Lee   Then how comes he's here?

Connor   I told him I'd just be his mate.

Lee   You really want that for a mate? You are one sad bastard.

Connor   That's when he started drinking. I feel sorry for him. He's all on his own.

Lee   Is it any wonder?

Connor   All Danny ever wanted was for his mum to put her arm round him and tell him that everything was going to be all right. But she couldn't. So I had to do it.

Lee   Don't mean you've gotta do it to Ben an'all.

Lana *is crying now.*

Lana   We all did it.

Lee   Look what you've done now.

Connor   I'm sorry.

Lee   Yeah. Just coz you stuck your prick up his arse, don't mean you've got the monopoly on feelings.

Connor (*teary*)   I'm sorry.

Lee   Oh, don't you start an'all.

Lana   D'you know the first thing he did when he moved to London?

Connor   'Feed the Bird'?

Lana   He liked all the lullabyes. 'Liverpool Lullabye', 'Hushabye Mountain'. I go up to the top of the hill and play that to myself.

Connor   Ben's gonna be on his own. Mary Poppins ain't gonna come in and sing 'Feed the Birds', Caractacus Potts isn't gonna sing 'Hushabye Mountain'. He'll be on his own. And it's not nice, it's vile.

Lana   Danny had you.

Connor   But he was still on his own. And so was I. And so will you be, and so will you be.

Pause.

I'm pissed. Take no notice.

Lee   What was that funny name? Sang about the mountain?

Lana   Caractacus Potts.

Connor   Dick Van Dyke.

Lee   That's a fucking stupid name.

Connor   Is anyone else cold?

Lee   We could walk along the front and find wanker rent boy. Try and find a pub. Get something proper to eat.

Lana   I'd like that.

Connor   You go on ahead. I'll follow you on.

Lee   Well, don't be too long. I'm not relishing the propect o'more boozing with your boyfriend.

Connor   He's not my boyfriend.

Lana   Coming?

Connor   I just wanno have a think for a while.

Lana and **Lee** *have cleared up the picnic and exit, carrying the bits.* **Connor** *stays there, staring out to sea.*

Danny *enters with a bag and a rug and sits down on the beach. He lights up a cigarette and swigs from a bottle of whisky, the rug covering him. The lighting changes and we go into:*

Scene Eleven

Beach.

Several years before. New Year's Day. Late at night. **Danny** *sitting on the beach under the rug. He is reading another letter.* **Connor** *approaches.*

Connor   I tried your door.

Danny   Funny thing to do for a straight boy.

Connor   Who told you that?

Danny   Your brother.

Connor   Well, he's a bit of a wanker then, in'e?

Danny   He doesn't know?

Connor   Depends how you'd define 'know'. He's been told. He just don't admit it. I can't be arsed to fight when I'm on me own. It's easier when I'm with someone. If I'm single I can't force him to see it, can I?

Danny   I hate being on my own.

Connor   You ain't.

Connor *sits down alongside* **Danny**.

Danny   Fucking hell. All these years. Me best mate's boyfriend's brother's a bender.

Connor   That's a bit of a mouthful, innit?

Danny   As the actress said to the bishop.

Connor   Boom boom.

Danny   My cousin Joanne. She was going to Crete one year. Or somewhere like that. She didn't have much money. She was going with a gang o'mates. And my mum said, 'How will yous afford the hotel?' And she goes, 'Oh, we'll probably sleep on the beach.'

Connor   Is that what you're doing?

Danny   I've never done it before.

Connor   You've got a fucking screw loose, it's freezing.

Danny   I was so jealous of our Joanne. I thought, 'One day, I'm gonna sleep on the beach.'

Connor   Bit tricky in Liverpool.

Danny   Well, this is hardly Crete. I should make a list.

Connor   Of what?

Danny   All the things I promised myself I'd do and never got around to.

Connor   Go on then.

Danny   No pen.

Connor   Tell me.

Danny   It's stupid.

Connor   I feel like I'm treading water. Another day gone and what a waste. But really, you can do whatever you want, can't you? It's just. Being arsed. Always putting off 'til tomorrow. Innit, love?

Danny   Are you warm enough?

Connor   I'm all right, mate.

Danny   You just called me love.

Connor   Did I?

Danny   And then mate.

Connor   No law against it, is there?

Danny   No.

Pause.

Connor   What would you rather I called you?

Danny   I'm drunk.

Connor   You don't seem it.

Danny   No?

Connor   I am.

Danny   Pissed?

Connor   Had a few cans in me room. Working up the courage to come and find you.

Danny   Sometimes the world looks better through a haze of drugs and drink.

Connor   What's up?

Danny   Another time.

They kiss.

Why doesn't this feel wrong?

Connor   It's legal.

Danny   It's a public place.

Connor   It's dark.

Danny   Have you ever fancied sleeping on the beach?

Connor   No.

Pause.

But I will.

He gets under the blanket.

And just because you've snogged me, don't think you're shagging me when my back's turned.

Danny   Why? Would you rather see my face?

Connor   Shut it. I'm not that sort of girl.

Danny   Don't worry. I haven't had an erection since 1983.

Connor   Weird, innit? I've heard so much about you from Lana.

Danny   We mustn't leave it so long next time.

They settle down to go to sleep. **Connor** *moans.*

I never did nothing.

Connor   No. I need a piss.

Connor *gets up and goes upstage, back to the audience to piss.* **Danny** *lights two ciggies, and glances at the letter.* **Beryl** *enters stage left. She has a letter to post. As she reads her letter,* **Connor** *finishes pissing and rejoins* **Danny** *on the beach under the blanket. They smoke together.*

Beryl   'Dear Daniel, What wonderful news! Your father and I are both very proud of your getting into London University with such pleasing grades at A level. See? *Educating Rita* was right. It's never too late. Have you thought about what you want to do at the end of it? There was a discussion on the radio about social work last night that was very interesting. Is that what you do with a sociology degree? That's what Harry Secombe seemed to think. Did I tell you? Silly me! Harry Secombe was up here on Monday filming that telly programme *Highway*. I managed to grab a word with him in the Puddled Pony and he was very impressed with your educational progress. So well done you! You'd adore the ponies here, Daniel. They're so sweet and approachable. I've made names for the four I see on my way from the cottage to the doctor's surgery. I've called them Shingles, Judy, Merryweather and Bergerac. They love me because I keep sugar lumps in my clutchbag and feed them every time I pass. The doctor seems to think they're a vital part of my adjustment to life in the country. How kind of you to send your cousin Raymond ten pounds for his birthday. Sadly your father ripped it up accidentally when he was tearing a letter he had printed in the *Settle Argus* out about addiction to tranquillisers. I mended it with my trusty Singer and your cousin put it

wisely in his savings account. He's really shot up. I think it's
the Yorkshire air, and his cheeks have never been so rosy.
He's the tallest in his football team and has earned himself
the nickname 'Tallest' at the youth club. Are you any taller?
Me and your father aren't. Anyway, son, I hope you like
university and meet lots of nice people. I've met a few here
by attending a creative cookery class. Enclosed is a recipe
for Eggs Californienne. So if I can meet some, so can you!
Bye for now anyway, Love and God Bless, Mum. Kiss.'

She sits down on the ground. **Lana** *approaches.*

Lana   Hello? Hello. Erm. Are they your horses?

Beryl   They're ponies.

Lana   Oh, right. Are you. Oh, gosh. Are you Beryl May?

Beryl   Who sent you?

Lana   Nobody. Allow me to introduce myself. I'm Lana
Stuart. I think I'm a friend of your son's.

Beryl   You think?

Lana   Do you have a son?

Beryl   I. No. Why?

Lana   Are you related to Danny May?

Beryl   Where is he?

Lana   London. Erm. I hope you don't mind me . . . I was
up in the area for a christening and . . . I'm sorry.

Beryl   Are you Danny's girlfriend?

Lana   No.

Beryl   No.

Lana   I was at university with him. And now. Now we're
not at university but we're still good friends.

Beryl   Do you live in Settle?

Lana   London. I'm up here on a visit.

Beryl   You've already said that, haven't you.

Lana   Would you like a cigarette?

Beryl   I don't know you.

Lana   Erm. Well, as I said my name's Lana. Stuart. I've got a boyfriend called Lee. Bond. Not James. My hobbies include: conversational Spanish, Thai cooking and the occasional night out.

Beryl   Say something in Spanish.

Lana   *Hola guapa, como usted? Por favor.* I'm not very good.

Beryl   My son's going to be a social worker.

Lana   Actually he's a waiter. A very good one.

Beryl   Are you a social worker?

Lana   No. After university I did a bit of temping, hither and thither. Ended up in a PR company. Phil Drill and Westcott.

Beryl   What's PR?

Lana   Well, like, say one of your clients is the Wombles. They're one of ours. Well, you sort of promote them. So far I've done a Wombles Reunited Tour of the Channel Islands – special guest Dime, the Dollar tribute band. And a Dana Sings TV Theme Tunes CD which was very popular in Reykjavik. As of May I'll be working hand in glove with our sister company Phil Drill and Sanderson on the PR for Hepatitis B. Sorry. I'm a bit nervous.

Beryl   Why?

Lana   Oh, I'm always nervous. Don't be offended.

Beryl   But why are you nervous today?

Lana   I didn't tell Danny I was coming to see you. And, well, I didn't know how you'd react.

Beryl   I'm not allowed to see Daniel. My husband won't let me. He doesn't even know I write. I'm a terrible mother.

Lana   At least you write. I think Danny needs at least that.

Beryl   I was a good mother once. Oh, this is when he was very little. I'm excellent with small children. I have a very good singing voice. They used to call me the Southend Soprano. Daniel and I shared a love of old musicals. And if he couldn't sleep I'd sing to him.

Lana   Oh, that's lovely.

Beryl   But my doctor says you can't recreate the past.

Lana   Your doctor?

Beryl   I either leave my husband and see my son or I stay put and don't. You see, I can't leave my husband. I'm a woman of very few means. Also, I have my nephew to think about, he's been left in my care.

Lana   Gosh, it's very Jane Austen. Or maybe it isn't.

Beryl   Does he talk about me?

Lana   Well. Yes. Of course.

Beryl   Are you going to tell him you've seen me?

Lana   Probably not. Will you keep writing?

Beryl   I'll just mention I met someone with red hair. Then it's ambiguous. You know, I miss Liverpool. I'm not used to all this fresh air. But it's supposed to be very good for you. Do you see all those molehills?

Lana   Gosh, yes. It's amazing.

Beryl   Isn't it? But do you see any moles?

Lana   No.

Beryl   No. Me neither.

The light fade. As they do Savage Garden's 'Truly Madly Deeply' plays, starting at the chorus, taking us into the next scene.

Scene Twelve

*Pub/***Lana** *and* **Liam***'s lounge.*

'Truly Madly Deeply' is playing on the juke box. **Lana**, **Lee** *and* **Connor** *are sitting at a table, finishing off a pub meal. There is a spare place and unfinished meal for* **Ben**, *who has gone to the loo.*

Lee   You oright, babe?

Lana   Fine. I was just thinking.

Lee   That Ben's been in the Gents for hours.

Connor   He's probably puking his guts up.

Lee   Well, don't you wanna go and see how he is?

Connor   It doesn't feel right.

Lee   Well, you're the one who said you wanted to look after him.

Connor   No. Us three sat here. And the empty seat.

During the following, till **Danny***'s entrance, there is a sound and lighting change and we are transformed back a few years to* **Lana** *and* **Lee***'s lounge for a dinner party.*

Lee   Here, listen to this. I couriered a kidney today.

Connor   You curried a kidney? I didn't know you liked offal.

Lee   Couriered.

Lana   A live one?

Lee   I thought, blimey, this is life and death. I nearly bloody shat myself. I go to this address in Harley Street and they hand me this package and the bird goes, 'You gotta be careful with that.' I felt like saying, 'I'm always bloody careful. Five years I've ridden that bike and not a fucking scratch. Best record in the company.' Be careful! Anyway, I looks at the package and on the top in bloody felt tip it says, 'Careful. Kidney Inside' and this address in Bayswater.

Danny *enters and sits with them. He finishes off the meal in front of him.*

Lana   OK?

Danny   Great.

Lee   I thought, it's only for a bloody transplant, innit? And I thought, well, they've obviously chosen me coz I've got the perfect track record. So I'm going like the clappers down Oxford Street, when from nowhere . . . Bosh! Some cunt of a taxi driver's slammed his breaks on to pick some rich bitch up with her fucking fur coats and I go slap bang in the back of him. Me bag goes flying through the air. The parcel come streaming out of it and . . . plop. Lands in the middle of the fucking street. The lights change and some cunting bus driver with a big red nasty-looking monster of a 38 drives flat over the top of it. I tell you what, I shat. I curses the driver, me bike's fine, and runs over to me parcel. Flat as a fucking anorexic's tits.

Danny   It's lovely, Lana.

Connor   Go on then.

Lee   Well, I'm thinking 'This kidney's fucked, innit?' Try telling that to your boss. Try telling that to the poor sod in Bayswater with no fucking kidneys waiting for his new one. So I rang me controller – he's a fucking waste of space – and break the news. Well, he just laughs, dunn'e?

Lana   God, that's terrible. You should report him.

Connor   Bastard!

Lee   Turns out it was a dead kidney anyway.

Connor   Who wanted that?

Lee   Checked the name on the parcel. A Mister D. Hirst. Fucking Damien Hirst. The artist. I tell you what he was not happy when I dropped it off. He was more upset than if he'd needed it to slap in his guts. Had a right go at me.

Lana   What did you say?

Lee   What d'you think I said? 'Learn to fucking paint!'

Danny   That was gorgeous, Lana. Thanks.

Connor   Yeah, babe. Spot on.

Lee   Who fancies a little line? Got some in specially.

Lana (*clearing the plates away*)   We've got cheesecake yet.

Lee   We can have it later.

Lee *exits*.

Lana   Your brother's turning into a coke head.

Connor   D'you want a hand with that?

Lana   No, honestly. If we ever have kids . . . they'll ask them at school what their daddy does. And they'll say, 'Coke.'

Connor   I'll give you a hand.

Lana   No. Please. I'm the hostess. You're our guests.

She exits with some of the plates etc.

Connor   What?

Danny   It's another world, isn't it?

Connor   What?

Danny   Well, I was just wondering when would be a suitable time to proffer my piece of news.

Connor   Danny.

Danny   When then? When's it ever a good time? Maybe you're right, I dunno. We see a lot of them, Lana's my best friend, Lee's your brother . . . I just thought . . .

Connor   There's some sort of friction between them tonight.

Danny   Isn't there always?

Connor   Maybe they've got desire discrepancy.

Danny   Desire discrepancy?

Connor   Just a little term I picked up to describe our . . . predicament.

Danny   Desire discrepancy.

Connor   Yeah. It was in a magazine. Apparently it's one of the most common causes of relationship difficulties.

Danny   You're so inappropriate.

Connor   I can't be inappropriate. My behaviour can be, but a person can't be inappropriate.

Danny   God, that was a big mistake.

Connor   What?

Danny   Bringing literacy to the cockney working class.

Pause.

It is inappropriate to rake up a minor problem when we're having a night round at your brother's.

Connor   A minor problem?

Danny   Oh shut up.

Connor   When was the last time you kissed me? When was the last time you held me? When was the last time you voluntarily touched my cock?

Lana *enters with her pièce de résistance, a huge cheesecake on a tray.*

Lana   Cheesecake!

Connor   What would you say was the most common cause of relationship difficulties, Lana?

Lana   Oh, erm. Money?

Connor   Would you say it was desire discrepancy?

Lana   Desire discrepancy? That sounds like fun.

Connor   It's fantastic, isn't it, Danny?

Danny   This looks lovely, Lana.

Lana   What's desire discrepancy?

Connor   Well, say me and Danny had it. It might possibly mean that he was frigid and that I'd want sex more often than on birthdays and bank holidays.

Lana   Right. Oh, we have that problem all the time. Do you have it too?

Connor   Oh, we have a fabulous sex life. Very regular. Once in a blue moon.

Danny   And what he's forgetting to tell you is that there are reasons.

Lana   Oh, I have a very low sex drive.

Connor   Like?

Danny   Like I'm HIV-positive and I'm petrified about passing it on to you because I fucking worship you.

Lee *enters proudly, carrying a mirror with four huge lines of cocaine on it.*

Lee   Now what have I got here? It's good stuff this. Got it off a bird at work. It's really crystally.

Lana   Oh, for Christ's sake!

Lee   What have I done now?

Lana   Put that away!

Lee   Eh?

Lana   Put it . . . (*She grapples with him for the mirror.*)

Lee   You stupid fucking . . . watch it!

She knocks the mirror out of his hands. It falls to the floor. The coke's gone everywhere.

Lana!

They all sit there ignoring him.

What?! What?!

Lana   Danny, I'm so sorry.

Lee   D'you know how much that stuff costs?

Lana   Lee! Please . . .

Lee   I thought we was having a line.

He goes down on the floor, trying to gather up the coke.

Connor   Lee. It's Danny. We've been meaning to tell you something.

Lee   Don't wanna know, mate.

Lana   It's important.

Lee   I don't give a shit.

Connor   Well, you fucking should, all right?

Lana   I don't believe this.

Lee   D'you think I'm stupid? D'you think I ain't already guessed? I'm not deaf, I'm not blind, and I'm not thick. D'you think I ain't already worked it out? Going down the hospital. I know what the problem is.

Connor   Say it.

Lee   You say it, Connor. It's about fucking time.

Danny   I'm HIV-positive.

Lee   Why didn't you tell me?

Connor   Danny weren't ready.

Danny   I can speak for myself.

Lee   D'you think I ain't seen how much you've changed?

Lana   Lee, that's dirty.

Lee *is rubbing the coke from the carpet around his gums.*

Lee   It was the same with when you started seeing each other. Oh no, don't tell Lee. Lee can't handle it. Let's let him find out by catching us down the beach. Nice one. And lately you've been going round like there's a fucking cloud over your head. I fucking love you, Connor. You're the best brother in the world.

He starts to cry, uncontrollably, it almost comes from nowhere, like he's been bottling it in for months. **Connor** *goes to hug him.* **Lee** *elbows him away.*

Get off me! Fuck off!

He sits back at the table, crying.

Lana   How long have you known?

Danny   Two years.

Lana (*to* **Lee**)   You never breathed a word of that to me.

Lee   I'm allowed me own little thoughts, in'I? And don't tell me you didn't know. I can't believe he never told his Siamese fucking twin joined at the perm.

Lana   Thanks.

Lee   Well, didn't you?

Lana   Was it that test you told me about?

Danny   Had to sort it out in me own head first.

Lana   I thought I was your best friend.

Danny   I'm sorry.

Lana   You're always bloody lying to me, as if I can't take the truth.

Lee (*to* **Connor**)   Are you all right?

Danny   Connor's fine.

Lee   Are you, mate?

Connor   Yes.

Lee   I just get so scared that he's gonna die. He can't fucking die, he's younger than me. D'you know what I mean?

Danny   Lana . . .

Lana   You don't have to wrap me up with cotton wool, you know. I know you all think I'm stupid but I'm not.

Lee   D'you use condoms and that?

Danny   Yes. I don't think you're stupid, Lana.

Lee   Is that enough?

Connor   We hardly ever have sex anyway.

Lana   You told me your mum and dad were dead when I first met you.

Lee (*to* **Danny**)   You fucking give it to him and I'll fucking kill you.

Danny   I give it to him and I'll kill myself. (*To* **Lana**.) Lana, I told everyone that. I didn't know we were gonna end up being best mates.

Lana   You're all a bunch of inverted snobs.

Danny   If I said me parents were alive it meant I had to go into the ins and outs about how they'd cut me off.

Connor   Oh what, like you don't go on about it now?

Danny   Is it better to lie then?

Lana   Obviously!

Lee   What's fucking going on, eh?

Lana (*to* **Danny**)   Are you all right?

Danny   I think so.

Lee   They might find a cure, mightn't they?

Connor   That's the only headline I'd like to read in the *Sun*. Cure Found.

Lee   Look, just don't have sex.

Lana   Lee.

Lee (*to* **Danny**)   Promise me, right, that you won't have sex with him again.

Connor   And promise me you will.

Pause.

Danny (*to* **Connor**)   I promise.

Lana   I've got a confession to make.

Lee   You're a fucking lesbian. I knew it.

Lana   Oh, nothing. (*The rest of the plates.*) Just get rid of these.

Connor   Eh?

Lee   Babe?

Lana   It's nothing. God. You're so pushy. (*Explodes, to* **Danny**.) Oh all right, I've met your mother!

Danny   What?

Lana   Oh no, that's a lie. Maybe I'm in shock. Yes. I'm in shock. I've just had some very bad news about my best friend.

Danny   What did you say that for?

Lana   I don't know.

Connor   You can't have met her. He hasn't even seen her for years.

Lana   I know. I'm going mad.

Lee   Sit down, love. I'll tidy them away in a minute.

Lana *sits down.*

Lana   What I really mean is, you probably feel that you decided to tell me that your parents were alive, but you didn't. I coerced you into it. I found a letter once. Signed Mum.

Connor   I wish I'd lied about something, I feel really left out.

Lana   Cheesecake?

Lee   Oh, fuck the cheesecake, Lana.

Lana   Yes, you'd rather do that than fuck me these days. What is it we've got again?

Connor   Desire discrepancy.

Lee   You been mouthing off about our sex life? Have you? You might wanno know the ins and outs of what they do in the bedroom, but I don't want them knowing about us.

Lana   Well, it would be a pretty boring conversation, wouldn't it?

Lee   Shut up!

Lana   You know, it's a shame. I was spoilt hanging around with Danny at college. I really did think I'd meet a man who would listen to me, value my opinions, tell me I was beautiful. Help me choose my clothes.

Lee   Well, if you want that from a man, move in with the little AIDS victim.

Danny   You fucking bastard!

Danny *lunges at* **Lee**. *He knocks* **Lee** *to the floor.* **Connor** *gets in there and splits them up.*

Connor   Oi, get off him, you.

Danny   Piss off.

Connor   That's my fucking brother.

Danny   Oh, and he's more important to you than me?

Connor   Grow up.

Danny   Well, you know what you can do if you're fed up with not having sex every three seconds, don't you?

Connor   Watch porn, I usually do.

Danny   You haven't got a fucking clue, have you?

Connor   What about, darling?

Danny   See this? (*Tries to get his ring off.*) You can fucking keep this!

Lee   I'm sorry, all right? It just fucking slipped out.

Connor   Ha ha! He always does this. I bought him that. Won't it come off, love?

Danny   I'll chop me fucking finger off if I have to.

Lee   I'm fucking sorry, Danny. It's just. She's winding me up. I don't like my sex life being talked about. I am. I'm sorry. I was bang out of order. Don't take it out on him!

Danny   Ha ha!

The ring has come off. He throws it at **Connor***, who makes no attempt to pick it up.*

Connor   You're so predictable.

Lana   Danny, don't go!

Danny (*to* **Connor**)   You're staying here tonight.

Connor   Good. Won't have you waking me up every five minutes saying 'I'm gonna die!'

Danny (*to* **Lana**)   And I don't know how you can live with the likes of its brother.

Danny *exits.*

Lana   Danny!

The lighting and sound change and we are back in the pub. **Ben** *returns from the toilet.*

Lee   You've been gone hours.

Bee   I don't feel very well.

Lana   The waitress took your plate. It had gone cold.

Ben   I'm not very hungry. (*To* **Connor**.) Take me home.

Ben *sits down.* **Connor** *reluctantly puts his coat on.* **Lana** *and* **Lee** *stare at him. The lights fade.*

Scene Thirteen

Beyond the pearly gates.

Danny *is asleep on his cloud.* **Judy** *is knitting in her boat. He wakes up.*

Judy   Hi there!

Danny   I fell asleep.

Judy   Self-induced audio sensory deprivation. Don't you just love it?

Danny   They haven't been back?

Judy   Nope.

Danny   I know who you are.

Judy   You wouldn't be the first.

Danny   I've seen all your films. I think.

Judy   Me too. But I bet you never went to the premieres.

Danny   When I grew up me mum named all our dogs after you.

Judy   Gee, thanks.

Danny   Well, two. First there was Judy the springer spaniel. Road traffic accident. Then there was Judy the mongrel. We had to have her put down.

Judy   You'll have to introduce them to me.

Danny   Well, they're dead.

Judy   Well, ain't that a shame. Look. It's a blanket now. (*Her knitting.*) So. Your mother was my number one fan, huh?

Danny   I'd rather not talk about her.

Judy   Why not?

Danny   I'd just rather not.

Judy   I think, Danny, that you might have to.

Danny   Why?

Judy   It just might help.

Danny   Me?

Judy   Your progress.

Danny   My passing on?

Judy   Give it a go.

Danny   I think someone's coming.

Judy   What?

Danny   There is. The water's moving.

Judy   This is most irregular.

Danny   They might be coming back to tell me thingy, if I've been passed.

Judy   It's far too early. Maybe someone died.

Danny   Can you see them?

Judy   I can see a shadow. (*Calls.*) Hey, why aren't you in a boat?!

The overture from Mary Poppins *starts to play. A bright light, then* **Connor** *and* **Lana** *appear, walking on the water, dressed head to toe in white, dressed as the attendants of the pearly gates. They carry clipboards. They looks up to* **Danny** *and smile.*

Judy   Has he been passed? Has he been passed?

Connor   Danny! It's me! Connor!

Danny   Connor!

Judy   Hey! Who's fuckin' fantasy is this?!

Blackout. The music plays us into the interval.

Act Two

Scene One

Beyond the pearly gates.

Judy, **Danny**, **Connor** *and* **Lana** *as before.*

Connor   Why am I here? I'm here to tell you that he'll never get passed on.

Danny   Connor, don't say that!

Judy   He will! He has to!

Connor   Oh, to make you feel better?

Judy   You want him hanging up on that cloud there for the rest of his death?

Connor   This isn't my headspace, darling, it's yours.

Judy   How insensitive can a person be?

Connor   You can't even be yourself in your dreams, can you? You have to be some camp gay icon to make it more bearable. D'you wanna know why he'll never get passed on?

Judy   Don't listen, Danny!

Connor   Because you were a dreadful mother.

Judy   I don't know what you're talking about. I have two daughters who are both huge. And my one and only son . . .

Connor   Oh, this is ridiculous!

Danny   Connor?

Connor   It's true, Danny. That's what this is all about. Whether she cut it, and we all know she didn't. Not by a long stretch of the imagination.

Judy   At least my imagination is vivid!

Connor   You're just a sad old woman, Beryl. With nothing to say for yourself.

Danny   Her name's not Beryl. Don't you recognise her?

Connor   Oh, so you've fallen for it?

Judy   Some boyfriend he turned out to be. One last chance to say hello and all he can do is ignore you and pick on me!

Connor   Pick on you? You ruined that man. Ruined him.

Judy   I loved him. What am I saying? I'm Judy Garland!

Danny   That's not my mum, Connor! You know my mum. You saw pictures. Our flat, Judy. It was covered in photos of my mum. Every nook and cranny. She loved me and I loved her.

Connor   You're taking this a bit far, aren't you? You'll do anything to make yourself feel better. Inventing little images of our life together and pretending you were a part of it.

Judy (*to* **Lana**)   You're the woman in PR.

Lana (*different voice*)   Oh no I'm not.

Danny   It's like a fucking pantomime.

Judy   Who taught you to swear?

Connor   Make your mind up who you are, Beryl!

Judy   Well, who's she then?

Lana   I bear the body of the woman in PR, but the body is inhabited by the spirit of another.

Connor   Little set-up you'd understand, Beryl.

Danny   Don't call her that!

Judy   So who's inhabiting your body?

Lana   The spirit of Esther Finnegan. Do you remember me, Danny?

Danny   Finnegan?

Lana   Between the years of Our Lord 1973 and 1975 I taught at the Hunts Cross County Primary school in the city of Liverpool, England. I wore my hair gelled and in a bun, and my glasses wouldn't have looked out of place on Dame Edna Everage.

Danny   Miss Finnegan?!

Lana   I was having an affair with Barbara Bewley, gym mistress, but that is not important right now.

Judy   What do you want? Coming round here, walking on the celestial waters, masquerading as an Attendant of the Pearly Gates . . .

Lana   I want to say that you took parental inadequacy to new depths.

Judy   But why?! Liza's fine really . . .

Lana   You did the unspeakable. You never let your child see the aurora borealis. Better known as the northern lights. You let them make do with . . . Blackpool!

Judy   My kids wanted for nothing. They did so!

Lana   However, I have come to rectify that. With a click of these fingers all will be redeeemed.

Judy's *boat starts to move.*

Judy   I'm gonna report you. Fifteen years I've been the Keeper of the Stars, never before have I been spoken to by a Pearly Gates Attendant in this way! I will! I'll report you!

Connor   Running away, Beryl?

Judy   I'm protecting Danny. Wait there! Don't move, Danny!

Danny   I don't think I can!

Judy's *boat disappears.* **Lana** *clicks her fingers. Lights flicker across the stage.* **Danny** *watches in awe.*

Lana   Come. We must leave now.

Danny   Don't you wanna stay and watch the lights?

Connor   Bye, Danny.

Danny   Connor, look. Isn't it fabulous?

Connor   Good luck, Danny.

Lana   You're going to need it.

Lana and **Connor** *walk back across the water.*

Danny   Connor, look! Isn't it fabulous?

Blackout.

Scene Two

Kensington Gardens.

Ben *in overalls, sweeping up leaves.* **Lee** *cycles past on his bike and stops.*

Lee   I thought it was you.

Ben   Oright?

Lee   Long time no see.

Ben   Yeah, well, I think I was getting on Connor's tits.

Lee   You were getting on everyone's tits.

Ben   I didn't know you were a courier.

Lee   I didn't know you'd gone back to work.

Ben   Got bored of twiddling me thumbs. Full glass, empty life.

Lee *chuckles to himself.*

Ben   What?

Lee   Just enjoying the sweet irony that you work in Kensington Gardens. After all you said about Princess Di.

Ben   She weren't the only person who died last year.

Lee   No. But you would've had to clean up all them flowers.

Ben   That was her flat up there. Seen her a few times. On the phone.

Lee   Ever see her in the nude?

Ben   And here was me thinking you liked her coz of her attitude to AIDS.

Lee *takes out a packed lunch. He sits down to eat.*

Lee   Mind if I join you?

Ben   Whatever.

Lee   Always eat me packed lunch here if I can. Been coming here for years. Desperate for a glimpse of Di. Then when all those flowers were here it was a good place to sit and think.

Ben   Plenty of thinking time in this job.

Lee   Don't it get boring? Raking all these lumps over.

Ben   They're not lumps.

Beryl *rushes on with a letter to post.* **Ben** *stops sweeping and he and* **Lee** *watch* **Beryl***.*

Beryl   'Dear Daniel, I don't know if you're aware, you probably aren't, it's a well-kept secret. But the whole of North Yorkshire is constructed on top of a system of underground tunnels known officially as Rankins. Having never visited them myself I cannot offer a vivid description, but I do see, daily, evidence of their existence. What some people idly pass off as molehills, I know to be ventilation turrets for the rankins. Indeed, the phrase "to make a mountain out of a molehill" actually derives from the phrase

"to make a molehill out of a rankin". The North Yorkshire
system, or grid, was originally built in the early 1960s as an
emergency evacuation site for use in the event of the nuclear
bomb. I firmly believe that your father is planning to plant a
series of bombs at strategic Rankenstraisses – the German
term for major rankins – thus causing the majority of North
Yorkshire to collapse. It has now become blatantly obvious
to me that Auntie Jan is not gallivanting round the world
but that he is keeping her hostage in Rankenstraisse F. I am
of course shielding this information from your cousin
Raymond, but I think the truth will out eventually. Your
father has secret contacts in various capital cities around the
globe and has trained them meticulously in imitating Jan's
handwriting. I was almost fooled. I find no alternative but to
turn your father in to the police, thus ensuring the
protection of several North Yorkshire beauty spots, and the
lives of millions of people. It's not so much the people that I
care for, but when I look from my kitchen window and see
the glory of the local mountains, I fear for his sanity. I
realise now that his reaction to your sexuality was indeed an
excuse to relocate from Liverpool and destroy North
Yorkshire. I plan to turn him in on Thursday after my
creative cookery class. Mum. PS Don't mention this to
anyone.'

She rushes off.

Ben   I've got to go. Will you see Connor?

Lee   Tonight.

Ben   Tell him to give us a ring. I'm back to me usual self
now. Will you tell him?

Lee (*nods*)   I'll see you, mate.

Ben   You're all right, you are. For a straight bloke.

Ben *makes to go.*

Lee (*camp*)   Who you calling straight? You wouldn't believe
where that saddle's been!

Ben *exits.* **Lee** *sits there for a while. He gets his mobile phone out and looks at it. It rings. He answers it.*

Lee   Hello? Where are you? I'm by a big tree. No to the left of that. Oh, I can see you now. Over here. That's it.

Danny *enters on mobile phone.*

Danny   I don't know why I've agreed to do this. (*Puts phone away.*)

Lee   You can meet a mate for a sandwich, can't you?

Danny   What've you got?

Lee   Peanut butter.

Danny   Vile.

Lee   Keeps the energy up.

Danny   I can't remember the last time we spent any time alone.

Lee   Obviously there's an ulterior motive. He's sorry, Danny.

Danny   I know. He's told me. He's left about fifty-five messages on the answerphone.

Lee   He loves you.

Danny   I know. He's told me that an'all. Look, it's been a bit of a difficult time, that's all.

Lee   Why?

Danny   Stuff with me mum.

Lee   Right. Look. We're going out tonight. Why don't you join us?

Danny   When you say 'we', I take it you don't mean you and a bunch of couriers in cycling shorts. I might be tempted then.

Lee   Come out with us, Danny. It ain't the same without you.

Danny   He's got you to say all this, hasn't he?

Lee   No.

Danny   He doesn't understand what I'm going through.

Lee   He wants to.

Danny   Why? Why should he? I wouldn't.

Lee   Well, would you rather be on your own?

A lighting change. 'People of Love' by Amen blasts out.

Scene Three

Heaven.

The northern lights now turn into the light display at the club. **Lana,** **Lee** *and* **Connor** *are dancing. They each have a bottle of water, or alcoholic drink, and are smoking.* **Lana** *and* **Connor** *are off their tits.* **Lee** *'s on the way. They move from the dance floor to a quieter area to stand and talk.*

Lee   Has your E worked?

Lana   I dunno.

Lee   Has yours?

Connor (*to* **Lana**)   Has anyone ever told you you look like Isla St Clair?

Lana   No.

Connor   In a 'you don't look anything like her' sort of way.

Lee   I ain't felt nothing.

Connor   Neither have I. In a 'fucking hell I'm buzzing my nut off' sort of way.

Lana　Well, you look like Larry Grayson.

Connor　Do I?

Lana　In a 'you don't at all actually' sort of way.

Connor　Isla St Clair. Top bird.

Lana　They should bring her back.

Connor　Where from?

Lana　Wherever she is.

Connor　Where is she?

Lana　I don't know. Possibly the Isle of Mull. (*Starts to panic a bit.*) Shit. I don't know. (*Calls out to people around her.*) Does anyone know where Isla St Clair is?!

Lee　Calm down.

Connor　Danny might know.

Lee　If he ever gets here.

Lana (*calling out*)　Look, are you sure none of you know where Isla St Clair is?

Connor　Where d'you think you go when you die?

Lana　Don't know.

Connor　I saw this bloke with a T-shirt saying 'When I die, I'm going to Jamaica'. Isn't that brilliant?

Lana　I want to go to heaven. Sit around all day playing the harp.

Lee　I reckon. Nothing happens. That's it. The end.

Connor　I reckon you just sit around all day taking bucket loads o'drugs and getting off your tits.

Lee　No, mate, that's what you do now.

Danny *enters, smoking a spliff.*

Lee   Oright, mate? Glad you could make it. You had an E yet?

Danny *blows a kiss and* **Lana** *catches it and wipes it on her lips.*

Lee   Ask a stupid question.

Danny (*to* **Connor**)   Oright, twat?

Connor   Brilliant.

They hug.

Lana   What do you think, Danny? Not that I'm singling you out. For any specific reason.

Danny   What?

Connor   Where d'you go when you die?

Danny   My mum always said that when you die you go to Hushabye Mountain.

Lana   Sweet.

Danny   I heard that song in *Chitty Chitty Bang Bang* and when I asked her what the fuck it meant, that's what she said.

Lee   Bollocks. Yous're all of your tits.

Danny   When I'm feeling like this, no one outside this club knows how to live. And here's me, with this time bomb inside o'me and I know what living's all about.

Lana   How did 'Hushabye Mountain' go?

Danny   I forget.

Lee   It's a big hill.

Connor   It's practically a mountain.

Danny   Where all your old mates are, and you hang out with them. Without a care in the world. And you just wait for all your other mates to get there. And they do.

Connor   That's brilliant. But you're all right, aren't you?

Danny   I feel great.

Lana   Danny? Did you say earlier that your mum was Isla St Clair?

Danny   No.

Lee   Don't be daft, he ain't got a Scottish accent.

Lana   Well, he could have been educated down here.

Lee (*starting to rush*)   Oh, here we go!

Danny   She's not Isla St Clair.

Lana   Isn't she? Does she look like Isla St Clair?

Danny   A bit.

Connor   Is she a folk singer?

Danny   No, she's tone deaf.

Lana   Oh, God, does she have to wear a hearing aid?

Danny   She has to wear two Danish pastries over her ears. She's only allowed to take them off on Sundays.

Lana   God, you don't realise how lucky you are, do you? Can you do sign language?

Danny   Semaphore.

Lana   God. With hankies and things?

Danny   Postage stamps. She lives in a doll's house.

Lana   Blimey.

Connor   No, Barbie.

Danny   She sort of abandoned me, Lee.

Lee   I know.

Lana   Were you an abandoned baby?

Danny   No.

Lana   No, neither am I. I used to live in a plastic bag though.

Connor   What sort?

Lana   Waitrose. I'm perennially middle class.

Danny   Every now and again she drops me a line.

Lana   What, your mum does coke?

Danny   No. A letter. Filling me in. I haven't really got any family. Except Connor. And my mates.

Lee   You're family to me, Danny.

Lana   And me.

Lee   Whatever happens we'll be there for you. Right, Lana?

Lana   Yeah.

Danny   Who needs family anyway?

Lana   Nobody. Except everybody.

Danny   But I appreciate what you're saying. And I'd just like to say, well, thanks. Thank you. I've just got to kiss you all if that's OK.

Lana   God, I'd really like that actually.

Danny *kisses* **Lana**, *and they have a really good hug. He goes to kiss* **Lee**.

Lee   God, I really feel I've got to say this right, but, I'm just so glad we introduced you to Connor. Coz if we hadn't, we'da never have had such blinding nights out. But we did. And we have. And I'm not just saying this coz I'm on an E or anything. But. I know I can be a cunt and all that but. I do love you, Danny. I mean. Life ain't always easy to understand. But like, who cares? Coz like, it's about what you get up to. And . . . all that shit. It's about . . . who's along for the ride. I really fucking mean that. What's AIDS, you know? It's just a fucking glitch, innit? Fucking hell, I'm rushing my tits off. But I know what I'm saying. It's like. AIDS. Fuck it. We'll fucking beat it. And even if you fucking die. We'll all still fucking love you. I mean, I don't wanna sleep with you or nothing. I mean, not coz you've got the HIV or nothing. I'm into birds. It ain't because of your blood or nothing. I mean, what's blood? It's just water, innit? And how much water have we drunk in our lives? And how would we know if someone had pissed in it? I mean. Love. It's fucking top, isn't it?

Lana   So, anyway, Danny. Let me run this by you again. You haven't seen your mum for ages. Right?

Danny   Yeah?

Lana   So it is possible . . .

Danny   Aha?

Lana   That she could have turned into Isla St Clair.

The music stops abruptly and there is a lighting change. We find:

Scene Four

Psychiatric hospital.

Beryl *sits in her hospital gown, holding her next letter.*

Beryl   'Dear Daniel, I'm not really sure why I'm here. To be totally frank, I'm not really sure where I am. I don't really know whether this letter will get to you. I sleep a lot, which is nice, because my dreams are in glorious technicolour. Your father has won. North Yorkshire will collapse at some time in the future. Now that I'm here he says that Auntie Jan's going to come home. Obviously he has panicked and is releasing her. It wouldn't surprise me if he's brainwashed her and she colludes with the travelling tale. Raymond is, of course, delighted. Oh, the naivety of youth. Your father is using this whole episode as an excuse to blame you. The general consensus of opinion is that I am

mad. Obviously, to the outside world, that is how I appear.
But the sadness of it is that I am not. I am enlightened. I am
also very angry. They'll be laughing on the other side of
their faces when it actually does happen. The psychiatrist
asked me some unspeakable things about my sex life and
when I said it was more like a sex death he accused me of
being in denial. My retort about never having been to Egypt
went right over his head. I've decided I will abstain from
speaking. This will make life a lot easier. Can you imagine
how your father is fairing without his chief cook and bottle
washer? That is some little reward. I have a tape recorder in
my room and would be very pleased if you could send me
the collected works of Judy Garland. They said she was
mad. Funny how it's always the women. The question I ask
myself is: What was her husband up to? I am sick. Sick of
your father. I can get better away from him. But time alone
will tell which of us was right. Mum.'

Scene Five

Connor's *flat.*

Connor *stands before several cardboard boxes in a new flat. He gets
the remote control and aims it at an unseen stereo. 'People of Love' is
playing on his stereo. He sits on the floor and starts going through the
boxes. The first houses a load of videos. He pulls them out, one by one.*
Beryl *enters and watches him. She takes the remote control and aims
it at the stereo and the music goes down.*

Connor   When are you gonna leave me alone?

Beryl   Nice pad.

Connor   I couldn't afford the rent on the other place. Not
on me own.

Beryl   I'm cold.

Connor   Tough.

Beryl   You think you're such a martyr, don't you. So
bloody perfect.

Connor   No I don't.

Beryl   So critical of me. That's nothing new. Had it all my
life. Even now I've stopped speaking, still they criticise.
What do I have to do?

Connor   I don't think I'm perfect.

Beryl   Mister Goody Two Shoes.

Connor   I shouted at him.

Beryl   So?

Connor   When he died. Not particularly proud of that.

Beryl   What did you shout?

Connor   Fucking bastard or something. I weren't really in
me right mind.

Beryl   You're still not. Why else would I be here?

Connor   I made them keep his ring on. I said, 'Yeah.
Can't throw it at me now.'

Beryl   How did he look?

Connor   Fabulous. We'd had a weekend at the seaside.
Did him the world of good. No, he looked dead peaceful.
He is.

Beryl   I've told you.

She tuts. Brief pause.

What are you doing?

Connor   Sorting these out.

Beryl   They're his.

Connor   Not any more. *Carry On Screaming.*

Beryl He saw that for the first time with me. Bonfire night. He loved that bit where Fenella Fielding looks through the picture. Remember? The picture of the woman on the wall, and the eyes move and she's looking through it? Spying on them.

Connor Yeah.

Beryl (*quoting*) 'Do you mind if I smoke?' He loved *Song of Bernadette* as well. And we're not even Catholics. (*Sees another box.*) Have you looked in here yet?

Connor Eh?

Beryl This one.

Connor Where did that come from?

Beryl You tell me.

Connor I've been storing all the stuff at Lee and Lana's. I must've picked it up by mistake when I got this lot. What's in it?

Beryl Don't know.

Connor What? (*He opens it.*) They're all addressed to him. At Lana and Lee's . . . What the . . . (*He opens a letter.*) Why?

Beryl He loved me.

Connor Why there?

Beryl You were dead set against it.

Connor So he was scheming behind me back?

Beryl It wasn't scheming.

Connor So he did write to you.

Beryl Well, you'd've really approved, wouldn't you. Letters every other week from me.

Connor He said he never.

Beryl We've all got secrets, Connor.

Connor   I haven't. I never had none from him. God, you must've been having a right laugh behind my back.

Beryl   I had no idea. I thought that was your address. Don't have a go at me.

Connor   Bastard.

Beryl   Don't be angry with him

Connor   Why not? All we ever did when he was alive was row. If it was that important to him he should've told me.

Beryl   He tried to.

Connor   I thought it was bad for him. Specially when he was ill. This one's for me.

Beryl   There are three for you actually.

Connor   What do they say?

Beryl   See for yourself. Do you miss him?

Connor   What sort of a question's that?

Beryl   Do you?

Connor   I miss kissing him.

Beryl   You sound like a pop song. They play pop songs all the time in that place. There's always a radio on somewhere. Drives me mad.

Connor   I miss putting me arms round him. I miss telling him everything. I miss having a laugh.

Beryl   Rowing?

Connor   Even that.

Beryl   Me too. You don't always get what you want, do you?

Connor   Now who sounds like a pop song?

Beryl   I should go.

Connor   You're not gonna come back, are you?

Beryl   That's up to you, isn't it?

Lee *enters with two cups of tea. He's dressed in his cycle courier outfit.*

Beryl   Not another Buddhist!

Connor   My brother. Leave me alone.

Beryl   Be grateful for small mercies. At least I've come as myself today. Next time I might be Fenella Fielding.

Lee   Fuck, I've lost me ring.

Connor   Eh?

Lee   Me wedding ring, where is it?

Beryl *picks a ring up off the floor.*

Beryl   You give it to him.

She hands it to **Connor**.

Connor   Here.

Beryl *leaves.*

Lee   Thank fuck for that. Musta dropped off when I was carrying this lot up.

Connor (*swigs tea*)   There's no sugar in it.

Lee   D'you take sugar?

Connor   I've been staying in your flat for six months, Lee. Shows how many times you put the kettle on.

Connor *exits.* **Lee** *plays with the ring in his hand and then slowly slips it on to his finger. As he does the lighting changes and we come up on:*

Scene Six

Hospital ward.

A year before. **Danny** *asleep in bed.* **Lee** *standing at his side. Eventually* **Danny** *wakes up.* **Lee** *is still dressed for work in his cycle courier outfit.*

Danny   How long have I been asleep?

Lee   Half-hour? You all right, mate? Can I get you anything?

Danny   Where are the others?

Lee   Getting a coffee.

Danny   Have you come straight from work?

Lee   No, I usually dress like this.

Danny   I'm dead thirsty.

Lee   Here.

Lee *pours him a glass of water and passes it to him. As* **Danny** *drinks,* **Lee** *is fighting tears.*

Danny   Hey. Stop it.

Lee   Hay fever. I don't usually get it.

Danny (*the water*)   Ooh, that's nice.

Lee   You know. When you and Connor first . . . I said . . . I mean, it was bang out of order. When you and him. That day I found you in the cottage. I seen red. I shouldn't have said what I said.

Danny   I can't remember to be honest.

Lee   Yeah, well, I can. I said if you fuck him up, I'll fuck you up.

Danny   And I have.

Lee   No, you ain't. You've made him the happiest man on God's earth. It was like he'd won the lotto when he met you. I just want you to know, it's been playing on me mind. I didn't mean it.

Danny   We've got a lot in common, me and you. We love the two same people. You're gonna take care of them, aren't you?

Lee   Yeah, mate. Don't you worry your head about them two. What's up?

Danny   How is it possible to feel this ill and yet get a twang of jealousy?

Lee   What you jealous of?

Danny   You. You're gonna spend more time with them than me.

Lee   They're boring bastards. You ain't gonna miss nothing there, mate.

Danny   It's nice here, isn't it?

Lee   S'all right, yeah. I'm. I'm gonna ask Lana to marry me, Danny. Usually, in the old days. I'd go to her dad and ask for his daughter's hand. But we don't get on. You know that. I don't respect 'em, Dan. Coz they're toffs. I know Lana's a toff, but she's the least snobby person I know. She sees through all the class bullshit. Well. I don't need their permission to marry her. Or even ask her. But I do feel I wanno ask the person closest to her. Danny. How would you feel about me asking Lana to marry me?

Danny   What are your prospects?

Lee   Better than yours. Worse than Richard Branson's.

Danny   You're better looking than Branson. Oh, go on then, you've twisted me arm.

Lee *gets up and kisses* **Danny** *on the forehead.*

Lee   I don't usually do that unless I'm on an E.

He hugs **Danny**. **Lana** *and* **Connor** *enter with coffees.*

Connor   Hiya.

Lana   You're awake! Are you comfortable? D'you want me to plump up your pillows for you?

Danny *shakes his head.*

Connor   When you get out of here. I'm taking you away for a few days. Somewhere nice.

Danny   We're skint.

Lana   We'll have a whip-round.

Danny   But. If only we'd had more. Scraping by to get a few drinks and a few E's of a weekend. Buying shit bread and cheap cling film. There's so much you wanna do.

Lee   You ain't giving in just yet, mate.

Danny   Who said I was?

Pause.

You know my problem? I believed all the hype. Not the usual shite. Get a semi-detached in suburbia, wife and kiddie and that's your key to eternal happiness. I believed the movies. The musicals. Everything's OK in the end. See? Even me dreams are tacky.

Connor   That's not tacky.

Danny   But no one was ever skint in the movies I liked. No one did a two-bit job in a Soho caff to get by.

Connor   We've done all right for ourselves.

Danny   I know. But we coulda done better. I was the first one in my family to go to university. Big deal. That didn't teach me about this.

Lana   Mildred Pierce worked in a caff. Sorry.

Pause. **Danny** *has fallen asleep.*

Lee   Is he breathing?

Connor   Yeah.

Lana   I said we'd stay with them if he wants to go home.

Lee   Course.

Danny *wakes.*

Danny   When are yous two gonna get married?

Blackout.

Scene Seven

Psychiatric hospital.

Beryl *with another letter.*

Beryl   'Dear Connor, I hope I've spelt that right. I am concerned that you have not written back to me since you came to visit. I realise that it must be painful for you thinking back to your time with Daniel. But please take the time to reply at some point. I still receive nightly messages from You Know Who saying Danny has not been passed for passing on. Or is it over? I'm not quite sure. In order to do this you need to tell me what sort of mother I was so that I can tell her and she can tell the relevant authorities. Can you do this soon? It is not me I am worried about. My guilt will never subside. I have lost everything and now it is too late to make it right. I worry about him. I fear the worst. But you know more than I. He will have told you. You must speak up honestly, and soon. I cannot pass on the relevant information, good or bad, unless you tell me. I hope life is treating you well. Yours sincerely, Beryl May. PS Enclosed is a tape that Danny sent me. I got the nurse to copy it for you. I thought you might like it.'

During this **Connor** *has entered and read the letter. He picks up a remote control and aims it at an unseen stereo. Pachelbel's 'Canon'* *begins to play. This plays under* **Beryl***'s reading of the letter and swells louder as the scene changes to:*

Scene Eight

Danny *and* **Connor***'s lounge.*

Connor*'s sitting on an armchair with a pad and pen.* **Danny** *is on the floor going through some CDs.* **Danny***'s pretty frail. Pachelbel's 'Canon' is playing.*

Danny   Pachelbel's 'Canon'. I think it's called. Hang on. (*Rifles through some CDs.*) See? It's really nice.

Connor   It's off an advert.

Danny   It's classical.

Connor   What's wrong with 'I've Been To Paradise But I've Never Been To Me'?

Danny   Just write down Pachelbel's 'Canon'.

Connor   How d'you spell Pachelbel?

Danny   Don't worry about that for now.

Connor (*writing*)   'I've Been To Paradise But I've Never Been To Me' was brilliant at the beginning of *Priscilla Queen of the Desert*.

Danny   Sung by a drag queen it's ironic. But the song is inherently misogynist.

Connor   I think you're making a big mistake.

Danny   D'you wanna do this or not?

Connor   Yeah.

Danny   Maybe I should do it on my own.

Connor   I don't mind.

Danny   No, it's all right. If you don't wanna think about my funeral I quite understand.

Connor   Well, can you blame me?

Danny   And can you blame me for wanting to plan it? It's the last vestige of control I can have over my life, my death. I've got fuck all control over anything else that's happening. D'you know what I'm saying, Connor?

Connor   Yeah.

Danny   Do you? Coz I don't know whether you do.

Connor   I don't want a row.

Danny   Just coz you wear a little red ribbon and you're going out with someone who's positive. Does that mean you've got insight?

Connor   Yeah.

Danny   Into what exactly?

Connor   Into how difficult it is for you.

Danny   Oh, and so you know how it feels to have a life-threatening illness?

Connor   I know how it feels to live with someone who has.

Danny   I didn't ask that.

Connor   What d'you want me to do? Go out there and share a dodgy needle? Go out there and have unprotected sex? Even better, stay in here and have unprotected sex! Just so's I can understand exactly what's going on in your head?

Danny   I just don't want your sympathetic wink and your patronising 'I know how you feel'. Coz you don't. And I hope to God you never will.

Connor   I never say that.

Danny   I shoulda known you'd be crap at this. Coz sticking your head in the sand's something you've got a fucking degree in.

Connor   I thought we were planning your funeral.

Danny   Oh, we were. Until some bright spark pipes up with 'I know, let's plan both our funerals'. Just so's it's that little less real for you. Coz you know you've got ages on me.

Connor   That's bollocks, Danny. I thought it'd make it easier for you if we did 'em both at the same time. And then you'd feel you had some input into mine an'all.

Danny   I'm dying, Connor.

Connor   You're all right.

Danny   And when I'm gone you'll probably meet someone else.

Connor   I'm dying an'all.

Danny   But not as quickly as me.

Connor   I won't meet anyone else.

Danny   I want you to.

Connor   Why?

Danny   Coz you should be happy. You look fucking awful when you frown. And then they'll have some input into your funeral.

Connor   I don't want their input, I want yours!

Pause.

Danny (*passes him CD*)   That's how you spell Pachelbel. And I want 'Liverpool Lullabye' somewhere.

Connor   Cilla Black's a Tory.

Danny   And 'Northern Lights'. Or did they have dodgy politics as well?

Connor   They were all in the BNP and killed black people and queers.

Danny   Did they?

Connor *grins cheekily. They try not to giggle.*

Connor   Your funeral's turning into a musical.

Danny   I love you, Connor. And I'm only gonna say this once. You've gotta realise that one day soon I'm gonna get ill. And I'm not gonna be doing your head in for ever. And don't try and be funny coz I'm being serious. It could be tomorrow, next week, next year, five years. Are you listening to me?

Connor   Yes.

Danny   Good. Put that down. Come and rub me neck.

Connor *goes behind him and massages his neck.*

Connor   Is it stiff?

Danny   No, but something else is.

Connor   You're insatiable.

Danny   You can't deprive a dying man of his nooky.

Connor   Can't I?

Danny   Take me to bed.

Connor *helps* **Danny** *up.* **Danny** *takes* **Connor**'s *face in his hands and kisses him. They kiss passionately.* **Connor** *pulls away.*

Danny   What?

Connor   Nothing. Come on.

Danny   What?

Connor   I don't want it to be the last time.

Danny   Neither do I. And change that CD. I don't want me fucking funeral music while I'm reaching nirvana.

The lights fade.

Scene Nine

Lady Chapel.

Connor *lighting a candle before a mosaic shrine to the Virgin Mary in a Catholic church. A nun comes in,* **Sister Bernadette**. *She kneels to pray.* **Ben** *enters.*

Ben   I thought it was you. I was coming out the hospital and seen you coming in here.

Connor   I better find the priest. Tell him to lock up the communion wine.

Ben   I didn't know you were religious.

Connor   Me brother's broken his leg. Come off his bike. I'm driving him home. Thought I'd pop in here, kill some time. I thought you were a Buddhist.

Ben   I am.

Connor   You just say you are.

Ben   No, I've got back into it. Come in here to think sometimes.

Connor   I'm sick to death of that place. Had to get out. Just went up to Danny's old ward. It's full of old women. They've changed it all around.

Ben   They've shut Radley down as an AIDS ward.

Connor   I got so used to the view from up there. If it was happening now I'd get a different view.

Ben   You wouldn't get any view at all, Connor. They shut Radley down coz there weren't enough patients.

Connor   What?

Ben   It's the combination therapy. Seems to be keeping us healthier, longer. Don't mean they'll never open it again. But for the time being it's right encouraging.

Connor   I don't fucking believe it. (*To* **Sister Bernadette**.) Sorry.

Sister   Sorry?

Connor   Sorry.

Sister   Open your mouth more. I'm deaf. Lip-reading.

Connor   Nothing.

Ben   Every time I come in for me check-up me T-cell count was creeping up. I've just got the results of me viral load test. Me HIV's just above undetectable.

Connor (*getting upset*)   That's brilliant.

Ben   It's weird.

Connor   Too fucking right.

Connor *looks away, trying to cover up the fact that he is crying.*

Ben   I'm sorry, Connor. You don't need to hear this.

Connor   I do. I do.

Ben   It's so peaceful here. D'you reckon she really is deaf? (*To* **Sister Bernadette**.) Ay, love, where d'you get that frock, it's gorgeous.

Connor   Shut up.

Ben   I used to hate going on that ward. People always start crying when I'm around.

Connor   I'm not crying for you, you egocentric . . .

Ben   The middle-aged nurses. All dead shocked looking after me. I was the youngest fella they'd had up there. I could tell what they were thinking when they seen me. I coulda been their son. But I haven't been admitted in over a year now. I've spent the last three years thinking me time was up. Out I did was a preparation for death. And now. Now some tosser's gone and moved the goalposts. I can't really take it all in.

Connor   Aren't you happy?

Ben   I'm sort of in shock really.

Connor   Well, you should be happy.

Ben   I was a bit out of control when I were knocking about wi'you lot. I'm sorry about that. Connor, they've closed three AIDS wards in London coz they couldn't fill the beds. We're all being managed at home.

Connor   Care in the community?

Ben   Don't you care?

Connor   Course I care! Don't mean to say it's fair.

Ben   Eh?

Connor   You! Look at you. You could land head first in a barrel of shite and come out smelling of CK1. (*To* **Sister Bernadette**.) Sorry. (*To* **Ben**.) Let's go outside.

Ben   I have to light a candle. I always light a candle after an appointment now.

Connor   Why?

Ben   I'm a drama queen.

Connor *watches* **Ben** *light a candle.*

Ben   It's not my fault Danny's not around for it.

Pause.

How are you anyway?

Connor   How d'you think?

Ben   Should I go then?

Pause.

I'm sorry, mate.

Connor   Yeah? Well, so am I.

Ben   They reckon one day HIV'll be a manageable illness like diabetes.

Connor   Oh, you know all the snippets of gossip, don't you. Like the time you were going round spouting conspiracy theories.

Ben   They do.

Connor   Do they? Well, it's a shame that there had to be so many guinea pigs along the way who never found that out.

Ben   D'you know my dream? They'll have to change the Lighthouse into a job centre for all of us who thought we were going to die. Maybe that's why I light a candle.

Pause.

I've got an acting job next week.

Connor   Well, life's just brilliant, isn't it?

Ben   It's all right sometimes.

Connor   For you maybe.

Ben   And what about you? You're young. You've got your health. You've got the whole of your life ahead of you. I thought I didn't. Now I just don't know. You say I could fall in a barrel load o'shite and come out smelling o'roses. Maybe. Who knows? But you, Connor, you never fell in it in the first place.

Connor   Leave me alone.

Ben   Oh, go and lie down in a darkened room and suck your thumb and feel sorry for yourself. Things never do get better, Connor. You taught me that. They just get different. Take some of your own medicine for a change.

Pause.

I was mad about you, you know. I didn't just fancy you. I wanted you to look after me. I'd get so jealous of Danny.

Coz he'd had all of you. Daft, int it? Being jealous of a dead person. And now I know why. He didn't mess things up. Don't fret. I'm not gonna start stalking you.

Pause.

D'you want to go for a walk?

Connor   I've gotta pick Lee up in a bit.

Ben   Can I call you?

Connor   I've moved.

Ben   Right. I'll see you around then.

Connor   Have you got a pen? I'll give you me number.

Ben   No. It's OK, Connor. See you.

Connor   See you.

Ben *starts to walk away.*

Ben   Ay.

Connor   What?

Ben   Funny-looking bird that Jesus's mam, weren't she?

They chuckle. **Ben** *exits.* **Connor** *watches him go. He kneels down to pray and starts to cry. While he's not looking there is some movement around the shrine to the Virgin Mary. A secret door where her face is slides across and we see a woman's face peering through. It's like in* Carry On Screaming. *The woman,* **Mary,** *speaks with an Irish accent.*

Mary   The cheek of it. I'm not that ugly.

Connor *looks up. He sees* **Mary**'s *face. He looks round to see if the* **Sister Bernadette** *is looking; she's got her head bowed in prayer.*

Mary   Pass us one o'them candles, quick.

Connor *gets up and passes a candle to* **Mary** *who has a ciggie hanging out of her mouth. He lights it and she smokes. He replaces the candle.*

Mary   Ta, love.

Connor   When's this gonno end?

Mary   Well, that's kind of up to you now, isn't it?

Connor   I'm going mad, I know I am.

Mary   Talking of which. Is that batty old cow still writing to you?

Pause.

Have you written back?

Connor   I can't lie.

Mary   A good Catholic. Pleased to hear it.

Connor   Well, what d'you want me to say? 'Yeah, you were a great mam. Well done, love.'

Mary   All a mother can give is unconditional love. A shoulder to cry on and an arm round you to steady you when you feel wobbly. What d'you reckon?

Connor   Well, she never done that.

Mary   But you did. From where I'm standing he had the best mother in the world.

Connor   I thought that was you.

Mary   For me son's sake he had you. Quick, I've got to go, the priest's coming. Remember what I said now.

She disappears and the painted face slides back. **Sister Bernadette** *gets up.*

Sister   Every day I come and pray. For a sign from Our Lady. Like me namesake, Bernadette of Lourdes. A miracle. To get my ears back. Every day the same. Looking at Our Lady's face. Every day the same blank expression. May the Lord be with you, my child.

She exits. A **Priest** *enters carrying a tray held by ribbons round his neck, like a cinema usherette. On the tray are small statues of Our Lady, Catholic novelties, pens, etc.*

Priest   Statues of Our Lady! Rubbers with the Sacred Heart of Jesus on them. Can I be interesting you in anything now?

Connor   No thanks.

Priest   How about a small donation to the restoration of the mosaic of Our Lady there? The face needs a bit of work.

Connor   All right then.

He gets a pound out.

Priest   A pound! I'm rich! Well, I can't let you go away empty-handed, can I? What do we have that's worth a pound? I know. One sheet of letter paper with the church's emblem on the top, one matching envelope and a biro. Don't say the Catholic Church isn't generous now.

He moves off.

Nine-inch Our Lady's! Holy Water from Lourdes. Get it all here for under a fiver!

The **Priest** *exits.* **Connor** *looks at the paper, envelope and pen in his hand and smiles.*

Scene Ten

Parliament Hill.

Lana *and* **Connor** *smoking a joint on a bench at the top of the hill.*

Connor   The view's brilliant.

Lana   Who was it said? Someone said. Sitting at the top of Parliament Hill is like. Like looking down into a huge breakfast bowl. And at the bottom of the bowl, is like . . . London.

Connor   Oh, Lana, you're so middle class. What's a fucking breakfast bowl? It's just a bowl.

Lana   I used to be really embarrassed about being middle class. Everyone on my course at uni. They were all so streetwise. Always taking the mickey out of my voice. Then Danny came along. He said, 'You're not middle class. You're camp.' I was delighted. Me. Camp. He said, 'Anyone called Lana has to be camp.' I'd never met a gay person in my life before. And suddenly I was Lana Lasagne. Camp as tits. He was the first person in my life to make me feel good about myself. I hated having red hair. He said, 'It's not hair. It's your sunset.' We drove everybody mad on our course. We refused to speak normally. We insisted on being Beverley from *Abigail's Party*. I remember the tutor asking why I'd handed an essay in late and I said it was because I had 'really beautiful lips'. Danny nearly wet himself. We talked for hours on the phone. Just doing stupid voices. I haven't done a stupid voice in years. It was Danny who told me to go for it with Lee. I thought he wouldn't look twice at me. Danny said, 'He's mad about you.' If it wasn't for him I'd probably be living in the Home Counties, making chutney, waiting for hubby to get in. Danny thought Lee was sexy. I was hardly surprised when he fell for you. The gay version.

Connor   So Danny was using me to get to Lee?

Lana   Danny was sexy. I was in love with him. This is twelve years ago, mind you. Well, who wouldn't fall in love with a man who said your hair was a sunset?

Connor   The bastard never said that about me.

Lana   Here's Lee. Look at him. Great big lolloping lump. Danny was right. He is mad about me. So romantic. Carrying our ice creams up the hill for us.

Connor   He'll probably trip up and drop 'em.

Lana   Don't be horrible.

Connor   I don't believe in romance. Life's not like that. Like when I first met Danny. And we were gonna sleep the night on the beach.

Lana   That's incredibly romantic though.

Connor   'Til the fucking tide came in. We were straight back to his room then.

Lana (*calls*)   Hurry up, Lee! (*To* **Connor**.) Life is like that.

Connor   No. You think everything's fine, and then you wake up, and you're soaking wet.

Lana (*about* **Lee**)   Look at him. Isn't he gorgeous?

Connor   He's all right.

Lana   You love me, don't you?

Lee (*off*)   What?!

Connor   It's coz you've got really beautiful lips.

From now on **Lana** *continues her Beverley from* Abigail's Party *voice. Sometimes* **Connor** *joins in.*

Lana   Oh, they're really beautiful. You should see my downstairs lips.

Connor   Beautiful?

Lana   Really beautiful. They're nice and dainty.

Connor   Fantastic.

Lee *enters, out of breath, with three ice creams.*

Lee   Don't say I never give you nothing.

Lana   Oh, Tony, I'm going to get ice cream over my really beautiful lips.

Lee   My bird's turning into a drag queen.

Connor   You'll have to stop her knocking about with so many puffs.

Lee   Yeah. Turns you queer. Give us some of that.

Connor *passes* **Lee** *the joint. They each sit eating their ice creams.*

Lee   It's all dribbled down me fingers.

Lana   Don't be rude, Tony.

Connor   Isn't it a beautiful day?

Lana   It's really beautiful actually.

Connor   Really beautiful.

Lee   Blinding view, innit.

Connor/Lana   Really beautiful.

Lana   Like my lips.

As they sit there admiring the view the lights come up on:

Scene Eleven

Psychiatric hospital / Beyond the pearly gates.

Beryl *sits in a wheelchair.* **Kevin**, *her nurse, approaches her with a letter.*

Kevin   It's your lucky day. Thank you. It's nothing.

Beryl   Thank you.

Kevin   You what?

Beryl   Thank you, nurse.

Kevin   Actually it's Kevin. As in Rowlands. Apparently I was conceived when Dexy's Midnight Runners were on the radio. 'Come On Eileen', remember that? That was my mother's name.

Beryl   Thank you, Kevin. You're Scottish.

Kevin   Moved down here to be with my girlfriend.

Beryl   I moved here too. From Liverpool.

Kevin   So much in common.

Beryl   Would you mind pushing me?

Kevin   Where d'you wanna go?

Beryl   Anywhere. Just push.

Kevin   Nay problem.

He starts to push her.

Beryl   That's too fast.

Kevin   Sorry.

He wheels her slowly towards the back of the stage. As he pushes her she opens the letter. The lights fade as we hear the voice of a woman begin to sing 'Hushabye Mountain' from Chitty Chitty Bang Bang. *The lights fade on* **Connor**, **Lee** *and* **Lana** *eating their ice creams and on* **Beryl** *and* **Kevin**.

The lights rise softly at the back of the stage.

It is **Judy** *who is singing. She tucks* **Danny** *up in the boat, covering him with her shawl. He has the stars as a night light. She puts up a small sail on the boat. She has a cigarette on the go.*

A breeze has begun to blow. The sails are filling with air. The lighting has got darker. As **Judy** *sings, the boat begins to move. The moon shining over the water sends light twinkling all over the stage.* **Danny** *is falling asleep.*

Judy *continues singing.*

We can't tell in which direction the boat is heading. **Danny** *is asleep.* **Judy** *has a drag on her cigarette. The lights fade.*

Out in the Open

Out in the Open was first performed at the Hampstead Theatre, London, on 15 March 2001. The cast was as follows:

Tony	Mark Bonnar
Iggy	James McAvoy
Mary	Linda Bassett
Kevin	Sean Gallagher
Monica	Michele Austin
Rose	Vilma Hollingbery

Directed by Kathy Burke
Designed by Michael Taylor
Lighting by Chris Davey
Sound by Dean Whiskens

Characters

Tony, *Scottish, thirty-three. His partner Frankie died six months ago.*
Iggy, *Mancunian, twenty-one, looks like a rent boy.*
Mary, *Londoner, fifty-five. Never shuts up, nervous. Frankie's mum.*
Kevin, *Londoner, thirty-three. An alcoholic. Frankie's best mate from school.*
Monica, *black, thirty, a bit overweight. A waitress who wants to act.*
Rose, *a friend of Mary's. In her sixties, a big drinker.*

Setting

The play is set over one long weekend in the back garden of Tony's ground-floor flat in Dalston, London, summer 2000. There is a set of French windows into the living room of the flat and an entry up the side of the house that leads to the street. The garden wouldn't look out of place on an episode of *Ground Force*. There is a step up from the house, and the raised area is covered in tasteful decking. Night lights hang on the wall in jars. There is a water feature and a barbecue. Nice benches and a table fitted into the design, matching the decking. Plants in pots. Fairy lights. The cordless phone seems to live on the garden table.

Act One

Scene One

Friday night.

*The lights come up on **Tony**'s garden, night-time. A hot summer's evening. The light is on in the living room and fairy lights light the decking, along with night lights and candles. **Tony** and **Iggy** sit on cushions on the ground. **Tony** has a bottle of lager. **Iggy** is drinking something fizzy from a glass.*

Iggy   Why are you on edge?

Tony   I'm not.

Iggy   You said you were.

Tony   I'm full of shite.

Iggy   You are single, aren't you?

Tony   What? Well, that's just it, you see. My boyfriend's inside. He's got a terrible temper on him. (*Beat.*) Yeah. I'm single.

Iggy   But someone else lives here?

Tony   Only my lodger. He's out. I think. Maybe I should go and check.

Iggy   Have you always been single?

Tony   No. No, I was with someone for seven years. Look at the size of your hands. Hold them up.

They hold a hand up against hand to compare sizes. They rub hands.

Iggy   What happened?

Tony   He died.

Iggy   Shit, I'm sorry. Was it recent?

Tony   Six months ago. Is that recent? It feels recent.

Iggy   Shit. What was his name?

Tony   Frankie.

Iggy *wretches.*

Iggy   Sorry.

Tony   You all right?

Iggy   It's this. (*Indicates the glass.*) It's minging. What is it again?

Tony   Dioralyte. Try this. (*Passes him the beer.*) So do you have a bloke?

Iggy   No one'll have me.

Tony   I don't believe that for one second.

Iggy   I just split up with someone.

Tony   Long-term?

Iggy *shrugs.*

Tony   Who did the ditching?

Iggy   Him.

Tony   He's a fool. Did you never show him your eyes? It's Frankie's birthday today.

Iggy   How old would he have been?

Tony   Thirty-three. Ancient.

Iggy   It's not ancient.

Tony   How old are you? Don't tell me you're still at school.

Iggy   Fuck off, twenty-one. I'm at college me. Photography.

Tony   The camera never lies.

Iggy   How old are you?

Tony   Forty-five next birthday. I know I don't look it.

Iggy   Really? God. You only look about thirty-eight.

Tony   I'm thirty-three.

Iggy   Good job I go for older men then, innit?

Tony   Was he old?

Iggy   I don't wanna talk about him.

Pause.

Tony   So what brings you to London?

Iggy   Felt like it.

Tony   I remember the days when I did things just cos I felt like it.

Iggy   Wanted to get him out me system.

Tony   But why did you end up in that pub? I'da thought a pretty boy like you would've been heading up to Soho.

Iggy   I was. Then I got the shits. D'you go there often?

Tony   Is that you chatting me up?

Iggy   No. It's a question.

Tony   Dunno. Couple of times a week. We used to go together. Had our own quiz team. The Dalston Darlings. I only go now when the boredom sets in. When I'm sick of fiddling with my decking. This isn't a garden by the way, it's therapy.

Iggy   D'you miss him?

Tony   Of course I do. He was my best pal.

Iggy   I'm a nosy twat, aren't I?

Tony   You're a very beautiful twat, I'll give you that.

Iggy   I think you're pissed, mate.

Tony   Is Iggy short for Ignatius?

Iggy   Sadly.

Tony   Good Catholic lad, eh?

Iggy   Oh yeah.

Tony   Would it be possible to see you naked at any point this evening?

Iggy   What if I tell you to fuck off?

Tony   You won't tell me to fuck off. I bought you a pint. You came home with me. I tried to cure your shits.

Iggy   Yeah and you made me fucking sick.

Tony   You have a duty to let me see your naked form, it's only fair!

Iggy   You're fucking barmy, you.

Tony   I'm sorry. It's a while since I've done this.

Iggy   Have you not had anyone else since him?

Tony   To be honest I've not fancied it. 'Til now.

Iggy   Sounds to me like you're getting over him.

Tony   You're over him too. His ashes are buried right under you.

Iggy   Fuck off!

Tony *laughs.*

Iggy   Freak.

Tony   Sorry.

Iggy   What was the funeral like?

Tony *gets up angrily.*

Tony   Oh, it was great. A real laugh. What d'you wanna know about my boyfriend's funeral for? Turn you on, does it? All this talk about death? Bit of a necrophiliac, are you?

Iggy   I'm only trying to be nice.

Tony   It rained. OK? There was a lot of crying.
Particularly from me. Almost wailing at one point. Nicole
Farhi and snot, not an attractive combination. Kevin, my
lodger, he was at school with Frankie, he did a reading.
Another friend Monica sang 'Here Comes the Flood' by
Bette Midler. His mother was inconsolable, she still is. We
had the wake back at his favourite restaurant in Smithfields,
and later on we all went to a club.

He starts to cry.

This isn't right. This is so not right.

Iggy *steps over and takes* **Tony***'s face in his hands and slowly kisses
him. They snog for a while.* **Iggy** *pulls away tenderly.*

Iggy   Sorry. Couldn't help meself.

Tony   I haven't been with anyone your age since . . . well,
since I was your age.

Iggy *gets up and walks to the French windows. He stands there and
looks at* **Tony***, trying to look all sexy.*

Tony   Where d'you think you're going?

Iggy   Where's the bedroom?

Tony   Tired?

Iggy   No.

Tony   You can't possibly fancy me.

Iggy   I asked you a question.

Tony   I'm not very good at describing.

Iggy   Well, perhaps you better show me.

Tony   OK.

Iggy *sniffs and looks down at his trainers.*

Iggy   I think I've trod in something.

Tony   Oh, that'll be next door's cat, sorry. Slip your
trainers off.

Iggy *slips his trainers off.*

Iggy   I've not had a bath today.

Tony   Is that supposed to turn me on?

Iggy   D'you have a shower?

Tony   Into the hall, second door on your right.

Iggy   I thought you were crap at describing.

Tony   I'm afraid there's no lock on the door.

Iggy   Pervert.

Iggy *goes inside, leaving his trainers outside.* **Tony** *rests his head in
his hands. He sits there for a while, lost in thought. He gets up and
blows the candles out, then switches the fairy lights off. He looks up to
the heavens and smiles. He calls out to the sky.*

Tony   You bastard!

Blackout.

Scene Two

Saturday morning.

The next morning. **Tony** *comes out in his dressing gown with a
dustpan and brush and a mop. He goes to brush away the cat shit on
the decking. The French windows are open and the telly is on. It's a
warm sunny day.* **Iggy**'s *trainers sit on the floor outside the French
windows where he left them last night.*

Tony (*shouts to neighbours*)   You should sew that cat's arse
up! How would you like it if I came over and crapped on
your grass?

He sweeps the shit into the dustpan and throws it over the fence.
Mary *bounds through the gate with three plastic bags. Two contain watermelons, one contains shopping.*

Mary   Oh no! He hasn't done it again, has he?

Tony   Mary?!

Mary   Hello, darling. Oh and all over your lovely decking look. What you done to your hair?

Tony   I'm just up.

As she speaks he goes about mopping the decking.

Mary   You ever tried Maurice on the high street? He's good. No, he is good, darling, trained in Paris. But don't, whatever you do, get saddled with Kisha-Louise. What she's doing in a salon of that calibre I'll never know.

Tony   Did you want a cuppa?

Mary   Ooh no, darling. I only popped in to give you these. (*She empties two large watermelons on to the table.*) I seen 'em up Ridley Road, darling. They got your name on 'em.

Tony   Where?

Mary   It's a saying, darling.

Tony   It's a joke, Mary. Sit down, I'll stick the kettle on.

Mary   No, I can't stop. Honestly, darling. I'm looking in on me lady with the leg, darling, and I'm late as it is.

Tony   Well, if you're sure.

Mary   Mind you, I've come all this way. And I don't suppose I'll get a bus straight away, bastards.

Tony   Tea?

Mary (*grabs his arm and pulls him close*)   What's that funny one you give me last time, darling?

Tony   Sage.

Mary   Have you got any left? Cos I'll have normal if I'm putting you out.

Tony   You're not. It's a glorious day, isn't it?

Tony exits with the watermelons. *Mary* gets a joint out of her handbag and lights up.

Mary   That's the only word for it. (*Spying* **Iggy**'s *trainers*.) Oh, Tony. You got yourself a new pair o'pumps, darling? Ooh, they're nice and fancy. Here, you'll never guess what. Bloody optician says I need a new pair o'glasses. I can stick with what I got for reading, but I need another set for watching the bloody telly. 'Blimey!' I said. 'I'll have more glasses than Stringfellows.'

Kevin *comes in, pissed, just woken up.*

Mary   Oh, Kevin. No work today?

Kevin   No.

He picks up a bottle of Hooch off the garden table.

Mary   How's your lovely old nana keeping?

Kevin   She's got shingles.

Mary   What, round her trunk?

Kevin   Yeah.

Mary   Cor, that's nasty. Send her me best, won't you?

Kevin   If you want.

He exits. **Mary** *starts mopping the decking.* **Tony** *comes back out.* **Kevin** *sits watching the telly indoors during the following.*

Tony   Mary, I can do that.

Mary   Oh, shut up. Want some o'this? (*Offers him the joint.*) Go on, darling. I hate smoking it on me own.

Tony   No, I'm trying not to.

Mary   Oh, me too. But see, it's me rheumatoid arthritis, darling. I'm not supposed to carry anything heavier than a bag o'sugar.

Tony   Well, what were you doing buying two fucking watermelons?

He goes back inside. **Mary** *calls the next speech through to him.*

Mary   I had this terrible dream last night, Tony. Horrible it was. I'm up John Lewis in Brent Cross and I'm in the basement, when the woman next to me in the queue sets fire to herself. And it starts to spread. So I leg it up all the escalators to get to the roof.

Tony *comes out with a bowl of hot soapy water and a scrubbing brush. He goes about cleaning the dirt off* **Iggy**'s *trainers.*

Mary   Then I has to jump off the roof, on to this big stack o'sofas. And all the firemen there was off *London's Burning*. But I can't stand *London's Burning*. What d'you reckon that means? They were really nice actually. Specially the Greek one. I was about to have a little cuddle and that with him only I woke up.

Tony   Who's the lady with the leg?

Mary   Three doors down, moved in last month. I only get her a few bits, she's ever so grateful. Had a ramp built up to her porch. I said to her, I said, 'Council didn't waste no time with you, darling. Shame they weren't like that with my wonky bath.' Eighteen months it took to level it out. I had a deep end and a shallow end. You taken your pills today, darling?

Tony   Aye. Why's she had a ramp built? That's pretty postmodern, isn't it?

Mary   She can't manage steps, darling. She's got one o'them funny wheelchairs what look like them golfing car things. Sort o'thing Magnum drove. She's got one o' them for going the post office only I won't let her. Cos she drinks, darling. She thinks I don't know. But I found fifteen miniature vodka bottles up her entry. She's a dangerous driver. She's had three crashes since she moved in.

Tony   She goes on the road in it?

Mary   Well, she's not supposed to, obviously. But she's so fucking paralytic she can't see where she's going. And we've got that school round the back of us. I worry for them kiddies. Anyway she won't be going out in it again. I hid the keys. (*Pats her pocket.*)

Tony   She sounds like a laugh.

Mary   Oh, she's lovely, Tony. No she is lovely. Showers her home help with toffees, coasters, you name it. Just, you know, bit of an alky. And I mean, between you and me, she smells a bit. Home help says it's got a name.

Tony   Oh well, if she's in a wheelchair maybe it's difficult for her. You know, like . . . washing and stuff.

Mary   No, apparently she's always had it. Persistent Fish Odour Syndrome. Tries to cover it up with Charlie, bless her. But fuck me she is rank. Nice though. Lost a son in the Falklands, so we usually have a natter about that side o'things. Husband used to hit her.

Tony   That's terrible! And her in a wheelchair.

Mary   Reading between the lines . . . he put her in it. Oh, I shouldn't say things like that. He ain't here to defend himself.

Tony   Dead?

Mary   Birmingham. Well, the outskirts.

Tony   I'll check the kettle.

Mary   Yeah, hurry up, darling. I'm on a schedule. And make sure you wash your hands!

Tony *exits.*

Tony (*off*)   You're not stopping long, are you? I'm supposed to be in work in an hour.

Mary   I went up the grave yesterday. Nice flowers. You're ever so thoughtful, darling.

Tony (*off*)   I've not been up for a few weeks.

Mary   Ain't you? Well, who put the flowers there?

Tony (*off*)   I don't know.

Tony comes in and gives her a cup of tea.

Mary   But yesterday was the thirteenth, darling. You said . . .

Tony   I got tied up at work.

Mary   But it was his birthday, darling.

Tony   I know it was his fucking birthday, Mary. What did you want me to do? Go up there and bake a cake? I got tied up at work. I might go later.

Mary   This phone's filthy.

She gives it a wipe with her cloth.

Tony   I was going to go.

Mary   What got you tied up at work then, darling? I hope they ain't working you too hard. When I met your manager at Frankie's send-off I thought she had a touch of the Adolfs about her. Right bossy cow.

Tony   One of my team's got shingles. So I'm covering for him.

Mary   Ooh, that's a debilitating disease, shingles. Kevin's nan's got that, ain't she. Cor. There's a lot of it about, Tony. You wanna make sure you don't get it. It's like being punched in the side with a crowbar, you know.

Kevin *comes out in sunglasses with his Hooch.*

Mary   'Ere, Kevin. One of his team's got shingles an' all.

Kevin   Great. What's a doppelgänger?

Mary   Type o'German sausage, innit?

Kevin   Is it?

Tony   No. It's a looky-likey. Why?

Mary   Is it? Oh.

Kevin   They just said it on the telly. Didn't know what it was.

Mary   What you been doing with this phone, Kevin? It's filthy. Look at the colour of that!

Kevin   I've been making dirty phone calls, Mare.

Mary   You didn't call me, did you? Years back? I got an heavy breather the day Princess Diane died. Some people have got no respect for the dead.

Kevin   Yes, it was me.

Mary   I blew a whistle down the phone. Frankie said I should've asked him out. Cheeky little git. You been up Frankie's grave, Kev?

Kevin   No.

Mary   Only there was some nice red roses up there yesterday. Thought it mighta been you.

Kevin   Well, it weren't.

Mary   Oh well. Probably Monica.

Kevin   Monica's in Greece.

Mary   The musical?

Kevin   The country.

Mary   Oh, cos she had that audition.

Tony   That was for *Mamma Mia!*

Mary   She'd be good in that. She's got a lovely voice.

Kevin *grunts.*

Mary   Kevin!

Tony   What I wouldn't give to be lying on a beach just now.

Mary   She sung lovely at Frankie's send-off. D'you know who she reminds me of? She's like a black . . .

Kevin   Bella Emberg?

Mary   Jane MacDonald. Now she can sell a tune.

Tony   I think she's back today.

Mary   That's what Monica wants to do. She wants to get on one o'them docusoaps. She'd be lovely in one o'them. She'd be lovely in a lot of things.

Tony   Frankie always fancied Mykonos.

Mary   Did he?

Pause.

Kevin   Didn't they leave a card or nothing?

Mary   No. Looks lovely though, Kevin. You should get yourself up there. All them flowers. Call yourself a friend. And I took tiger tulips. I'm so pleased we went for that marble in the end.

Kevin   I don't need to go to no cemetery to remember him.

Mary   There's a new grave two doors up. Looks lovely. They went for the photograph on the headstone. Lovely looking woman. Got a look of Gloria Hunniford about her. I do think it's nice to put a face to the name.

Tony   Mary . . .

Mary   Don't shout me down, darling.

Kevin   That's so tacky!

Mary   I still say . . .

Tony   Mary!

Pause.

Kevin   Why's it called doppelgänger?

Tony   I dunno. I think it's a German word.

Kevin   God, couldn't we even think up one of our own?

Tony   We did. Looky-likey.

Mary   Give it a little clean, you know. Found this fabulous marble cleaner up Windsor last week. Had an excursion. Saw the castle then went to a garden centre. Lovely stuff for your garden there. And I found this marble cleaner. I thought, 'I'm having some o'that!' Brought the grave up lovely.

Kevin   I think I'm getting a cold sore.

Mary   Oh. That'll be your herpes back with a vengeance. Oh, I better be off. Use those watermelons wisely.

She stands.

D'you know? The menopause don't half make you dizzy. (*Kisses* **Tony**. *To* **Kevin**.) I'm not kissing you, you dirty bugger. You taken your pills today, Tony?

Tony   Yes.

Mary   Well don't forget. Oh. (*To* **Kevin**.) Will you be seeing Dodgy Rog this week?

Kevin   Maybe.

Mary   That stuff's fantastic. Purely medicinal.

Kevin   I'll get some more.

Mary   OK. I get paid Friday so I'll sort you out then.

Kevin   Whatever.

Mary   And don't work too hard up that shop, Tony!

Mary *exits.* **Kevin** *is still standing in the doorway.*

Tony   You look like shite. What time did you roll in?

Kevin   You ain't my nan.

Tony   I'll tell you when. Five o'clock. Who did you bring back?

Kevin   I don't have to answer to you.

Tony   Can you remember?

Kevin *thinks.*

Kevin   I met him up the heath.

Tony   Is that supposed to be funny?

Kevin   Oh, I'm sorry. No, I am, I'm really sorry. How you feeling today?

Tony   Kev, I don't mind you having fellas back but for fuck's sake keep the noise down next time, eh? I'm going back to bed.

Kevin   I thought you was going to work?

Tony   I lied. OK?

Tony *picks up the trainers and goes in.* **Kevin** *looks up at the sky.*

Blackout.

Scene Three

Saturday afternoon.

A few hours later. **Monica** *sits in a deckchair, rolling a cigarette. She wears a friendship bangle round her wrist. On the table sit two presents in brown paper bags from a gift shop. The trainers have disappeared.*

Monica   I've decided.

Kevin (*off*)   What?

238 Out in the Open

Monica   I'm gonna be a performance poet.

Kevin *comes out with a cup of tea and a bottle of Hooch.*

Kevin   Why?

Monica   I wrote some poetry in Mykonos.

Kevin   Is this mine?

Monica   Yeah it's a present. I think you'll like it actually.

Kevin (*unwrapping present*)   Is it a gay Mecca?

He has unwrapped a cup.

Monica   It's a cup. It's got a picture of me on it.

Kevin   You narcissistic bitch. Was there millions of queens there?

Monica   Yeah. Well, a few. There were quite a lot in the gay bars. Met a nice couple from Stanmore. They were cool. Had some really mellow chats with them. They bought me this on the last night.

Kevin   A shoelace?

Monica   It's a friendship bangle. (*Gets photos out.*) Look. That's them. The one on the left's Colin, the one on the right's Vince. We're going to have a reunion on Monday.

Kevin   They're a bit old for you, aren't they?

Monica   I think one of the most interesting things about foreign travel is you really let your barriers down.

Kevin   How old are they?

Monica   I don't know, but they've been together eighteen years. Eighteen years! I said, 'I've gotta hand it to you guys. You're setting a really good example to younger lesbians, gay men, transgendered and questioning people.'

Kevin   They look like the fucking Chuckle Brothers. (*Handing photo back.*) Are you still a dyke?

Monica   Yeah!

Kevin   But have you slept with a bird yet?

Monica   Do I have to pass a test or something? Being a lesbian's not like driving a car, you know.

Kevin   Well, you'd pass the written but I won't hold me breath for your practical.

Monica   And what if I slept with a woman in Mykonos?

Kevin   No you never! You never! I don't believe it!

Monica   Why is that so incomprehensible to you, Kev?

Kevin   Did she have a name? Or was it anonymous? In a lezzie back room.

Monica   Don't tar me with your brush, Kev.

Kevin   So where was it?

Monica   Look, I'm not saying I did, right?

Kevin   So you're still a lesbo virgin?

Monica   How's Tony? I've been so worried about him. I almost phoned him from Mykonos.

Kevin   He seems to be bearing up.

Monica   I was thinking about him non-bloody-stop. Poor Tonio. It's like his right arm's been wrenched off. The next few years are gonna be so tough for him. Facing the future. All alone. Every time I think about it I just crumble. I've gotta be strong. If only for him.

Kevin   He doesn't have to be alone. He's got us.

Monica   Yeah. Yeah. Oh, God, you can be really sweet when you want to. Yeah he's got us. And how's Mary?

Kevin (*tuts*)   Don't ask.

Monica   It can't be easy for her, Kevin.

Kevin   It isn't easy for any of us.

Monica   True, but there's different issues if it's your own kid. She carried him for nine months, don't forget. D'you know how many weeks that is? It's something like thirty-six. Maybe if you had a child you'd understand.

Kevin   Oh yeah and that's really likely.

Monica   I'm gay. Does that mean I can't have kids?

Kevin   I'd be a crap dad.

Kevin *squints up at the sky and yawns.*

Monica   Colin and Vince would love to father a child.

Kevin   You didn't offer them your eggs!

Monica   I'd love kids.

Kevin   But you're on the Pill.

Monica   I'm a lesbian, Kevin. It'd be pretty redundant.

Kevin   You used to be on the Pill.

Monica   God, I was having a really positive day 'til I came round here.

Kevin   What you gonna be at this reunion? The main course?

Monica   I wouldn't actually have to fuck them, you stupid idiot. I'd artificially inseminate myself with Colin's sperm.

Kevin   Eugh! (*Looks her up and down.*) You'll need more than a fucking turkey baster. You'll need a good set o'bellows up you.

Monica   D'you know one thing I realised in Mykonos?

Kevin   You'll never be a size twelve?

Monica   I hate sarcasm.

Kevin   You know where the door is.

Monica   It's a gate actually.

Kevin   You know where the gate is.

Monica   I'm waiting for Tony to get up. Now can I have your undivided attention please? Cos I've got something really major to tell you.

Kevin   Oh, *Mamma Mia!* phoned while you were away. They want you to play the lead.

Monica *looks gobsmacked.*

Kevin   They didn't really.

Monica *gives him daggers.*

Kevin   Sorry. Was that really cruel?

Monica   Have a drink, Kevin. You're so much nicer when you're drunk.

Kevin   Why?

Monica   Sit down.

Kevin   You're a fucking control freak.

Monica (*dismissively*)   You sound like my therapist. Sit.

Kevin   I don't wanna sit.

Monica   OK, we'll stand.

Kevin   No. I wanna sit.

Kevin *sits.* **Monica** *shuts the French windows quietly.*

Monica   I met someone in Mykonos who really freaked me out.

Kevin   Who?

Monica   I didn't think it was him at first. I mean, you don't expect to bump into someone from home in bloody Mykonos.

Kevin   Who?

Monica   Not that I really knew him as such. Depends on your definition of 'know', I guess.

Kevin   Oh, for God's sake, Mon, cut to the quick. Who?

Monica   Brett.

Kevin   Brett?

Pause.

But you don't know Brett. None of us do.

Monica   I've seen photographs of him. When Frankie took him to Belgium he took a whole film. Thirty-six bloody pictures.

Kevin   Oh well. It's in the past, isn't it. He can't hurt no one now.

Monica   It just really freaked me out. Seeing him. You know.

Kevin   What did he look like?

Monica   Well . . .

Kevin   The way Frankie went on you'da thought he was shagging Michael Owen. Was he fit?

Monica   See for yourself.

She hands him a photo.

Kevin   Monica.

Monica   What?

Kevin   You've got your arm round him.

Monica   Yeah, my camera's got a self-timer.

Kevin   You mean you spoke to him?

Monica   Can I have that back please?

Kevin   I don't believe you.

Monica   Please.

Pause. **Kevin** *stares at the photo.*

D'you wanna hear some of my performance poetry?

Kevin   No.

Monica   I bought a biro from the beach taverna shop and wrote them on postcards. Tony!

Tony *comes out of the French windows, still in his dressing gown.* **Kevin** *puts the photo in his pocket.*

Tony   Hiya. Monica! You look gorgeous!

Monica   Oh, God I've really missed you, Antonio McBonio. Come here, you sexy beast.

Tony   God, you're looking great. Isn't she looking great, Kev?

Kevin (*Scottish*)   Aye, she looks fab.

Monica   Present! Open your present! It's not much. Mykonos really cleaned me out. It's a lot more expensive than it looks.

Kevin   How much was it? 50p?

Tony *too has unwrapped a mug.*

Tony   Oh, fab.

Monica *rubs* **Tony**'s *arm and groans earnestly.*

Monica   How are you, Toe? You OK? You OK, poppet?

Tony   I'm fine.

Monica   Ah! You're so brave. I'm so proud of you, you know.

Tony   So come on. How was it? Tell all!

Monica   Yeah, it was a really cool headspace.

Tony   You didn't get bored?

Monica   I wrote poetry. My hotel had some really interesting shit in it.

Tony   Did you meet anyone nice?

Monica   Yeah, some really great guys from Stanmore. I've got to go there on Monday. We're having a reunion.

Kevin (*at the same time as she says reunion*)   Baby.

Monica *gives* **Kevin** *daggers.*

Monica   We're having a reunion.

Kevin (*at the same time again*)   Baby!

Monica   God, it's nothing definite, right? I don't know if I'm centred enough yet to bring some bloody kid into the world. I mean, I'm skint for starters. And my landlord's threatening to evict me.

Tony   Why?

Monica   Cos I didn't pay my rent when I was in Mykonos. Capitalist wankstain.

Tony   Are they photos?

Monica   Yeah. Did you know that Mykonos is Greek for windmill?

Tony   Let's see.

Monica   OK, but I've got to vet them.

Tony   Oh, Monica, we've all seen your tits before.

Kevin   The whole fucking country's seen your tits.

Monica   That documentary about breasts is up for a BAFTA.

Kevin   I've never seen so many saggy old mams in me life.

Monica   I don't show photographs to misogynists.

Tony   I'm not a misogynist, show me.

Monica   OK, but I have to vet them. I did some nude sunbathing and I've got some issues about who I expose my labia to. That's me with clothes on with Colin and Vince. Stanmore.

Tony   Talk me through this nasty blouse?

Monica   Oh, Colin and Vince bought it for me. I think they were having a bit of a giggle.

Tony   God, I can't abide T-shirts with slogans on.

Kevin   What does it say? Learner Lesbian?

Monica   Kev. You're starting to do my brain in!

Kevin   Let's see, what does it say?

Tony   'You can't keep a good woman down.'

Kevin   You can if you hold her head under the water long enough.

Monica   Give me that. Give it to me.

She snaps the photo out of **Tony**'s *hand. Grabs her bag.*

I'm outta here!

Kevin   You are the weakest link. Goodbye!

She takes a sip of her tea and then throws it over **Kevin**. *She exits via the back gate.*

Tony   Oh, I've only just mopped this!

Kevin   Stupid fucking bitch!

Tony *goes inside to get the mop.* **Monica** *comes back in.* **Kevin** *goes inside to wipe down.* **Tony** *comes out and mops up.*

Tony   Get out my way, I'll do that.

Monica   He gives gay men such a bad name, you know. It's dangerous spouting bullshit like that. I know he only does it to wind me up, but it's no excuse. (*Shouts in the direction of the house.*) Wanker!

Tony   Keep your voice down. Jesus! I'm surrounded by bloody kids.

Tony *goes inside.* **Monica** *looks for the photo of her and Brett.* **Kevin** *comes out.*

Kevin (*Scottish*)   Tony says I've gottie apologise to yee.

Monica (*hushed*)   Where's my fucking photograph, you cunt?

Kevin (*hands it over*)   You wanna rip that up.

Monica   Oh, stop worrying. Tony doesn't know what he looks like. Tony doesn't even know he exists.

Tony *calls from inside.*

Tony   Who?!

Monica *and* **Kevin** *look back towards the house.* **Monica** *is shitting herself.*

Monica   What?

Tony   Who don't I know exists?

Monica   Oh, it's not important.

Tony *comes out.*

Kevin   Tell him.

Monica   Kevin!

Kevin   Well, I will then. She's tryina set you up on a date, Tony. I told her it was too soon. He ain't gonna want another fella yet. You stupid fucking bitch!

She's a bit taken aback by his lie, and his attitude. She comes back at him.

Monica   I know it's too soon, you vulgar cockney twat! (*To* **Tony**.) I just happened to mention someone gay in passing. And he's got them married off to you already! (*To* **Kevin**.) You twisted sick psychopath!

Kevin   You were going on and on and on about how fantastic they were and how they really got off on the Scottish accent, you boring beached whale!!

Tony   Who? Who are you talking about?

Kevin   Yes, do remind me again, Monica. I've already forgotten – it was so boring.

Monica   Oh, just someone who comes in the caff.

Tony   Does he have a name?

Kevin   Yes, do tell, Monica. We're all ears.

Monica   Of course he has a name. Randolf.

Kevin *laughs.*

Kevin   Randolf?

Tony   Well, thanks for the concern. But. Well, maybe I don't need to meet someone new.

Kevin   That's exactly what I said. Frankie's only been dead six months! God, Mon, you're so insensitive!

Monica   I just mentioned that he liked Scottish accents. That's all. I wouldn't set you up with anyone, Tony, I know it's wholly inappropriate.

Tony   I mean, maybe I already have met someone.

Monica   What?

Kevin   You're joking!

Monica   Really?

Tony   Why d'you think I went back to bed? I'm shagged. Literally.

Monica   Right. Oh I see. You've had sex with someone. God, is that all?

Kevin   You pulled down that vile pub?

Tony   Aha.

Kevin   You vile slut, Antony Graham. What are you like?! Eugh, was he septic?

Tony   No, you cheeky bastard.

Kevin   When did he get off? I'll have to disinfect the house.

Tony   About five minutes ago.

Kevin   It weren't Billy the barman, was it? He gave me lice.

Tony   No.

Kevin   Well, who was it then?

Tony   No one you know.

Kevin   Good in the sack? Did he break your back?

Monica   Why does everything have to be measured by sex, Kevin? You're such a stereotypical gay man, you do my head in.

Tony   Well, aren't you happy for me?

Monica   Sure.

Kevin   If you're happy I'm happy.

Monica   Ditto.

Tony   Good.

Pause.

'Are you seeing him again, Tony?' Yes, thanks for asking. We're gonna go clubbing tonight.

Kevin   Eugh, do you have to drone on about your vile trade. So you got a fuck last night. So what?

Tony   He wasn't vile.

Kevin   You don't hear me banging on about last night's meat, morning, noon and night, do you?

Tony   No.

Kevin   No, cos I'm not boring.

Tony   No, cos you can't remember.

Monica   Er . . . guys? Can I ask something? Are you ready for this?

Tony   For what?

Monica   Another relationship?

Tony   Monica?

Monica   Toe?

Tony   Are you ready for a slap?

Kevin   Attaboy, Tony!

Monica   Tony!

Tony   Am I not allowed to meet anyone else? I thought yous two'd be really happy for me.

Monica   I am happy for you.

Kevin   I'm delirious.

Tony   I wish I could fucking believe you.

Kevin   What you worried about us for? It's your life.

Monica   Yeah. (*Directed at* **Kevin**.) I think it's really cool actually. Way to go, Toe!

Kevin   I haven't got a problem with it at all. I mean, it's not like we're Mary, is it?

Monica   Oh, God! Don't tell her. I mean, it doesn't sound that serious.

Kevin   Monica! Are you encouraging Tony to lie?

Monica   Lies can be really positive, yeah? If you're . . . like . . . protecting someone.

Tony   And what if it is serious?

Monica   It's not.

Tony   Were you there?

Kevin   She was probably peering through the window, flicking herself off.

Monica   I think that's your department, Kev, actually. Oh, come on, Tony. One night? Serious? Pur-lease!

Tony   Anyway, it's not like I tell Mary my deepest darkest thoughts.

Kevin   It's none of her business, Tony. I wish she'd just give it a rest. Frankie wasn't even that close to her.

Tony   I know.

Mary *comes crashing in through the back gate. She is carrying a casserole dish in a plastic bag.*

Mary   Who, darling? I could hear your voices. Seemed silly to knock.

Monica   Mary! God, I've really missed you!

Mary   Who weren't our Frankie close to?

Kevin   Oh, you don't know her.

Mary   I know all Frankie's friends.

Tony   Oh, we're talking about someone else. Someone from down the pub.

Mary   Who? Was she at the funeral?

Tony   No.

Mary   Oh well, some friend!

Monica   I know. She's a fucking bitch guy!

Mary   Oh, I hate that. Don't you hate that, Kevin?

Kevin   I fucking loathe it, Mary, I'm so glad you asked me.

Mary   You have a nice time on your travels, Monica? Oh, it's lovely to have you back. That path could do with a sweep. Don't do it now, darling. Only popped round to bring you this. I can't stop. I made it for me lady with the leg but she turned her nose up at it. I thought, 'I bet Tony'll have that,' so I phoned you at Harvey Nicks.

Tony   Oh, I didn't have to go in in the end. His shingles disappeared miraculously.

Mary   I said, 'Is Tony in, darling?' She goes 'Oh, he ain't in today.' I goes, 'I'm glad. You're working him too hard as it is.' She just laughs. I thought, don't you fucking laugh at me. I said, 'How's that other lad's shingles then, darling?' She goes, 'Which other lad?' I said, 'Call yourself a manager!' and hung up.

She has produced a casserole dish.

Tony   Mary, I'm not supposed to take personal calls at the shop.

Mary   Well, I wanted to know where I could give you this. I thought, well, if you're up Knightsbridge all afternoon I could pop along. I've got me travelcard, seems a shame to waste it.

Kevin   What is it? Eugh, it's got egg in it.

Tony (*has a look*)   It's a Mary Special.

Mary   Frankie's favourite. Pasta, condensed tomato soup, tin o'tuna, tin o'peas, egg. I left the crisps out, darling, cos I know you ain't enamoured. I'm not gonna eat it. You can have it with a little salad or a baked potato. Mind you, that might be a bit starchy. Where was it you went again, Monica? Greece, wannit?

Monica   Mykonos.

Kevin   It's Greek for windmill.

Mary   Bet it's nice to be home though. Always nice to get back to your own toilet.

Monica   You can't throw paper down Greek toilets.

Mary   Lovely. You taken your pills today, Tony?

Tony   No.

Mary (*slaps him*)   What've I told you?

Tony   Yes, I have taken my tablets, Mary. You've asked me three times already! What d'you want me to do? Overdose?

Mary   Well, pardon me for taking an interest! You were always moaning that Frankie never took an interest. I'm only trying to reshake the balance.

Monica   They have little bins and you stick it in there.

Kevin   Stick what?

Monica   The loo roll.

Mary   What?

Kevin   What are you on about, Monica?!

Monica   They don't let you throw toilet paper down the toilet.

Mary   Who don't?

Monica   The Greek authorities. You can get into real trouble for it.

Mary   What, they have someone standing over you while you're doing your dirties? That's fucking disgusting!

Monica   No. There's just like . . . a little bin there.

Mary   Oh, that's really hygienic. What if you've got company?

Monica   I've got you a present actually.

Mary   Here, she's bought you a bloody bin, Tony!

Monica   I was going to leave it here for you.

Mary Me, darling?

Monica *hands her a gift-wrapped present.*

Mary Oh.

She bursts out crying.

Oh, you didn't have to do that, darling. You shoulda saved your money.

Kevin You ain't seen it yet. She give us cups.

Mary Oh, it's too beautiful to open. Oh, you're all so good to me. I dunno why, I'm such a burden. Oh, you open it for me, Kevin. I ain't got me glasses on. Don't rip it, darling, I'll use that paper at Christmas. Oh, you shoulda saved your money, Monica. Oh, she's a good girl. You're all good people. I dunno what I'd do without you.

Kevin *has unwrapped a sarong.*

Mary Oh, isn't that stunning? That is stunning. Look at that. Oh, will you look at that, Tony? You can say what you like about their toilet facilities, but the Greeks do a lovely line in scarves.

Monica It's a sarong.

Mary No! Is it?

Kevin Put it on.

Monica Yeah.

Mary What do I do with it?

Kevin Come here.

Kevin *ties it on her.*

Mary You cleaned your teeth yet, Kevin?

Kevin Yeah.

Mary You wanna suck on a Trebor. Oh, Monica, you've got an unusual eye, intya? Eh? Look at me like I'm on

Camber Sands. Oh, this is very exotic. Oh, come here, you. (*Kisses* **Monica**.) I'm gonna keep this on I am.

Kevin   You look like David Beckham.

Mary   Well, he's a lovely dresser.

Monica   It's really versatile.

Mary   Isn't it? Isn't it? It'd make a lovely picnic rug. Or a baby's blanket. You seen Dodgy Rog yet, Kev?

Kevin   Give us a chance.

Mary   My arthritis, Monica. Fucking nightmare. So did you have a little holiday romance in Mykonos, babe? Meet a nice Greek man with a boat?

Kevin   Monica's a dyke.

Mary   Fucking load o' rubbish.

Monica   I am, Mary.

Mary   Yeah, well, I'm a lesbian an' all then.

Monica *shrugs as if to say it's cool.*

Mary   You'll have to get me down them lady bars. Find meself a nice lady in a bowler hat like in that film.

Kevin   Which film?

Mary   Beryl Reid and Susannah Whatsit.

Kevin   *The Killing of Sister George?*

Mary   Ooh, that's a sinister picture. Innit though, eh? Eh? Put the willies up me, that did. 'Ere, there was that movie set in Greece. She was in it. That actress. Shirley Valentine. Oh, I like that Shirley Valentine. She takes a good part.

Kevin   Pauline Collins?

Mary   That's it. That's a lovely picture. You seen *Pauline Collins*, Mon? It's a lovely picture. You got that in your video shop, Kevin?

Monica   I went to the beach where they filmed that. That's where I met . . . people.

Mary   No! Was it lovely?

Monica   It's a bit touristy.

Mary   That's me that film.

Monica   Mykonos has all together become very touristy.

Mary   Like Soho, innit? What's the matter with you, Tony? Cat got your tongue?

Tony   No law against being quiet, is there?

Mary   You staying in tonight, Tony?

Tony   No, I'm going to Trade.

Mary   Lovely. I'm going up me club wi'Rose.

Monica   Which one's Rose again?

Mary   Used to be in the pub trade so she likes a bit o'that. (*Mimes drinking.*) Her fella went blind with his sugars. That's no way to lose your sight.

Tony   Is she the one who's the terrible gossip? Frankie said she was a scream.

Mary   Swears blind her fella's got a roving eye. But how can he? I'd get rid tomorrow, Tony, but she needs me, see. Are they your holiday snaps, Monica?

Monica   Kind of.

Mary   Got any of that beach?

Monica   No.

Mary   Oh well, don't bother getting them out. Look at the fucking time! I'm nipping over St Clements cos him upstairs got sectioned again. I only know cos his wife popped a note through. She's an angel, only she can't visit him today cos she's gone up Salisbury for a christening. I thought they only done them of a Sunday. Maybe they're Jewish, eh. You had any luck on the job front, Monica?

Monica   No.

Mary   Oh, that's a shame. You're Liza Minelli waiting to happen. See ya! Don't get up. Bye then.

She leaves.

Tony   I'm gonna get in the bath.

Tony *exits.*

Monica   God. So. What do you make of that, Kev?

Kevin   You're nothing like Liza Minelli.

Monica   About Tony's news!

Kevin   Well, good. I'm happy for him. It's his life.

Monica   Yeah, me too. It's great, isn't it? Yeah, really great.

He looks at her.

Blackout.

Scene Four

Sunday morning.

Kevin *is watching over the barbecue, which he has heated up. He puts some sausages and some bacon on it.* **Monica** *sits with two suitcases, an empty birdcage, a bin bag and a boogie box.* **Kevin** *is wearing sunglasses and a hat, which he takes off at some point in the scene, before* **Iggy**'s *arrival.*

Monica   Is Tony in bed?

Kevin   No, he ain't back from church yet.

Monica   Church?

Kevin   Trade. He's just phoned, he's on his way home. Told me to get some breakfast on. Said he's got company.

Monica   I'll pay you back for the cab as soon as I get paid. Are those Linda McCartney's?

Kevin   No, they're fresh.

Monica   You know. If this was America, right, I'd probably own a gun. They're like mobile phones over there. Everyone's got them. And I'd have pointed it straight between the eyes. And shot him. Dead.

Kevin   Who?

Monica   My landlord. Ex-landlord. Are these yours?

She helps herself to a cigarette from a packet on the table. She lights up.
Kevin *rolls his eyes.*

Kevin   Help yourself.

Monica   Great. I haven't got a fucking girlfriend. I haven't got a fucking job. And now I haven't got a fucking home.

Kevin   Have they sacked you from the caff?

Monica   That's not a job. I'm a fucking actress!

Kevin   You can say that again. You're not thinking of stopping here, are you?

Monica   In your dreams, Kevin! No, Cora from the café, her flatmate Rafferty's gone trekking in Nepal. So she's going to put me up. Only she's doing her shift at the café 'til five so I can't go round 'til then. God, I had such a good chill in Mykonos and now this.

Kevin   Well, maybe you shoulda stayed put and paid your rent rather than splashing out on two weeks in Greece.

Monica   I've been depressed. I had to get away to find me again.

Kevin   Well, you didn't find you, did you? You found Brett.

Pause. **Kevin** *continues cooking.* **Monica** *sits.*

Kevin What was he like?

Monica I wasn't going to talk to him. When he walked into that bar. I couldn't take my eyes off him. I didn't fancy him.

Kevin Well, obviously. You're a dyke.

Monica I was thinking. Oh my God, it's him. And I just kept staring. Everyone else was staring at the sunset. The Kastro Bar, it's this bar where you go to watch the sunset. Huge great picture windows. The view's amazing. It's like this big round orange ball of flame and fire, just like . . . dropping into the horizonesque watery ocean. He ordered a strawberry daiquiri and then lit up a Camel Light. And he looked so vulnerable. And this classical music was playing. I felt like I was in a Caravaggio painting or something. Then Colin and Vince started debating what music was playing and I said I thought it was the theme music from *The Mission*. And they said who was in that. And I said . . . Liam Neeson and Jeremy Irons.

Kevin Oh get the fuck on with it.

Monica And when I looked back . . . he'd gone.

Kevin But you spoke to him. You had your arms round him.

Monica The next day I went to Super Paradise Beach. Yeah, me and seven million others. And who comes and lies on the lounger next to me?

Kevin Fancy a spot in the shade, did he?

Monica It was like Frankie was sending me a sign or something. There must have been five hundred sun loungers on that beach, and he chose . . . Weird. So I spoke to him.

Kevin Fuck me, that is weird.

Monica He said he wasn't having that good a time in Mykonos. I said, 'Yeah, it's windy, isn't it?' and then he just came out with it. He and his boyfriend had always wanted

to come. But his boyfriend had died. And so he was . . .
doing it for him, so to speak.

Kevin (*incredulously*)   He called Frankie that? His
boyfriend?!

Monica   Well, to Brett he was. OK to us he was Tony's.
But to Brett. Brett was in love with Frankie. Frankie was
living with someone else, but Brett was in a relationship with
him all the same.

Kevin   Did you ever let on that you were a mate of
Frankie's?

Monica   No. We were never bosom buddies. I only
bumped into him about three times.

Kevin   So. He's going round thinking he was the love of
Frankie's life? And what does he think Tony was? The bit
on the side?

Monica   He loved Frankie.

Kevin   Shut up. He's just some little scally Manc you met
on holiday who shagged our mate a few times.

Monica   Brett didn't even have a chance to say goodbye.

Kevin   Frankie got struck by lightning, Monica! None of
us got a chance to say goodbye!

Monica   The first he heard that Frankie'd died was a
message from Mary on his answerphone.

Kevin   Mary knew Brett?

Monica   Mary phoned everyone in Frankie's Filofax and
let them know. Brett was in under 'Col the Carpenter'.
Code name. Brett got in one night to a message on his
answerphone saying Frankie McAdam wouldn't be needing
any more carpentry. What an image. Yeah?

Kevin   You should write a poem about it.

Monica   I have. D'you wanna hear it?

Kevin   Life's too short.

Monica   Why do you always have to be so horrible to me, Kev?

Kevin   Force of habit.

Monica   You used to be really cool with me when we did the pub quizzes. You were always complimenting me on my knowledge of contemporary politics.

Kevin   You know your Bush from your Gores I'll give you that.

Monica   I remember the exact day you started being horrible to me.

Kevin   The minute we met?

Monica   That night at Marvellous. In the toilets. When I told you your feelings for Tony would never be reciprocated.

Pause.

Kevin   What feelings? What are you talking about?

Monica   Oh, face it, Kev, you've always carried a torch for Tony.

Kevin   Don't be daft! Frankie was my best mate!

Monica   You were always threatening to tell Tony about Frankie and Brett, and don't think I don't know why!

Kevin   Because I thought he had a right to know!

Monica   Because you thought they might split up and you'd get Tony to yourself.

Kevin   That's bollocks! So why didn't I tell him then?

Monica   Because you liked the idea of it. And were too scared of the reality.

Kevin You're fucking mental, you are. I've been living with him for six months. Don't you think I woulda come on to him by now? If I was mad about him.

Monica Haven't you?

Pause. **Monica** *laughs.*

Kevin Of course I fucking haven't. Why? Has he said something?

Monica You've always tried it on with Frankie's boyfriends, Kev. You try it on with everyone.

Kevin I just get pissed, that's all. And when I get pissed I don't know what I'm doing. I ain't tried it on with Tony. He woulda said something. Has he said something, Monica?

Monica No.

Kevin I've gotta stop drinking. And I have. I didn't have a drink last night. I'm sick of finding meself in strange places at eight o'clock in the morning. Standing on the doorstep with me shoes on the wrong feet wondering how I got home. Losing me fucking bag. Losing me fucking memory. Getting flashbacks of people and lines of coke and rowing and . . . not knowing whether I've dreamt it or done it. Meeting people in the clubs who reckon they've had a big night out with you three weeks ago, and you don't know them from Adam. Or fellas coming up saying 'You were fucking rude to my boyfriend last week. He does not look like Gary Glitter.' And you look at the boyfriend. And they're right, he doesn't. Except for the fact he's got black hair. And then you remember singing 'Leader of the Gang' on a fucking table. And being vile. But convinced at the time you were hilarious. And other people saying, 'Ah, you're a lovely drunk.' When you know in your heart of hearts what they mean is: You're so vile it's entertaining.

Monica Is that why you stayed in last night?

Kevin Kind of. And I didn't really want to meet Tony's fella off me head.

Monica   It's weird, isn't it.

Kevin   I haven't laid a finger on Tony, Monica. If I had I'd remember.

The back gate opens and **Tony** *comes in, off his tits.*

Tony   What's all this stuff? Is it more presents? Oh, Monica, you didn't have to!

Tony *goes into the living room as she speaks and then reappears with a picnic rug or blanket and goes about spreading it out on the decking.*

Monica   Oh, it's just some of my stuff. I'm taking over Rafferty's room at the commune.

Tony   Guess who was in the club. You'll never guess who came to the club!

Kevin   Your new life partner? Well, where is he?

Tony   That bastard never turned up.

Off, we hear **Mary** *coming up the path.*

Mary   Where's he gone? (*Louder.*) Where've you gone?

Tony   We're out here!

Mary *comes through wearing her sarong.*

Kevin   I don't fucking believe it.

Mary   Put some sounds on, guy. Rose! Where's Rose?

Rose *comes in. She is tiny and splattered. She wears a summer dress with red wine down the front.* **Monica** *gets a CD out of her bag and puts it on her boogie box. It's Abba. She sits and sings along quietly to it, though with real feeling.*

Rose   I'm here.

Mary   Thought I'd lost you. Weren't that cab driver lovely?

Rose   Oh, he's a diamond. Oh yeah, d'you know who he puts me in mind of, Mare? Whatsisname. Used to be relief cellar man at the Elusive Camel. He had a terrible life. His Sharon was born with her pelvis back to front and no genitalia.

Mary   Get us a cup o'tea going. Me neck thinks me throat's been cut.

Rose   All her intestines was hanging out her stomach like a string bag. It's no life, is it?

Tony   Sod tea. Shall I raid the drinks cabinet?

Kevin   D'you want a bacon butty, girls?

Mary   Yeah, I've got the munchies.

Rose   I hope you're hygienic. All your meat's in the danger zone. I had to do a course when I ran the pub. Hygiene. We done lunches. Basic. Type o'thing Barbara Windsor does.

Tony *goes indoors.*

Mary   Someone roll a spliff.

Kevin   So you went to Trade, Mary?

Mary   Well, we was only round the corner. Down the Blind Beggar, as was. What's it called now, Rose?

Rose   I forget.

Mary   Anyway it was a bit of a late one there, so when they chucked out, she wanted another one, so I said, 'Why not try Trade?' I knew Tony was gonna be there. Nice, wannit, Rose?

Rose   Loud.

Kevin   Have you taken drugs, Mary? Popped a few pills?

Mary   Kevin! This is the one I told you about, Rose. Cheeky monkey, you are. Cheeky monkey!

Rose *starts tickling* **Kevin**.

Rose   Yeah, I thought it might be you. You've got a twinkle, int ya? What's going on behind them eyes, you dirty bugger?! (*Giggles like a schoolgirl.*)

Mary   Ah, they all loved my baby there. Said he was a king among doormen.

Rose   Mare. I was out of order earlier. I know it. I'm sorry, everybody, if I offended but. You know. I don't want these fuckers chatting to me just cos I'm old. And that was the vibe I was getting.

Tony (*from inside*)   Rose knows loads o'famous people, don't you, Rose?

Mary   Well, she used to run this pub near Victoria Bus Station so celebrities were always popping in en route to various destinations.

Kevin   Who's the most famous person you've ever met?

Rose   Salvador Dali.

Monica   Who?

Tony *comes out with a selection of drinks. He puts them down on the blanket. He has plastic beakers.*

Mary   I didn't like that fella you were speaking to by the toilets, Tony. He was all over you like a rash. I had a word. I said, 'Listen, love. He's grieving. Back off.' Well, you are.

Tony   Brandy and Coke?

Kevin   Please.

Rose (*to* **Kevin**)   You're making a right pig's ear o'that. Leave it to the professionals.

Kevin   No, you're all right, I'll do it.

Rose   Give it here! I've gotta do something or me hands'll seize up.

She elbows **Kevin** *out of the way and takes over the cooking.*

Mary   There was a lot of men in there tonight had their eye on you.

Kevin   So you were stood up, Toe?

Tony   Aye I was. I was supposed to meet him in there about midnight. He never showed. Searched high and low for him.

Mary   Who's this, darling?

Tony   Just a friend really.

Mary   Oh, it's good to have friends. You gotta be careful though. There's a lot of people out there who'll just want you for your money. Int that right, Ro?

Rose   'Ere, remember that Jap who was always sniffing around me?

Tony   Mary. It's obviously escaping your notice, but. I have no money.

Mary   You've got this lovely flat!

Rose   Made out he'd invented the wok, when they came all the rage in the eighties. Turned out he didn't have a pot to piss in.

Tony   Anyway it was only a friend, so there's nothing to worry about.

Mary   So why d'you search high and low for him?

Tony   Cos I wanted to see him.

Mary   Oh. That's nice. It's a great thing, friendship. It's great, isn't it, Monica?

Monica   Yeah it's the best.

Mary   Innit great, Kev?

Kevin   D'you know what it is, Mary? It's a tonic.

Mary   Ah! My Frankie had some lovely friends, didn't he, Rose?

Rose   Mmm, not half. Mind you, they had nice friends.

Mary   Who?

Rose   This lot singing.

Monica   Abba?

Rose   When they come in the Elusive Camel, their mates were so respectful of me.

Monica   What did they drink?

Rose   Abba? Pernod and black.

Mary   Oh, shut up, Rose. It weren't the real Abba. It was that Abba tribute band. Yabba Dabba Doo. They doubled as the Flintstones.

Rose   They weren't, they were the real thing!

Mary   Oh, shut up. Were they Swedish?

Rose   No, they were from Tunbridge Wells! I told you they were from Tunbridge Wells! I told that journalist!

Mary   Exactly! And what did he do? Laugh! (*About the joint.*) Fucking hell, that's strong.

Rose   Wash your mouth out. You're worse than Fern Britton. (*To the others.*) She's got a mouth on her. Cunt this, cunt that. I said to her, 'You don't speak like that on *Ready Steady Cook*! I think you should stick to halves!'

Mary   It wasn't Fern Britton! (*To the others.*) She's deluded.

Rose *leaves the confines of the barbecue with her sausage tongs and approaches* **Monica**.

Rose   What you staring at?

Monica   Me? Nothing.

Rose   I remember your mother. She threw a mean dart.

Monica   My mother doesn't play darts.

Rose   Oh, and why's that? Cos she broke her arm? And I suppose she told you she broke it falling on the ice? And I suppose you believed her. You silly whore.

Monica   Sorry?

Mary   Ro!

Rose   It was Big Alice Diamond what broke it cos she grassed up the Forty Thieves. Oh, the Old Bill said she was singing like they'd given her fucking canary seed once she got started. Dropped everyone right in it. Thanks a bunch!

Monica   My mother's called Phoebe.

Mary   D'you wanna have a dance, Tony?

Tony   No thanks, babe.

Kevin   Ah, it's a shame you got stood up, Tony. Are you gutted?

Mary   It was only a bloody little friend, Kevin. Who gets upset over a fucking little friend? Eh? He lost his lover less than a year ago. What's missing one little inconsequential friend compared to that? He's got a garden full of friends here.

Rose   Well, I wouldn't call it a garden. Where's your fucking lawn?

Kevin   I don't know why you don't just tell her.

Mary   Tell me what? What?!

Kevin   Well, maybe the fella he was going to meet was more than just a friend.

Mary   I don't understand what you're getting at, Kevin.

Tony   Kevin!

Kevin   Maybe Tony actually quite likes him.

Mary   Frankie's only been gone six months. He ain't even cold, darling. Tony ain't ready yet, darling. Are you, darling?

Tony   No, darling.

Mary   See?

Tony   Kevin gets his wires crossed sometimes.

Mary   Our Frankie used to say that. He'd say, 'Mummy. Kev don't half get his wires crossed sometimes.' D'you remember, Ro?

Rose   No.

Kevin   I don't believe for one minute that Frankie ever called you Mummy, Mary.

Mary   Was you there?

Kevin   I was round your flat often enough when I was growing up. The nicest thing I heard him call you was 'Bitch'.

Pause. This throws everyone. **Kevin** *laughs to make light of it.* **Mary** *giggles, embarrassed.*

Mary   You cheeky monkey. Eh? You cheeky monkey.

Rose   Cheeky monkey!

Monica   Kev, that's bang out of order. Just because your relationship with your mum was dysfunctional.

Kevin   Dysfunctional?

Monica   It doesn't follow that everyone's relationships are fucked up.

Kevin   What d'you mean, dysfunctional?

Monica   Well, your mum was a smackhead, wasn't she? I'd have thought that would make for a pretty dysfunctional relationship. I could be wrong.

Kevin   Who told you that? She's weren't a smackhead. She weren't!

Mary   Weren't she, darling? You hundred per cent sure about that?

Kevin   No. (*To* **Monica**.) Fucking hell, you wanna reassess your attitude.

Mary   That's why you lived with your old nan.

Kevin   No.

Monica   Well, sorry, right, but Frankie told me otherwise. He was obviously lying. Don't blame me, blame the gay community. Gossipy or what?

Tony   Can we have something else on?

Rose   You got any Badly Drawn Boy?

Mary   What did you say, Monica?

Rose   I knitted him that hat.

Monica   Sorry?

Mary   Did you call Frankie a liar?

Monica   Well . . .

Mary   A liar and a gossip?

Rose   That's her family all over. Stirrers.

Mary   When he ain't even here to defend hisself?

Rose   Don't tell her nothing!

Mary   Oh, that's really nice, that is, Monica. Tell me, Tony. Were you aware that my dead son was a liar and a gossip? Only Monica here reckons he was.

Tony   None of us are perfect, Mary.

Mary   Oh! So you'd agree? Anything else we wanna slag him off for while I'm here? Jesus, you won't even wait 'til me back's turned.

Kevin   He was a liar. About some things. We all lie.

Mary   That's a terrible accusation.

Kevin   No it's not.

Monica   Well, *somebody* told me your mum was a smackhead.

Mary   Oh, great, so pick on the person who ain't here to defend hisself to get the blame! Of course it's true. What else would explain your rottenness? Don't get me wrong, darling, I love you, you know I love you. But you are rotten at times, rotten.

Kevin   I don't believe this!

Tony   Can't we talk about something nice?

Kevin   My mum is nice! You're so full of shit, Monica!

Monica   I must have made a mistake. Sorry.

Mary   I hope so, darling. It ain't nice to hear about your dead son's negative aspects.

Monica   Look, Mary, I didn't mean to . . .

Mary   Mean to what, darling? Fuck me off? Well, you have.

Rose   D'you know who's lovely? Gargy Patel.

Monica   All I meant was . . .

Mary   D'you think it doesn't hurt? When I see horrible things written about queers in the papers? D'you not think every time I see an MP on the news spouting bollocks it don't cut through me like glass? 'My Frankie weren't like that,' I wanna scream. 'Come and meet my Frankie. He'll change your mind.' Only he can't now cos he ain't here. And every time someone's rude about gay lads on the box I take it personal. They're slagging off my son. And they didn't even know him. And you did. And yet you're more than ready to coat him.

She falls into **Monica***'s arms and sobs her heart out.*

Mary   When you've got kids you'll understand.

Kevin   Funny you should say that.

Monica   Drop it, guy!

Kevin   Oh, am I not supposed to tell anyone?

Mary   Eh?

Kevin   Sorry.

Mary   You're not pregnant, are you?

Rose   I knew it. I thought she was pregnant, only I didn't like to say in case she was just . . .

Monica   I'm not pregnant.

Kevin   Yet.

Monica   Drop it, Kev!

Rose   Now I ain't saying she's fat. Cos she ain't. She's glowing. And a lot of people glow when they're pregnant.

Mary   I was like a fucking Belisha beacon, Monica. Do you want little babies, Monica? Did you hear that, Rose? I'm gonna be a grandma!

She starts to cry again.

Monica   Look, you know. My mind isn't made up or anything. I mean, it's a big step. I don't know if I'm up to it.

Mary   Oh, it's easy, Monica. It's easy. It's like riding a bike. Can you ride a bike? (**Monica** *nods.*) Have a baby, Monica. You'd make a lovely mum, you would. Wouldn't she make a lovely mum, Rose?

Rose   Dunno.

Monica   But it's really painful.

Mary   When they hurt you? I know, darling. But the pros outweigh the cons. Believe me, babe.

Monica   No, I mean, like . . . giving birth.

Kevin   Can you still die in childbirth?

Monica   I don't know. Shit, can you?

Kevin   Fingers crossed!

Rose   I like him.

Monica   I'm going to the toilet.

Kevin *is pissing himself.* **Monica** *runs inside.*

Mary   Who's she having a baby by, Kevin?

Kevin   A couple o'saddos she met on holiday.

Rose   Trollop. And her the size of a house.

Mary   That's my baby girl you're talking about.

Rose   Oh, listen to you. 'She's one of my kids!' Another one you've adopted to make you feel better about Frankie.

Mary   Nothing's gonna bring him back, Rose.

Rose   Good. Cos all he did was cause you heartache.

Mary   Is somebody rolling a spliff or not? Where's your dope box, Tony?

Tony   In the living room.

Mary *goes indoors.*

Rose   It's true. But she don't like the truth. Never did. Her and Rula Lenska.

Monica *comes out and heads for the back gate.*

Tony   Where are you going?

Monica   Out. I can't bear the smell of all this burning flesh.

Kevin   See you, lesbo!

Monica   Fuck off, poufter.

Rose   Tell your mother she wants to learn to button her lip!

Monica *exits.*

Rose   Is she lesbian?

Kevin   She'd like to think she is.

Rose   Does her mum know? She'll go fucking spare.

Mary *comes to the French windows.*

Mary   Where's this bloody tin?

Tony (*to* **Kevin**)   Go and show her.

Mary (*to* **Rose**)   I'm not speaking to you.

Rose   No? Oh, that's a shame.

Kevin *goes inside with* **Mary**.

Rose   He was always breaking her heart, silly cow.

Tony   I know he was hardly an angel.

Rose   All she ever did when he was alive was moan about him.

Tony   Oh well. We all do things we regret in retrospect.

Rose   Dunno why you're defending her. She never had a good word to say about you. I had you down as a right monster.

Tony   What? What did she say?

Rose   How you was eating away at his money.

Tony   Me? Frankie was a fucking bouncer. I'm management material!

Rose   We all know he done funny things on the side. Bouncing never paid for this flat.

Tony   No, I did! We put it in Frankie's name cos I'm HIV. I'd never have got a mortgage.

Rose   She never liked that neither. Case you gave it to him. At first she thought you was making it up, to snare Frankie.

Tony   To snare him?

Rose   'Oh, he's always been a soft touch, my Frankie. Always been a glutton for a sob story. That boy's got him just where he wants him.'

Tony   Why on earth would me being HIV snare him? It'd put most people off.

Rose   Oh, am I being out of order? You can tell me. I can take it.

Tony   No. No, you're not. You're telling the truth. If I'm to be honest I . . . My head's pretty screwed up right now. I'm such a coward.

Rose   What you scared of?

Tony   People not understanding me.

Rose   Oh, who gives a toss what other people think?

Tony   I don't understand me.

Rose   If I'da spent me life worrying what every fucker thought about me, I wouldn't have had half the fun I've had.

Tony   Why does she have this hold over me?

Rose   She makes people listen to her. And they do. Even if she is speaking crap. She used to tell people I was an alcoholic. It got back to me. I spread it round she had a false leg. Well it was when she was always wearing them suede ski-pants.

Tony   Did she say any of that stuff to Frankie? About me. Not trusting me.

Rose   That was all they used to row about. He came down the pub and had it out with her. 'Stop coating my Tony,

you interfering bitch! You ain't welcome round my house!'
Looked like he was going to punch her. She was hiding
behind me Golden Wonder.

Tony   He said she refused to come cos his dad wouldn't
let her. She only started coming after he left her.

Rose   Siddie never stopped her going nowhere!

Tony   I wonder why he didn't just tell me.

Rose   Oh, he was probably trying to protect you. You
know her problem? She didn't bond with him when he was
a baby. Weren't her fault, the . . . (*Clicks fingers.*) didn't click.
That's sad when that happens. There's someone coming up
your back passage. (*Calls.*) Who is it?

Off, we hear **Iggy** *calling.*

Iggy   It's Iggy!

Rose   Iggy?

Tony   Oh fuck, is it?

Rose   Iggy? What sort of a name's that?

Iggy *comes in through the back gate.*

Iggy   All right, Tony?

Tony   What time d'you call this? I thought we were
supposed to be meeting in the club?

Iggy   Better late than never.

Tony   This is Rose. This is Iggy.

Rose   Oh, it's you.

Iggy   Sorry?

Rose   Ever been down the Elusive Camel?

Iggy   Er, no.

Rose   Oh, well, it ain't you then. What are you talking
about? Keep an eye on breakfast. I'm gonna have a kip.

Rose *lies down on the sun lounger.* **Tony** *keeps an eye on the barbecue.*

Iggy   Are you trashed?

Tony   I looked all over for you.

Iggy   I'm a wanker. What more can I say? Did you cop for any one last night?

Tony   No. You weren't there.

Iggy   What's it got to do with me?

Tony   Woulda been a bit embarrassing now.

Iggy   I'd sit out here 'til he went away.

Tony   D'you want a drink?

Iggy   I'll have this. (*Takes drink off table.*)

Tony   It's not yours.

Iggy   Is now.

Tony   I should be really angry with you.

Iggy   What you gonna do? Hit me?

Tony   But I'm not. I'm too angry with someone in there.

Iggy   I don't mind if you're angry. I'd be angry. I'd hit you.

Tony   You? You're a scrawny little fucker.

Iggy   Is this yours? (*Puts* **Kevin**'s *hat on.*)

Tony   No. It's Kevin's.

Iggy   Chuck us them shades.

Tony   They're not yours either.

Iggy   I'm in disguise.

He sits there in the hat and sunglasses that **Kevin** *was wearing earlier. He sits there, facing the sun.*

Mary *and* **Kevin** *appear at the French windows.* **Mary** *is proudly holding up a massive joint.*

Mary Look at the size o'that! Oh. Who's this then? We've got a visitor, Kevin.

Tony This is Iggy. My new little friend.

Kevin All right?

Mary Iggy? Oh, that's unusual, innit?

Tony The boy who stood me up.

Kevin You're wearing my hat and glasses, mate.

Iggy Sorry.

Kevin Nah, keep them. For now.

Tony Kevin, this is the beautiful Iggy.

Iggy Oright, mate?

Tony And Mary.

Iggy Hi, Mary.

Mary So you didn't come to the club last night.

Iggy No.

Mary It was fucking wicked.

Iggy You went to Trade?

Mary I'm never out of that place. You're probably wondering who I am.

Tony You're Mary. He's not deaf.

Mary I'm Tony's mother-in-law.

Tony As was.

Mary You look tired, Tony. You should have a lie-down. He should have a lie-down. Tell him, Kevin.

Tony I'm fine, Mary.

Mary *looks very sad. She sits on the step up to the decking and rests her head on her hand, staring contemplatively at the ground.* **Tony** *rolls his eyes.*

Iggy   You OK, Mary?

Mary   I'll be all right in a minute.

Kevin   What's the matter with you, Mary?

Tony   As if we didn't know.

Mary   Oh, I was just thinking. It's nothing. You all ignore me. I'll be fine. Eventually.

Iggy   You look dead sad.

Mary   I've lost me son.

Kevin   She's so careless.

Tony *giggles.* **Mary** *gives* **Kevin** *daggers then looks back to* **Iggy**.

Mary   I expect Tony's told you.

She reaches out and holds **Tony**'s *hand, not looking at him.*

Iggy   Yeah he did.

Mary   You'da liked him, darling. He was one of the best.

Iggy   I'm sure. I'm sorry, Mary.

Mary   It was only six months ago. He ain't even warm.

Tony   Cold!

Mary   Cold. It's nice that Tony's got good friends. His heart's breaking every second of the day. Ain't that right, Tony? Takes a long time to get over someone like my Frankie, ain't that right, baby boy?

Tony (*sarcastically*)   Years.

Mary *nods her head, sagely.*

Tony   May I have my hand back?

Tony *removes his hand from* **Mary**'s *grasp.*

Mary   You ever had a mum, Iggy?

Iggy   Yeah.

Mary   You treat her good, yeah?

Iggy   Yeah. I think so.

Mary   That's beautiful.

Tony   Actually, I think I will go to bed. Iggy?

Mary   Oh, I was just beginning to enjoy meself then.

Tony   Care to join me?

Mary   Don't go to bed, darling. We can all sit up and have a singsong. Does anyone know 'Edelweiss'?

Tony   We've been up all night. You're no spring chicken any more.

Mary *starts to sing 'Edelweiss'.*

Rose *sits up and joins in.*

Mary *gives* **Rose** *daggers.*

Mary   Did I ask you to join in?

Rose   I know her.

Mary   I've got a lovely voice. Coulda been professional. A gypsy once crossed my path with silver and said she seen big things for me in the opera.

Rose   Bollocks!

Rose *lies back down again.*

Tony   Maybe we should all call it a day.

Mary   Oh, Tony! I'm having too nice a time to go home.

Iggy   D'you live near?

Mary   No. I'd need to get the bus. What bout you?

Iggy   I'll walk you to the stop. I'm only round the corner.

Mary   Oh. So you ain't stopping neither?

Iggy   No.

Mary   Oh. Rose. Rose!

Rose *sits up again.*

Rose   She's another one with a mouth on her.

Mary   Rose, we're going.

Rose   I said, 'Bit of a comedown from jigging round that nunnery, you dirty strumpet.'

Mary   Rose, Tony wants his bed, darling, and Iggy's gonna walk us to the bus stop.

Rose   What about my breakfast?

Mary   Give us a kiss and tell me you love me, Tony. See you, Kev. Tell Monica bye, yeah?

Tony   See you. See you, Iggy.

Kevin   Bye then.

Iggy   I suppose you'll be wanting these.

He takes off the shades and hat.

Nice meeting you.

Kevin *gets the fright of his life when he sees* **Iggy**'s *face for the first time.*

Mary   Say goodbye, Kevin. Bloody hell, you're so rude.

She links **Iggy**'s *arm.*

What's your mum's name, darling?

Iggy   Denise.

Mary   Oh, that's a pretty name. She a bit on the young side?

Iggy *leaves with* **Mary** *and* **Rose**. *We hear them talking as they walk up the path.*

Iggy Forty-three.

Mary Oh, she's a baby. D'you hear that, Rose?

Rose What?

Mary Forty-three.

Rose Who?

Mary His mum. Denise.

Rose Well, if she's anything like Denise Van Outen she'll be lovely.

Mary She's just a baby. And how old's your nan?

Rose There's a bus. Leg it!

We hear them run off down the path. **Kevin** *and* **Tony** *sit there a while.*

Kevin Where did you meet him?

Tony The pub. Do I look disgusting or something?

Kevin Where does he live?

Tony Manchester. He's staying at a B&B round the corner. He couldn't bear to look at me for more than five minutes.

Kevin What did he say his name was?

Tony Why?

Kevin He just . . . reminds me of someone.

Tony Who?

Kevin I dunno.

Tony Don't you think he's cute?

Kevin He's all right, yeah.

Tony Please don't do a Mary on me.

Kevin It's difficult, you know.

Tony   Why is it difficult?

Kevin   I dunno. It just is.

Tony   Come here.

He hugs **Kevin** *to him.*

Kevin   You'll maybe never see him again, eh.

Tony   Don't sound so fucking pleased.

Kevin   Stop touching me.

Tony   Why?

Kevin   Cos I can't fucking bear it!

Tony *lets* **Kevin** *go.*

Kevin   No. Don't stop.

Tony *hugs him again.* **Kevin** *closes his eyes and savours it.* **Iggy** *comes back in.*

Iggy   Am I interrupting something?

Tony   Darling!

Iggy   Well, that was easy. Bus was already there. She weren't happy, was she? I kind o'got the impression that she didn't want me knocking about with you. It was only a little white lie. Don't mind that, do you?

Tony   No. You played that really well, didn't you? Who's a clever boy?

Iggy   Are you ready for bed yet?

Tony   I'm gonna take a shower. I won't be long. You keep an eye on my Iggy, Kev? And keep your mucky paws off. I'll be two ticks. (*To* **Iggy**.) He goes anywhere near you? Scream!

Tony *goes in.* **Kevin** *watches* **Iggy**. *He sits down and knocks back his drink.* **Kevin** *is staring at him. He shuts the French windows.*

Iggy   Have I got a welly on me head?

Kevin   What did you say your name was again?

Iggy   Iggy.

Kevin   Does anyone ever call you anything else?

Iggy   Like what?

Kevin   Like your real name?

Iggy   Ignatius?

Kevin   No. (*Beat.*) Brett.

Iggy *looks at* **Kevin**.

Blackout.

Act Two

Scene One

Sunday morning.

Kevin *and* **Iggy** *sitting there.* **Kevin** *is knocking back a drink. He's quite pissed now.*

Kevin   I've seen a photograph.

Iggy   People look alike. (*Takes a swig of drink.*)

Kevin   Don't you fucking drink that! What game are you playing?

Iggy   I'm not playing any . . . ! Who's this Brett fella?

Kevin   You can't pull the wool over my eyes!

Iggy   Was Frankie having an affair then?

Kevin   Hah! Did I say that?

Iggy   Does Tony know?

Kevin   No. Keep your fucking voice down!

Iggy   But you do. And you never told him. What sort of a friend are you?

Kevin   Not half as fucked up as you are. Shag the dead one, get the live one. You sick or something?

Iggy   I'm Ignatius. You're mistaken.

Iggy *makes to go in.* **Kevin** *bars his way.*

Kevin   Leave Tony alone.

Iggy   Why should I? What right have you got to tell me what to do?

Kevin   Because I'm a grown-up, you're a kid, and he's my mate.

Iggy   I dunno what the fuck you're talking about, mate. Now can I go in, or do I have to hit you?

Iggy *tries to push past* **Kevin**.

Kevin   Leave him alone!

Kevin *wrestles him away from the door and on to the decking.* **Iggy** *easily brushes him off, as he is so pissed.* **Kevin** *sits on the decking and starts to cry. He gets up, sits at the table, trying to hide it.* **Iggy** *watches this.*

Iggy   You know, Tony was right about you. You're fucking barmy, mate. Listen. Let's not say owt about this to Tony. If Frankie was having an affair. He doesn't need to know, does he? And as I'm not this . . . Brett character. I'm gonna go in, and forget this conversation ever happened. You're drunk, Kevin.

Kevin   Drinking doesn't make me stupid, you prat!

Iggy   Well, it makes you fucking paranoid! What's the difference?

Kevin   Musta been strange. Meeting Mary. The woman who gave your lover life.

Iggy   Are you on tablets? I think you should take some.

Kevin   No I'm not on fucking tablets! For Christ's sake, where do you get off?

Iggy   Look, I don't want a slanging match. I just wanna be with Tony, yeah? I certainly don't wanna fall out with his mates.

Kevin   Why? Why are you doing this?

Iggy   I'm down for a couple o'days. I meet a guy in a bar. We have a bit of fun. I go home. There is no 'why' about it.

Kevin   Nobody stays in Dalston.

Iggy   It's cheap.

Kevin   Unlike you, you're free.

Iggy   Jealous?

Kevin   Of what?

Iggy   That I've got Tony?

Kevin   Why would I be jealous?

Iggy   You're just making up stories to try and get rid of me. Cos you want him for yourself.

Kevin   Why does everyone think I've got a thing for Tony?

Iggy   Well, you seem a bit obsessed with him.

Kevin   He's my friend.

Iggy   If you want. (*Makes to go in.*)

Kevin   Brett was from Manchester.

Iggy   A lot of people are.

Kevin   You're the fucking image of him. You're his doppelgänger!

Iggy   Look. I'm sorry, but I'm not him.

Kevin   I hate all this.

Iggy   What?

Kevin   Lying. It's not right.

Iggy   So Frankie was seeing someone else?

Pause. **Kevin** *stares at* **Iggy**.

I won't tell Tony, if that's what you want.

Kevin   Yes.

Iggy   How long for?

Kevin   It doesn't matter.

Iggy   What a bastard.

Kevin   Frankie treated him like shit, you know. And he just took it. Monica thought he was a fool. I thought he had dignity. I've never had a relationship. Not proper. I dunno what I feel any more. But I know this much. I ain't waiting for the grieving widow to turn round and tip me the wink. I just get confused cos I'm lonely. D'you ever get lonely?

Iggy   Come on, mate. Calm down.

Kevin   Do you?

Iggy   Yes.

Kevin   You're called Iggy, aren't you?

Iggy   Yes.

Kevin   You're not Brett, are you?

Iggy *shakes his head.* **Kevin** *sits there, crying.* **Iggy** *goes to get* **Kevin**'s *drink and hand it to him. As he does,* **Monica** *returns, carrying a large bag and putting her mobile phone away.* **Iggy** *has his back to* **Monica** *at first.*

Monica   Hi, Kev! Look, I'm so sorry about earlier. Guess what? My really great friend Candice has just rung and there's this new musical and they're looking for really great black actresses who can . . .

Iggy *turns round to see who it is.* **Monica** *stands staring at* **Iggy**. *They stay staring at each other.*

Kevin   Oh, this is Iggy. Tony's new . . . friend.

Pause.

The bloke Tony was going on about. Iggy. Stood him up last night. This is him. He's sound as a pound.

Monica   What are you doing here, Brett?!

Pause.

Kevin   What?

Iggy   You two know each . . . ?

Kevin   This is Iggy. It is, it's Iggy.

Iggy   You're that bird from Mykonos.

Kevin   You said. You fucking bastard!

He lunges at **Iggy**. *He gets* **Iggy** *in the eye.*

Monica   Get off him! Kev, get off him! Oh God, he's really drunk.

Kevin   It's him. The twat that Tony's been seeing.

Iggy (*to* **Monica**)   Why didn't you tell me? I poured me heart out to you! (*Winces.*) Me fucking eye!

Monica   Look. I never lied to you, Brett. I just . . . didn't tell you the truth.

Kevin   I was right. I was fucking right. And you made me think . . . !

Monica   Oh, shut up, Kev, you're pissed.

Kevin   But . . .

Monica   Drop it, Kev!

Pause.

Iggy   I don't have to explain myself to you.

Monica   Fine. So I take it Tony knows who you are?

Pause.

Iggy   You're just as much a liar as I am.

Monica   I didn't follow you to Mykonos!

Iggy   You should have told me.

Monica   Well, that's the pot calling the kettle black.

Iggy   I didn't plan this.

Kevin   What did you plan? Come and stay in Dalston just to visit his grave?

Iggy And what's so barmy about that?

Monica What's barmy is you're shagging his boyfriend.

Kevin You can't tell him now. You've got to tell him but you can't tell him now. He's off his nut. It's not safe. You'll freak him out.

Monica I don't quite believe this is happening. As if my life couldn't get any worse. You wouldn't believe the day I've had.

Iggy I thought you were all right.

Monica I am.

Kevin She's one of the nicest people she knows.

Monica How did you think you'd get away with it?

Iggy Frankie said no one knew.

Monica Oh, he couldn't shut up about you. Not in front of Tony. Just.

Iggy I told you loads.

Monica I'm a good listener.

Iggy You don't give a shit about Tony. Neither of you do.

Monica I love Tony. Tony's, like, one of my closest pals.

Iggy So why didn't you tell him?

Monica I thought he'd never find out. What you don't know doesn't hurt you.

Iggy Well, he wouldn't, if you didn't tell him.

Monica Why, Brett?

Iggy All I wanted was to put flowers on Frankie's grave. Look at the flat he lived in from the outside. Go to the pubs he drank in. Look at it from my point of view. I loved him. And I didn't even know when his funeral was. All I get's a message on me machine saying. I just wanted to feel close to

him. Then I meets a bloke in a pub and he chats me up.
And he tells me his name, and I think . . . nah, can't be.
Can't be. So I asks him what street he lives in. And I know.
And he invites me back. For a coffee. But I know he wants
to fuck me. Everyone wants to fuck me.

Kevin   Bit full of yourself, aren't you?

Iggy   So I says to Tony I need a crap. So I goes to the bog
in the pub and I think, if I stay here. If I just stay here for
half an hour, he'll fuck off. He'll think I've got off. So I sit
there, on the bog. And I smoke a fag. I hears his voice.
Asking me if I'm all right. I said, 'I've got the squits.' I'm
thinking, if he thinks I've got a shitty arse he won't want me
to go back with him. He goes, 'I've got Dioralyte back at my
place.' This bloke ain't giving up.

Monica   You should have gone home.

Iggy   I wanted to see what Frankie's flat was like. I reckon
I can come back, have a drink, and get off. Have a quick
butcher's. So I've got a picture in me head. Then scarper.
Nobody's hurt nobody. And we come back. And the next
thing I know this guy's telling me about his dead boyfriend.
And he's my dead boyfriend. And I can't tell him. I want to.
I want to grab hold of him and say I know exactly how you
feel. I feel so close. I didn't set out to hurt Tony. Tony's all
right. I can see why Frankie was with him.

Monica   If you didn't set out to hurt him, you'll just go
now.

Iggy   And what excuse would I give? I can't.

Kevin   Easy. Say the usual crap blokes say. You're not
ready for this. Christ, he can't be ready for this, won't be
like you're speaking a foreign language.

Monica   I knew something like this was going to happen.
I'm quite psychic. No, really. The way I kept bumping into
you in bloody Mykonos. I saw you at the Kastro Bar. You
ordered a drink and then left.

Iggy   How did you know?

Monica   I saw a photo of you. When you went to Belgium. All those photos he took.

Iggy   Have you still got them?

Monica   He put everything with you on it. Photos. Address books. Keepsakes. Letters.

Iggy   I never sent him letters. I sent him emails.

Kevin   He used to print them out and keep them.

Iggy   Did he?

Monica   If I could just finish! He put them all in left-luggage at Paddington.

Iggy   Where are they now?

Monica   We don't know.

Iggy   But there'd be a receipt? The ticket for the left-luggage. He'd have a ticket for that, wouldn't he?

Monica   He kept it in his wallet.

Iggy   And where's that? What if Tony found it?

Kevin   When Frankie died. The guy who. The guy who stayed with him 'til the ambulance came. We don't know who this guy was. And. The police seem to think he. Well, they know. He went through Frankie's pockets. His wallet was missing. And his house keys. Tony had to get the locks changed.

Iggy   That's fucking sick. Robbing from a dead man? I wish you'd told me you knew him. What were you thinking?

Tony *opens the French windows, dressed in a towel, fresh from the shower.* **Iggy** *and* **Monica** *look round.*

Tony   Ah! My three pals bonding! This is what I like to see. Isn't he gorgeous?

Monica   Yes but what a shame he's got to get off so quickly. Oh shit. Sorry. You haven't told him, have you? I put my size sevens in it again!

Tony   What?

Iggy   Tony. There's something I've gotta tell you. I've. I've gotta go back to Manchester tomorrow.

Tony   I thought you were going back on Tuesday?

Iggy   I know but. I found out today I've got a job interview Tuesday. So I need to get back up tomorrow. It's a pisser, innit?

Tony   Better make the most of you while I've got you then. Come on.

Tony *makes to head back in.* **Kevin** *and* **Monica** *are looking at* **Iggy**, *wondering what he is going to do.* **Tony** *looks back, wondering why he is not following.*

Iggy   That's the other thing. I've gotta phone the bloke about the job tonight. Well, he's phoning me at the B&B, so I've gotta get off.

Monica   I'm going to get a drink. Kevin?

Kevin *shakes his head.* **Monica** *goes inside.*

Tony   What's the job?

Iggy   It's not very interesting.

Tony   What is it?

Iggy   Old-Time Portraits. Folk come in and dress up in Victorian clobber. Or Wild West. Or 1920s gangsters and have their pictures taken. Sepia wash. There's a new one opening near us and they need a photographer.

Kevin   Oh, I've seen them, yeah. Oh, I always wondered what sort of people worked in them places.

Iggy   It'll keep the wolf from the door. Get me through college a bit.

Tony   Kev, would you mind?

Kevin *gets up to go inside.*

Kevin   It was nice meeting you, mate. Good luck with the job.

Iggy   Cheers, mate.

Kevin *exits.*

Tony   So do I not get to see you again?

Iggy   D'you want to?

Tony   Course I fucking want to, Iggy. Course I fucking do. Does that scare you?

Iggy   I'd love to see you again, Tony. I just don't know that it's right.

Tony   Well, it's not wrong, is it? How is it wrong? Is there something you're not telling me?

Iggy   There's nothing wrong about it, it's just. I dunno. I don't know.

Tony   You don't fancy me.

Iggy   It's not that.

Tony   So you do fancy me?

Iggy   I've got to go.

Tony   Come round tomorrow. Before you go. Come round for your lunch.

Iggy *is crying.*

Tony   Don't cry. There's no need to cry. My cooking's not that bad.

They kiss. For a long time. **Monica** *comes to the French windows filing her nails. She watches them. They stop kissing.*

Iggy   I'll see you tomorrow.

Tony   Great. I'll take the day off work.

Iggy *nods and leaves.* **Tony** *watches him go.* **Monica** *steps out.*

Monica   Hey, you'll never guess what. I've got an audition tomorrow. My really great friend Candice phoned earlier. There's this new musical, and they're having trouble finding really great black actresses who can ice-skate. I said, 'Look no further, Candice.' I love that Candice, you know. She's quite fit actually. Great tits.

Tony   Lovely.

Monica   Oh, look, I'm sorry it didn't work out with little . . . thingy.

Tony   I'm a bit mixed up about all this, you know. This isn't what I'd planned. When I went the pub the other night. I didn't think that. Two days later I'd be. So confused. Nice, isn't he?

Monica   Is he?

Tony   Isn't he?

Monica   Whatever. Yeah, I guess he's kind of . . . sweet.

Tony   Eh?

Monica   Truth?

Tony   Go on.

Monica   I don't trust him.

Kevin *comes out.*

Kevin   Neither do I.

Tony   Why not?

Kevin   I dunno, I just don't.

Tony   You'd say that about whoever I got off with next.

Monica I mean, what was all that bullshit about having to go to a job interview? I mean, come on! That was just like . . . so invented!

Kevin Did you think so?

Monica Believe me. I know when people are improvising. And improvising badly.

Kevin Maybe he's just trying to let you down gently. He's only a kid.

Tony Why don't you trust him, Mon? Cos he's a scally?

Monica No. I'm really into auras and he has got such a disturbing one. It's a colour I've never seen before.

Tony Oh, shut up.

Monica Look, don't lose your heart or anything to him, babe. Yeah?

Tony I'm only having a bit of fun. I. If I'm honest, it doesn't feel right.

Monica See, I knew it. I'm probably just picking up some of your vibes, you know. Anyway he's going to be out of your life soon enough. That much I do know.

Tony But every time I look at him, I can't help myself. I want to hate him. Cos he's not Frankie. But I don't.

Kevin His eyes are too close together.

Tony His eyes are perfectly positioned thank you!

Kevin I've met lads like him before. That's all I'm tryina say, mate. And that sort are only after one thing.

Tony All right, so you can't stick him. I think it's up to me who I see. Don't you? You can't just cling on to the idea that I'll never get over Frankie. Cos I will. I have to.

Monica Does he know you're positive?

Tony Do we have to talk about everything all the time?

Kevin   What d'you see in him?

Tony   Isn't it obvious?

Kevin   He's cute, yeah, but . . .

Tony   Don't you think I like the danger?

Monica   So you agree he's dangerous? That's a good word for him actually.

Tony   Maybe I'm dangerous. Maybe what I feel for him is dangerous.

Monica   Right.

Tony   Christ, I've only known him since Friday night. And I'm all worked up about him. I took one look at him and said, this guy's trouble. But I don't care. You're right. He's too cute.

Monica   Oh, pass me the sick bag. Cute?! What's cute? Bunny wabbits? Furry little kittens? Yukola, Antonio McBonio. And remember rabbits crap everywhere. And cats, yeah, cats have claws.

She thinks she's been terribly profound. **Tony** *rolls his eyes and goes back inside.*

Blackout.

Scene Two

Monday afternoon.

Tony *sits at the table drinking a glass of wine. A bowl of salad on the table. Two plates. The remnants of a meal.* **Iggy**'s *sports bag on the ground.* **Kevin** *sits on the back step wearing a Blockbuster Video uniform. He is putting on a pair of trainers and a funny voice.*

Kevin   'That's due back Wednesday before eleven o'clock. That's due back Wednesday before eleven o'clock. That's due back Wednesday before eleven o'clock.' That's all I'll say for the rest of the day, you know. I could bring a bottle of wine back tonight. You might be feeling a bit funny.

Tony   Why?

Kevin   Well, he's getting off inn'e? He'll be out of your life for ever. Sort of thing.

Tony   Kevin, why do you have to make it sound so dramatic?

Kevin   Dunno. I'm just thinking of you really. He's taking his time. Is he having a crap?

Tony   I don't know, we didn't go into details, I was still eating.

Kevin   It's just I wanna get in and use the ear things. Last week me boss said I had dirty ear holes. Waxy.

Tony   Well, why don't you ask him how long he's going to be?

Kevin   I don't like to put people on the spot.

The back door goes and **Monica** *comes in, beaming. She is carrying a pair of ice-skates.*

Tony   What are you doing here?

Monica   Antonio? Audition? I don't want to tempt fate, but I really think that job is mine!

Kevin   That's what you said after *Mamma Mia!*

Monica   So?

Kevin   Well, that was months back, and you still haven't heard.

Monica   Yeah, but they still haven't said no!

Kevin   You poor deluded fool.

Kevin *goes indoors.* **Monica** *can't believe* **Kevin**'s *cheek.*

Tony   Well, he's kind of got a point. I'm not saying you're deluded. Oh, I'll shut up.

Monica   Do you want me to be stuck in that caff for the rest of my life? My first audition in seven months, and you have to be vile about it. Thanks a lot, Tony. Nice one, buddy!

Tony   How did it go?

Monica   They really liked my voice. They were fucking hooked actually.

She swipes his wine and knocks some back.

And I'm pretty sure the director was a lesbian. Fuck did she enjoy touching me.

She laughs cockily and takes one of his cigarettes.

Tony   What's it about?

Monica   It's really interesting actually. It's about this really fierce girl gang in Nottingham, and they hang out at this ice rink. I said, 'That is so uncanny, Pam, cos I spent the majority of my puberty at the Silver Blade in Basingstoke. It's in fact where I first realised I was a lesbian.' Well, you've gotta flirt. My character's called Trish. And she . . . God this is so exciting . . . she dies at the end! I love dying. And my blood slowly seeps over the ice of the rink. And the other gang members gather round and sing this song called 'The Red Rink'. That's the name of the show. *The Red Rink.*

Tony   What did they say?

Monica   When?

Tony   At the end. Did they say 'When can you start?' or something?

She gets her mobile out.

Monica   They don't come out with it outright, Antonio McBonio. But I bet this little baby's gonna ring any moment. Think I'll call Sheila.

Tony   Sheila?

Monica   My agent.

Tony   I thought she got rid of you.

Monica (*on phone*)   Hi, is that Ming? Ming, it's Monica. Book deal? No, Ming, it's Monica Monroe. Hi. Monroe. I used to be a client of Sheila's. Hi. I'm fine. Just about to do *The Red Rink*, I think. So! Fingers crossed! Oh, it's this really 'grrrrreat!' new musical about . . . Sorry? Well, yeah, I rang to speak to Sheila. Oh, right. When will she be out of it? No, I mean the meeting. God, that's a long one. It's just she said. Right. Could you tell her I called? Well, I just thought, what with me going into the show. I just thought she might be interested in . . . Right. Right. Oh, I see. Really? What . . . never? Right. Any specific reason? Sorry? Ming? Ming, I think I'm breaking up. (*Hangs up.*) I'm going to have to get a new phone.

Tony   So did you have to sing?

She pulls her dress over her face and sings 'Lord Here Comes The Flood', à la Bette Midler. As she sings, **Iggy** *comes out of the French windows. He is taken aback by her singing. He gets a bit upset.*

She drops her dress.

Tony (*to* **Iggy**)   You OK? Come here.

Iggy *sits on his knee.* **Tony** *hugs him.*

Monica   Oh, hi, Iggy.

Iggy   Is that what you sang at Frankie's funeral?

Monica   How did you know?

Iggy   Tony told me.

Tony   Monica's had an audition.

She takes one of **Tony***'s cigarettes. As she lights up:*

Monica (*showing off*)   I told them about Frankie.

Tony   Why?

Monica   Well, like my character gets stabbed, right, and like just dies there. Blood on the white-cold ice of the rink. And I said, 'You know, something similar happened to a really close friend of mine last year.'

Tony   Frankie wasn't stabbed, Monica.

Monica   But he died. And people gathered round. They were all really sympathetic.

Tony   Sympathetic? One of them went through his pockets!

Monica   No, the musical people. I told them about the pockets. They all looked horrified. I thought Pam was going to cry.

Tony   I'll expect a bouquet this afternoon then, shall I?

Monica (*Nottingham accent*)   Don't be facetious, Tony. (*Own voice.*) That's quite good, isn't it? (*Nottingham.*) That's really good. I'm doing a Nottingham accent, Tony. What do you think?

Tony   It's wonderful, babe.

Monica   Cheers, cock!

Iggy   Is Nottingham in South Africa then?

Tony *pisses himself laughing.*

Monica (*own voice*)   Oh yeah, that's right. Go on, laugh at me.

Tony   Lighten up, for fuck's sake. It was only a joke.

Monica   Nice meeting you, Iggy. Will we be seeing you again? I suppose it's going to difficult, what with your new job and everything. D'you know what I mean?

Iggy   Oh, you never know. Stranger things have happened.

Monica   What time's your train?

Iggy   Are you trying to get rid of me?

Monica   No! No! No! God, you're so paranoid! Jesus! What am I doing even mixing with you guys? I've gotta get me to Stanmore! Got an *A to Z* Toe?

Tony   In the bedroom, on the shelf.

She goes inside.

Iggy   She's right. I should be getting off really.

Tony   Get off with me.

Pause.

I never was very good at being serious. It was Frankie's biggest complaint about me.

Iggy   I know.

Tony   It's easier to play court jester. I thought I'd lost my sense of humour. But when I'm with you, right. It comes back, crap though it may be.

Beat.

What d'you mean, you know?

Iggy   It's something I've noticed.

Tony   What is?

Iggy   You'll have a laugh rather than be serious.

Tony   What are you? My fucking psychiatrist?

Iggy   You do it all the time.

Tony   You've only known me five minutes.

Iggy   Well, Frankie didn't like it, did he? You just said.

Tony   Do you have to go back?

Iggy   Well, I can't stay here for ever, can I?

Tony   Why not?

Iggy   Well, what about my job? I'm starting a new job soon.

Tony   Yeah, well, I reckon you made that up.

Iggy   Why would I make that up?

Tony   So you don't have to stay here.

Iggy   Tony, I came away for a long weekend. I didn't expect to meet someone.

Tony   And let's face it. You didn't. Well, no one special, eh?

Iggy   I don't understand what you see in me.

Tony   I could come to Manchester if you want.

Iggy   You've got work.

Tony   I'll take a week off. I took today off.

Iggy   There's things you don't know about me.

Tony   There's things you don't know about me.

Iggy   If you got to know me. You'd hate me.

Tony   Try me.

Iggy   I have to go.

Tony   I don't want you to. I could lie. Pretend. Say fine. Cool. Whatever. But it's not fine. It's not cool. And I'm sick to fucking death of that word whatever.

Iggy   I'm sorry.

Tony   These things. That if I knew about you I'd hate you. Tell me.

Iggy   No.

Tony   You think I'd never forgive you?

Iggy No.

Tony I will. I promise.

Iggy No.

Tony If I don't forgive you then I give you the right to stab me. How's that?

Pause.

Have you murdered someone? Is that it? Have you?

Iggy No!

Tony Well, it can't be all that bad then.

Iggy I don't need your forgiveness.

Tony Do you not?

Pause.

Iggy Bye, Tony. I'll phone you.

Tony Fine. Cool. Whatever.

Iggy *kisses him and then heads to the back gate.*

Iggy The chicken was nice.

Tony Very tender. The flowers were nice too.

Iggy *looks back.*

Tony The red roses.

Iggy Which red roses?

Tony The ones you put on Frankie's grave.

Pause.

Iggy Did you see me?

Tony I didn't need to.

Iggy How did you know?

Tony   About the flowers? Well, you were fucking him, weren't you?

Iggy   He told you?

Tony   No, he didn't have the backbone. I thought you had to go.

Iggy   How did you know?

Tony   I first saw you on March the first, 1998. Frankie was up in Manchester on business. Checking out some clubs for Trade. He phoned me in the afternoon. I was in a cunty mood and we had a row. Nothing major, but after I put the phone down I started to feel guilty. So I decided to be dead impulsive and get on a train. And go to his hotel. I get there in the . . . the evening. And the bloke on reception says he's gone out for dinner. Did he know where? Yes he'd made the booking. He'd gone to Mash. So I go to Mash. And I climb up the stairs. Oh, I'd forgotten to say I was looking devilishly handsome and carrying a big fuck-off bouquet of flowers. I tell the waiter I'm looking for Mr McAdam. He points out the table. There's a waiter standing at the next table. Frankie's sitting there with his hand outstretched. The waiter moves out to reveal that Frankie is in fact holding someone's hand. Your hand. He never held my hand in public. But he's holding your hand. And I hid behind the flowers. And I walked out, backwards. I went outside and stood where he couldn't see me, but where I could get a good look at you. And you were sat there. And you weren't saying much. So little in fact that I thought, this isn't the first time. In fact, this is worse. This has been going on for some time.

Pause.

Did you love him, Iggy? I don't want to call you Brett. Did you?

Iggy   I . . .

Tony   Did you love him?

Iggy   Yes I did.

Tony   And did he love you?

Pause.

Did he love you?

Iggy   He said he did. But he never left you.

Tony   We're not talking about me. We're talking about you two.

Iggy   I'm sorry.

Tony   It must have really fucked you off that he was with me.

Iggy   Maybe.

Tony   You didn't have a clue who I was at first, did you?

Iggy *says nothing.*

Tony   When I clocked you that night in the pub. I just wanted to be near you. Because you'd been near to him. When did you realise?

Iggy   I knew who you were from the off. I'm sorry, Tony. I should be going.

Tony   I still don't want you to go.

Iggy   I'm not Frankie.

Tony   No. But now we've got things out in the open.

Iggy   This is too weird. The whole fucking thing's weird.

Tony   I know you a little bit now. I know what he saw in you.

Iggy   Snap.

Tony   Why 'Iggy'?

Iggy   Middle name.

Tony   I really wanted to hurt you. I really wanted to hate you. And I don't. Thought I'd freak you out bringing you back here that night. And I never.

Iggy   Wanna bet?

Tony   You're a part of him. You were intimate with him. And I wanted to feel close to him.

Iggy (*shrugs*)   Snap.

Tony   And then it all changed. I liked you. And I thought, well, there's no harm in this. We'll have the conversation one day. He'll freak but he'll be fine. And then I think why am I doing this? Am I getting revenge on him? But I don't think I am. I really don't think I am. What did he say I was like?

Iggy   He said you were all right. Said you were good-looking. He showed me a photo. I said I wouldn't kick you out of bed.

Tony   And you didn't. Did he say he loved me? Please feel free to lie, if he said he didn't.

Iggy   I'm not lying. He did.

Tony   Did he tell you I was positive?

Iggy *nods.*

Tony   What did he say?

Iggy   Truth?

Tony   Now feels like as good a time as any.

Iggy   He said he couldn't leave you in case you got ill.

Tony   That tied to me, was he?

Iggy   But he was talking bollocks, want he?

Tony   Was he?

Iggy   Course he coulda left you. If it was that wrong, you and him. And from the sounds of things you've not been that ill.

Tony   Aye, I've been lucky.

Iggy   I used to pretend it fucked me off. I'm sorry, Tony. But I did love him. In my own little way.

Tony   You're not the only one. I knew he shagged around. I've shagged around. But we used to have this agreement. More than once and it's an affair. And that was breaking the rules. No way. But me. I'm a shithouse. A yes man. Didn't even question him. Just thought it would run its course. And nobody else knew. So I was only losing my dignity in your eyes. And you I never knew. He never finished with you, did he?

Iggy *shakes his head.*

Tony   How did you know he'd died?

Iggy   Mary.

Tony   For fuck's sake! Did she know about you?

Iggy   No, don't be soft. I was in his Filofax. Under a false name. She left me a message on me machine. I rang her back and she told me he'd died. Crying me eyes out in the middle of Canal Street. On me mobile. All these queens going past screaming, 'She's been jibbed!'

Tony   Oh, you poor wee sod.

Iggy   She said he was struck by lightning in some field.

Tony   It wasn't just any field, darling. It was Hampstead Heath. It was mortifying. Burying your bloke when he's died looking for a quick fuck. People laughing at the funeral. Saying what a great fan he was of outdoor pursuits. It's not like it hadn't crossed my mind. I asked Kevin. After he'd died. Whether he'd been having an affair. He seemed really shocked. I was glad. I thought I was Frankie's best mate really. And if he could keep it a secret from me, he could keep it a secret from them.

The doorbell goes. **Tony** *calls into the house.*

Kev? Could you get that?!

They stand there. The doorbell goes again.

Monica?! Sorry, Iggy.

Tony *goes inside. He lets* **Mary** *into the living room. She is carrying a flan dish.*

Mary   I phoned work, but they said you was poorly. I thought, 'He's bunking off.' I bet half o'London's bunking off today. It's glorious. I've carried this all the way on the bus. I made it for me lady with the leg only something happened.

Tony   Mary, this isn't really a good time.

Mary   Oh, all right, darling. I won't stay long.

Tony   You shoulda phoned.

Mary (*to* **Iggy**)   Oh, you're still knocking about, I see. What's your name again?

Iggy   Iggy.

Mary   That's the one.

At the same time as she says this . . .

Tony   Mary. Kev and Monica are inside. Would you mind just . . . I just need a few minutes with Iggy.

Mary   I had an apparition, darling. Hear me out.

Tony   Look, Mary, I'm speaking plain English, will you just get the fuck outta my face?!

Mary   Ooh! Who rattled your cage? You rattled his cage, Iggy?

Tony   I'm sorry but. This is. Oh, what's the fucking point?

Mary   I was just putting the spring onions in this when the face of Frankie appeared to me on me calendar. I've got this calendar with well-known Jewish people on it. Nothing special, 50p in the jumble. Anyway, this month's Vanessa Feltz. Only the face of Vanessa Feltz turned into Frankie and he said, 'Give the flan to my old man.' At first I thought he meant his dad. And then I realised.

Tony   Well, take your pick. We're both here. Unless there was someone else as well. Someone we don't know about. It's possible, I suppose.

Mary   I ain't never had an apparition before. You ever had one, darling?

Tony   Mary, Iggy and I are talking.

Mary   About Frankie? Oh, he don't half miss him, Iggy, you know. You can't blame him, babe, you can't blame him. (*To* **Tony**.) Go nice with a baked potato. You've got chives somewhere here. You could bung a few o'them in, babe.

Tony   Iggy misses him too, Mary.

Mary   Do you? Why? Did you know my Frankie? Oh, thank God for that! I thought yous two was getting it on and that. And I don't mean to be horrible, darling, but I thought it was a bit early, you know. I mean, he ain't even cold yet, darling. How did you know him, darling?

Iggy   Oh, you know.

Tony   No, she doesn't, Iggy. Why don't you tell her?

Iggy   I knew him from Manchester.

Mary   He went there a few times on business. Doing stuff for Trade. They done a few nights up there and they liked Frankie to go up and case the joints, you know. He was very well respected in clubland.

Tony   He went there a lot on business. And managed to combine it with pleasure.

Mary   Oh, we all like a bit of pleasure, darling. Don't deny him a good time.

Tony   And he was the good time that was had by all.

Iggy   Fuck off.

Mary   No need for swearing, darling. Is there, Tony? Tell him, Tony. (*To* **Iggy**.) I don't like your tone.

Tony   Iggy and Frankie were . . .

Iggy   I should go.

Tony   Don't you dare leave me now!

Mary   Where are those chives, darling?

Tony   Frankie was having an affair, Mary. Your flawless perfect son was having it away with Iggy.

Mary   No. No.

Mary *is kneeling down at the chives. She gets a pair of scissors out of her handbag and starts cutting some up.*

Tony   Tell her. She won't believe me. But then you've never believed anything I've said, have you, Mary?

Mary   Eh?

Iggy   It was nothing special.

Mary   Fucking load o'rubbish.

Tony   It wasn't that special? How fucking dare you say that?!

Mary *stands up with a bundle of chives. She hands them to* **Tony**.

Mary   There you go. Is that right, Iggy? Was you seeing my Frankie an'all?

Iggy   Casual.

Mary   Nice lad, darling, wann'e?

Tony   Fucking lovely! The best guy in the land!

Mary   I don't think Tony's very happy about it.

Iggy (*leaving*)   See you.

Mary *grabs hold of him.*

Mary   I don't think you're going nowhere, darling. Give the bloke some respect if you were . . . having it away with his old man. The love of his fucking life, darling. Now I'm gonna let go of you and you're gonna stay. You got that?

Iggy *wrestles with her.*

Mary   Do I have to spell it out to you?

Iggy *stands still. She lets go. He stays there.*

Mary   Sit down.

He sits.

Iggy   You're a fucking hard bitch, aren't you? Frankie was right.

Mary   Me? I'm soft as marge, darling.

Tony   It's got to have been serious! Don't you understand? Cos if it wasn't serious with you it wasn't serious with me!

Mary   This really needs to go in the fridge, Tony.

Tony   Well, put it in the fucking fridge then!

He guides **Mary** *and her flan quite forcefully inside.*

Mary   Don't manhandle me, darling!

She is gone.

Iggy   What d'you want me to say? That he was leaving you for me? That's bollocks! But it weren't just casual. I loved him and he loved me, just not as much as you. But I still loved him. And it broke me fucking heart knowing he'd gone. And I never said goodbye. And I never went the funeral. And I'd never seen his grave. And I never knew his mates. And they never knew me. What else d'you want me to say?

Tony   I'm jealous. I want to be all those things to you too. I want you to think. Yeah, Frankie was great. But Tony's better. Cos deep down I know. He was a fucking wee shite. A fucking liar. And it's so easy to lie. It's fucking brave to be honest.

Tony *is crying now.* **Kevin** *comes out.*

Kevin   Everything all right? Mary's crying in there. Going on about some calendar.

Tony   Fuck Mary. You were right all along about her, Kevin, she's a fucking waste o' space. Just like her son.

Pause.

Kevin (*to* **Tony**)   What's he said to you? What's he told you?

Iggy   I haven't said a thing!

Kevin   You've fucking told him, you bastard!

Tony   Told me what?

Pause.

Told me what?

Iggy   Tell him, go on.

Kevin   What have you said?

Iggy   I ain't said out, mate. I didn't need to.

Tony   What you talking about?

Iggy   See, you might think you've got good mates, Tony. But they knew all along.

Kevin   I told you to get out. I knew you were trouble, you lying bastard!

Iggy   Oh and you're not? You fucking psycho!

Tony   You knew?

Kevin   Go on, get out! Get out before I knock you out.

Tony   You stay there, Iggy. You knew?

Kevin   Knew what?

Iggy   He knew me the minute he clapped eyes on me. Why d'you think your mates have been so keen to get rid of me?

Tony *sits down.*

Tony   You knew?

Kevin *shrugs.*

Tony   I asked you. I asked you the night of the funeral. You told me not to be so stupid. *You* told *me*. Not to be *stupid*! You of all people!

Kevin   I didn't know for sure.

Iggy   Don't lie!

Tony   Monica?

Kevin (*to* **Iggy**)   Look at all the trouble you've caused!

Tony   Monica knows?

Kevin   Oh, she got all the gory details.

Tony   How long have you known?

Kevin   Don't be angry with me, Tony. Please. I hate meself, Tony. I do. Don't be angry, with me, Tony. It ain't fucking worth being angry over. He was a cunt. You're right. I'm a cunt. You're a cunt. We're all cunts.

Tony   Do you get some sort of perverse satisfaction out of seeing me suffer?

Kevin   No. Course I don't. How can you say that? I love you, Tony.

Tony   Fuck off!

Tony *headbutts* **Kevin**. **Kevin** *falls back. He sits there clutching his head.*

Kevin   I do!

Tony   Why? Because I'm the only person who'll put up with you?

Kevin   No, because you're my mate.

Tony   I don't need mates like you. Mates is about honesty. I can keep any fucking secret I want from a lover. But not from a mate.

Kevin   Well, that's a bizarre type of psychology. Don't hit me!

Tony   Take a look in the mirror, darling. That's bizarre fucking headwork. D'you know why I never told you or Monica? Cos I thought you'd be disappointed in him.

Kevin   You knew?

Tony   Course I fucking knew. I'm not stupid.

Kevin   I wanted to tell you. But each day I never made it harder and harder.

Tony   Don't lie to me, Kevin.

Kevin   Frankie said he was going to finish it. Frankie said it wasn't worth hurting you over.

Tony   Save your breath and get Monica.

Kevin   I'm late for work.

Tony   I said go and get her.

Kevin   She'll freak.

Tony   I'm freaking, Kevin, just get her now!

Kevin   Yeah. Yeah. I'm going, I'm going.

Kevin *goes inside.*

Tony   I think maybe you should get out of the way, darling.

Iggy   I don't wanna leave you.

Pause.

Come to Manchester.

Tony   I can't think about that right now. Sorry.

Iggy   I'll be in the pub. Where we met. I'll wait an hour. Then I'll get off. I know it's fucked up. But I like you. Let's live dangerously.

Iggy *picks up his bag and goes.* **Monica** *comes to the door, shitting herself. She has an* A *to* Z *in her hands and her bag.*

Monica   Listen, I'm going to have to make this really quick. Do you know how far Stanmore is?

Tony   I know you were Frankie's friend.

Monica   Listen, Antonio Mc . . .

Tony   Don't call me that. I don't like it. I've never liked it. But, 'Oh no,' said Frankie. 'She thinks the world of you. Give her a go.' And you? You used to spout all that bullshit about how good pals we were. Bollocks. I've been made a cunt of.

Monica   I don't like that word. Much.

Tony   I don't like you much. And d'you know why? Cos you're a fraud.

Monica   If anyone's a cunt round here it's Brett. Where is he?

Tony   D'you know why you've never heard from *Mamma Mia!*, Monica? Because you probably did their heads in. Like you probably did their heads in today. 'Oh, I'm a lesbian, right.' Like it's going to impress them. Well, go and fucking lick someone out and stop pretending you're my friend.

Monica   That's pretty offensive, Tony.

Tony   I don't give a fuck, you fat talentless bitch.

Monica   I'm outta here.

Monica *goes out.* **Kevin** *comes to the door.*

Kevin   Tony.

Monica *marches back in again.*

Monica   Hang on a mo. Talentless? Talentless? You make it up as you go along, you do. If I was (*Mimes inverted commas.*) 'talentless', why did you ask me to sing at the funeral? That priest was in tears, guy!

Tony   He was probably shagging Frankie as well then.

Kevin   You're being silly now.

Monica (*chuckles*)   A psychiatrist would have a field day with you.

Tony   Ah, but I don't see a psychiatrist, darling, you do. I'm pretty much together, thanks.

Monica   Well, I think it's pretty rich actually.

Tony   What's pretty rich?

Monica   That you're so angry with us. When you should really be angry with Frankie.

Tony   Oh, don't pass the buck, Monica.

Kevin   Well, it's not us that had the fucking affair. I didn't jump on Brett the first time I seen him.

Tony   Don't call him that.

Kevin   Why not? It's his name!

Monica   Because if you call him that it's proof of what a hypocrite you are! You've met him, you like him, you've stuck your cock in his mouth and liked it, and you feel guilty. You feel bad. And so you're taking it out on us. Fine, babe. Whatever. Where is he?

Tony   If you weren't a woman . . . .

Monica   I always knew you were a misogynist.

Tony   Oh, don't make me laugh. I don't hate all women. I just hate you.

Monica   Displacement!

Tony   OK, I hated Frankie. Hated him not telling me. And I was jealous. But see I've had years to work through that one. And ever since Frankie died, all you've done is done my head in.

Monica   I'll tell you what you hate, Tony. You hate the fact that you fancy your boyfriend's bit of trade. That's all. And hey, it's no big deal. You'll get over it. I have. You're gay. Be gay. Live up to the stereotype, babe! Have no scruples! Doesn't bother me!

Tony   No wonder you were both being so vile about Iggy yesterday. Got a weird aura, has he? Eyes too close together? You were just bloody well protecting yourselves. Encouraging me to get rid of him to ease your guilty consciences.

Monica   Whatever!

She sits down and consults her A to Z. **Kevin** *edges round and sits next to* **Tony** *and tries the softly-softly approach.*

Kevin   Don't be pissed off with me, Tony, please. I never made Frankie have an affair.

Tony *pushes him away.*

Tony   You fucking stink! You always fucking stink!

Kevin *gets up, angrily.*

Kevin   Why did you carry on seeing him when you knew full well who he was? And you reckon I'm fucked up?

Tony   I don't have to answer to anybody here. I'm not in the wrong.

Kevin   No, Tony. You never are.

Monica   Listen, can we continue this another time? I'm
supposed to be in Stanmore. Colin and Vince beckon!

Tony   Actually, no, let's not continue this another time. In
fact, let's never continue anything ever again.

Monica   Sorry?

Tony   And one way you can do that, Monica, is by never
darkening my garden again.

Monica   Oh don't be such a drama queen. I'll give you a
call tomorrow. You'll be so over this by then.

She leans in and pecks him on the forehead. He pushes her away.

Tony   You're so thick-skinned, aren't you? Nothing ever
really affects you, does it?

Monica   I'm incredibly sensitive actually. It's one of my
most endearing qualities. As you'd know if you ever
bothered to find out. (*Winks and clicks her teeth at* **Kevin**.)
Wish me luck!

She leaves. **Kevin** *stands there.* **Tony** *looks at him.*

Kevin   Do you think I'm in love with you? Do you think
I'm that sad?

Tony   Why should I think that?

Kevin   Cos I'm not.

Tony   I wish you were.

Kevin   What? Why?

Tony   Maybe you'd have told me sooner.

Kevin   I wish I fucking was. Then it would have made this
simple. I wouldn't have been torn like I was.

Tony   I don't really care, Kevin. So save your breath.

Kevin   I'm late for work.

Tony   I think maybe you should investigate finding somewhere else to live.

Kevin   Maybe if I did love someone I'd have a reason to stop drinking.

Tony   Don't do that on my account. It's the only thing that makes you interesting.

Kevin   We'll talk later. I could get a video out. A bottle o'wine. I could get a gram of coke. We can talk. Or we'll skip the wine. And the charlie. We can make this right, Tony. I know we can.

Tony   I don't want to.

Kevin   Don't say that.

Tony   Why not? It's the truth. And the truth hurts. Me and you. But I've got to be honest. I do not want to sit in having some girlie chat with you like Ally McfuckingBeal, chewing over the events of the last few years. I'm hurt, Kevin. I thought you were late for work.

Kevin   I'll see you later.

Tony   Don't count on it.

Kevin *leaves.* **Tony** *sits there. He looks at his watch. He gives a big sigh.* **Mary** *appears at the French windows. She holds a spliff in one hand and a plate of flan and salad in the other.*

Mary   You still angry with me? I dunno what it is you think I've done.

He doesn't respond.

You ain't gonna shout at me again, are you?

He shakes his head. She comes out.

Mary   Frankie used to shout a lot. I think I might have frustrated him. You feeling peckish? I cut you up a bit of flan.

Tony   I've only just eaten.

Mary   What did you have?

She puts it on the table. She sits with him and lights up her spliff.

Tony   Roast chicken.

Mary   That was one thing I never had to worry about with Frankie. I knew you was feeding him properly. It's different when you're on your own, innit? You don't wanna make the effort. I always feel like I'm in a movie when I sit out here. You know, one o'them pictures where they're all in Italy. And they play tennis. Write letters home. In the twenties, or Edwardian. No it's lovely.

Pause.

Mary   Where's little Iggy then?

Tony *shrugs.*

Mary   Ah, has he done the dirty on you?

Tony   No.

Mary   Oh. Oh good. Nice-looking lad. Pleasant with it. There's a lot to be said for manners. Ah. My Frankie had good taste in men, didn't he, eh? I always said it. That bloke he was with before you. He was nice an'all. Gary.

Tony   Gary's inside for GBH, Mary.

Mary   He was provoked though, Tony.

Tony   Cut the crap, Mary, eh?

Mary   I'm only saying how my Frankie had good taste in men.

Tony *smiles.*

Mary   I dunno why. He was no oil painting.

Tony *laughs. She laughs too.*

Mary   Face like a bulldog chewing a wasp.

They laugh.

Oh, I shouldn't be cruel. His old girl can't have been no oil painting neither, eh?

Tony   Oh, she's all right.

Mary   D'you want some o'this? Oh, go on, I hate smoking it on me own.

Tony   I didn't think you had any.

Mary   It's yours, darling. Hope you don't mind. I was hoping Kev woulda seen Dodgy Rog, but what with it being so hot he'd taken his kids up Victoria Park. Well, you can't blame him. Where is everyone?

Tony   Kev's gone to work. Mon's gone to Stanmore. Iggy's gone the pub. I'm going out of my mind.

Mary   It's a busy life, innit? I often envy that Kevin. That's a lovely job, innit? Seeing all them pictures. I wouldn't mind a job like that. He don't drink at work, does he?

Tony   Iggy's waiting for me down the pub. Wants me to go up North with him.

Mary   There's a lot of crime up there. Guns. When my nice lady with the leg went up Manchester to see Daniel O'Donnell she had her handbag slashed. Someone come at her with a pair o'scissors. All she had left were the straps. And her in a wheelchair. There's something wrong there, int there, Tony? Int there though?

Pause.

Tony   I've just been quite vile to Monica and Kevin.

Mary   Oh well. Sometimes you can't do right for doing wrong. I feel like that sometimes.

Tony   I don't know whether I was just waiting for an excuse to jib them.

Mary   Ah, they're nice people, Tony. You're all nice people.

Tony   I feel like I've shed a skin. (*Suddenly hearing what she said.*) I'm not a nice person.

Mary   Oh, don't say that, you're one in a million, darling.

Tony   I'm boring. I go to work. I sell expensive clothes to richer people than me. I come home. I potter in my garden. Have the odd drink. Take the odd tablet. See the same old boring people, day in, day out. I am, I'm boring.

Mary   You wanna be grateful you've got that job. It's a swanky shop, Harvey Nicks. Frankie bought me that make-over there.

Tony   He never. I did. He'd completely forgot it was your birthday.

Mary   I had a glass o'champagne in the bar. The girl who done me nails said my cuticles were amazing. I know what she meant to say. They were amazing for a woman like me. From my background. Cheeky cow.

Tony   Iggy makes me feel exciting again.

Mary   I said, 'Don't judge a book by its cover, darling. I was very nearly an opera singer.' But like Frankie said. It's a shop for posh people. That's probably why you feel a bit funny, darling. Why you're snapping and that. Working all day surrounded by snobs. Ain't good for your psyche. Bound to get you down sooner or later.

Tony   It's time to move on, Mary.

Mary   You should get a job at Marks. That's a lovely shop. Their staff are always immaculate. If you worked up the Angel, you wouldn't have to get up 'til about half eight. Imagine that. Half eight! Life o'bleedin' Riley.

Pause.

Tony   It's time to move on.

Mary   You're lucky. You can. You can get another boyfriend. I can't get another son.

Tony I've gotta sell this flat.

Mary You can't do that, darling. You can move on, I can't. This is all I've got left of him. No one thought he'd leave it to you. I don't mean to be rude, darling, but we all know you're on your way out. Don't make sense, darling.

Tony You really don't know anything at all, do you?

Mary I know I ain't educated, darling. I left school when I was fourteen. That's the way it was in our house. It don't mean we're stupid though.

Tony This is my flat, Mary, and I'll do with it what I like.

Mary You don't wanna sell it when you've got it looking so lovely, darling. You've got a screw loose.

Tony *gets up and locks the French windows with his house keys. He looks back at her.*

Tony Why do you come here, Mary?

Mary To see you.

Tony You never used to like me.

Mary I didn't know you.

Pause.

Cos I miss him. Ain't nothing wrong with that, is there?

Tony It's not grief that's keeping you here, Mary. It's guilt. There is a difference.

Pause.

Mary You had any thoughts about what you're gonna plant out for next year, darling? There's so much stuff on the telly these days about it, you're spoilt for choice really.

He approaches her.

Tony Come here.

He gives her a hug.

Mary   What you doing?

Tony   Shut up.

He stands back.

Mary   You've got a screw loose.

Tony   Will you make sure you click the latch off when you go out.

Mary   Oh yeah. Blows open otherwise, dunnit.

Tony   I'm going the pub.

He pecks her on the forehead. He takes a last look at the place and then leaves. She calls after him.

Mary   Don't mind if I finish this wine off, do you?

Mary *sits smoking the spliff on her own, lost in thought. There is some wine left over from lunch. She picks up a glass and drinks some. Maria Callas starts to play. 'J'ai Perdu mon Eurydice.' The lights fade.*

Methuen Modern Plays

include work by

Jean Anouilh
John Arden
Margaretta D'Arcy
Peter Barnes
Sebastian Barry
Brendan Behan
Dermot Bolger
Edward Bond
Bertolt Brecht
Howard Brenton
Anthony Burgess
Simon Burke
Jim Cartwright
Caryl Churchill
Noël Coward
Lucinda Coxon
Sarah Daniels
Nick Darke
Nick Dear
Shelagh Delaney
David Edgar
David Eldridge
Dario Fo
Michael Frayn
John Godber
Paul Godfrey
David Greig
John Guare
Peter Handke
David Harrower
Jonathan Harvey
Iain Heggie
Declan Hughes
Terry Johnson
Sarah Kane
Charlotte Keatley
Barrie Keeffe
Howard Korder

Robert Lepage
Stephen Lowe
Doug Lucie
Martin McDonagh
John McGrath
Terrence McNally
David Mamet
Patrick Marber
Arthur Miller
Mtwa, Ngema & Simon
Tom Murphy
Phyllis Nagy
Peter Nichols
Joseph O'Connor
Joe Orton
Louise Page
Joe Penhall
Luigi Pirandello
Stephen Poliakoff
Franca Rame
Mark Ravenhill
Philip Ridley
Reginald Rose
David Rudkin
Willy Russell
Jean-Paul Sartre
Sam Shepard
Wole Soyinka
Shelagh Stephenson
C. P. Taylor
Theatre de Complicite
Theatre Workshop
Sue Townsend
Judy Upton
Timberlake Wertenbaker
Roy Williams
Victoria Wood

Methuen Contemporary Dramatists
include

Peter Barnes (three volumes)
Sebastian Barry
Edward Bond (six volumes)
Howard Brenton
  (two volumes)
Richard Cameron
Jim Cartwright
Caryl Churchill (two volumes)
Sarah Daniels (two volumes)
Nick Darke
David Edgar (three volumes)
Ben Elton
Dario Fo (two volumes)
Michael Frayn (two volumes)
Paul Godfrey
John Guare
Peter Handke
Jonathan Harvey
Declan Hughes
Terry Johnson (two volumes)
Bernard-Marie Koltès
David Lan
Bryony Lavery
Doug Lucie
David Mamet (three volumes)

Martin McDonagh
Duncan McLean
Anthony Minghella
  (two volumes)
Tom Murphy (four volumes)
Phyllis Nagy
Anthony Nielsen
Philip Osment
Louise Page
Joe Penhall
Stephen Poliakoff
  (three volumes)
Christina Reid
Philip Ridley
Willy Russell
Ntozake Shange
Sam Shepard (two volumes)
Wole Soyinka (two volumes)
David Storey (three volumes)
Sue Townsend
Michel Vinaver (two volumes)
Michael Wilcox
David Wood (two volumes)
Victoria Wood

Methuen World Classics

include

Jean Anouilh (two volumes)
John Arden (two volumes)
Arden & D'Arcy
Brendan Behan
Aphra Behn
Bertolt Brecht (six volumes)
Büchner
Bulgakov
Calderón
Čapek
Anton Chekhov
Noël Coward (seven volumes)
Eduardo De Filippo
Max Frisch
John Galsworthy
Gogol
Gorky
Harley Granville Barker
   (two volumes)
Henrik Ibsen (six volumes)
Lorca (three volumes)

Marivaux
Mustapha Matura
David Mercer (two volumes)
Arthur Miller (five volumes)
Molière
Musset
Peter Nichols (two volumes)
Clifford Odets
Joe Orton
A. W. Pinero
Luigi Pirandello
Terence Rattigan
   (two volumes)
W. Somerset Maughan
   (two volumes)
August Strindberg
   (three volumes)
J. M. Synge
Ramón del Valle-Inclán
Frank Wedekind
Oscar Wilde

Methuen Classical Greek Dramatists

Aeschylus Plays: One
(Persians, Seven against Thebes, Suppliants,
Prometheus Bound)

Aeschylus Plays: Two
(Oresteia: Agamemnon, Libation-Bearers, Eumenides)

Aristophanes Plays: One
(Acharnians, Knights, Peace, Lysistrata)

Aristophanes Plays: Two
(Wasps, Clouds, Birds, Festival Time, Frogs)

Aristophanes & Menander: New Comedy
(Women in Power, Wealth, The Malcontent,
The Woman from Samos)

Euripides Plays: One
(Medea, The Phoenician Women, Bacchae)

Euripides Plays: Two
(Hecuba, The Women of Troy, Iphigeneia at Aulis,
Cyclops)

Euripides Plays: Three
(Alkestis, Helen, Ion)

Euripides Plays: Four
(Elektra, Orestes, Iphigenia in Tauris)

Euripides Plays: Five
(Andromache, Herakles' Children, Herakles)

Euripides Plays: Six
(Hippolytos, Suppliants, Rhesos)

Sophocles Plays: One (*The Theban Plays*)
(Oedipus the King, Oedipus at Colonus, Antigone)

Sophocles Plays: Two
(Ajax, Women of Trachis, Electra, Philoctetes)

Methuen Student Editions

Jean Anouilh	*Antigone*
John Arden	*Serjeant Musgrave's Dance*
Alan Ayckbourn	*Confusions*
Aphra Behn	*The Rover*
Edward Bond	*Lear*
Bertolt Brecht	*The Caucasian Chalk Circle*
	Life of Galileo
	Mother Courage and her Children
Anton Chekhov	*The Cherry Orchard*
	The Seagull
Caryl Churchill	*Serious Money*
	Top Girls
Shelagh Delaney	*A Taste of Honey*
John Galsworthy	*Strife*
Euripides	*Medea*
Robert Holman	*Across Oka*
Henrik Ibsen	*A Doll's House*
	Hedda Gabler
Charlotte Keatley	*My Mother Said I Never Should*
Bernard Kops	*Dreams of Anne Frank*
Federico García Lorca	*Blood Wedding*
	(bilingual edition)
John Marston	*The Malcontent*
Willy Russell	*Blood Brothers*
Wole Soyinka	*Death and the King's Horseman*
August Strindberg	*The Father*
J. M. Synge	*The Playboy of the Western World*
Oscar Wilde	*The Importance of Being Earnest*
Tennessee Williams	*A Streetcar Named Desire*
	The Glass Menagerie
Timberlake Wertenbaker	*Our Country's Good*

Methuen Film titles include

The Wings of the Dove
Hossein Armini

Mrs Brown
Jeremy Brock

Persuasion
Nick Dear after Jane Austen

The Gambler
Nick Dear after Dostoyevski

Beautiful Thing
Jonathan Harvey

Little Voice
Mark Herman

The Long Good Friday
Barrie Keeffe

State and Main
David Mamet

The Crucible
Arthur Miller

The English Patient
Anthony Minghella

The Talented Mr Ripley
Anthony Minghella

Twelfth Night
Trevor Nunn after Shakespeare

The Krays
Philip Ridley

The Reflecting Skin & The Passion of Darkly Noon
Philip Ridley

Trojan Eddie
Billy Roche

Sling Blade
Billy Bob Thornton

The Acid House
Irvine Welsh

For a complete catalogue of Methuen Drama titles
write to:

Methuen Drama
215 Vauxhall Bridge Road
London SW1V 1EJ

or you can visit our website at:

www.methuen.co.uk

Lightning Source UK Ltd.
Milton Keynes UK
UKOW05f2143291113

222123UK00001B/4/P